Chapter Two

Few people can live in denial for their entire life without eventually reaching a breaking point. Unfortunately, we don't get to choose when we break, because if we did, I wouldn't have chosen September 11. It was a date far too important in the collective American consciousness. But however unintentional, the tenth anniversary of the day the two planes hit the twin towers happened to be the day when my own past collided with my present, creating a surge of energy that would propel me into an entirely different future.

It was a Sunday afternoon in 2011 and we were sitting in the corner booth of our local diner on the outskirts of a small Connecticut town, waiting for the commemorative rally of motorbikes to ride by. Opposite me, across a sea of decimated pancakes and spilled maple syrup, sat my husband, Charles, safely hidden behind a copy of the *Financial Times*. Next to him, five-year-old Alfie was using the seat as a trampoline, holding on to the back of the booth for support as his little bottom bobbed up and down, while under the table Lily and Rose, my three-year-old twins, were hiding in a camp they'd made by draping a jacket over their father's knees.

In the corner was Freddie, perched on the shelf behind the banquette with his nose pressed against the diner window. The eldest at six, he'd been on the lookout since we'd arrived, a sweetly redundant act of dedication since it was unlikely we might accidentally miss the sight of two thousand motorbikes roaring through the middle of town.

On the other side of the diner a family I knew from the children's school was getting ready to leave; the husband was wearing a pair of pressed khakis, the wife a quilted jacket, her hair shaped into the sort of neat shoulder-length bob that implied she'd asked an expensive hairdresser for something easy to manage. She waved at me across the diner. I knew what she saw when she looked at me: the extrovert, charming Englishwoman who hosted the best dinner parties; the devoted wife and mother who attended school PTA meetings, well-presented and slim in expensive jeans offset with a lot of jewelry, subtle eye makeup, and a mane of long blonde hair. She didn't know that once upon a time brunch for me had been a fry-up with a gang of bikers down at the local greasy spoon in London, my face caked in dirt from an open-faced motorcycle helmet, my body shaking from alcohol withdrawal. But that had been a lifetime ago, before the disaster itself, before I married Charles.

A pudgy hand appeared from under the far side of the table, groped around on top until it found a knife, and then disappeared again. I twisted down and rescued the knife from Lily's grasp before she cut through one of Charles's shoelaces. Rose had got bored of the camp and was lying on the floor on her belly, making swimming motions. I pulled her up by the armpits and plopped her down on the seat beside me, but she immediately slithered off again like a cartoon jellyfish.

Charles sighed, stretched his arms, cricked his neck, and then went back to his newspaper.

"Mummy, what did your motorbike look like?" Freddie asked from the top of the banquette.

"Which one?"

"The fastest one."

"It was red. An Italian classic."

"Will you get another one?" Alfie asked.

"I don't think so, darling."

"Why not?"

"I can't take you to your soccer games on the back of a motorbike, can I?"

"I'm going to get a bike when I grow up," Freddie announced.

"No, you're not," Charles said without looking up. "No motorbikes, no drugs, no tattoos."

"No tattoos?" Alfie asked.

"Or I won't pay for college."

I squirmed in my seat, remembering the guys I hung out with before I met Charles, the oil-stained, leather-clad bikers who needled their own tattoos, set their own speed limits, and laughed at the cops with the invincible confidence of white boys in a country where police don't have guns.

"I wish I had a bike," Freddie sighed. "Then I'd be cool."

"I wish I had a bat," Alfie said in sympathy. "Then it could bite me and I'd turn into Batman."

Charles reached over and absentmindedly picked a piece from Alfie's waffle, licking the syrup off his fingers before returning to his newspaper. Freddie started drawing circles in the fog his breath left on the windowpane. For a moment the whole scene—with Charles as the father and husband and me as the mother and wife—felt like a performance, as if I'd accidentally walked into the wrong play and picked up the wrong script and got stuck here playing the wrong part for all eternity. I didn't know why it all felt so wrong; all I knew was that I missed motorcycling so much that sometimes I still dreamed about it. Sitting astride my bike, using my weight to push down aggressively on the kick start, vainly pulling back on the throttle, my frustration mounting as the bike refused to move.

"Mummy, they're coming!" Freddie cried, pressing his hands against the windowpane.

I looked over at Charles. He didn't seem to be in a hurry.

"Shall I take them outside?" I asked.

"Sure," he replied, turning the page of his newspaper. "I'll wait for the check."

Out in the parking lot I lined the kids up on the low wall that bordered Main Street, standing behind them to make sure they all stayed safe. We heard the rumble of the engines in the distance, then glimpsed the first glint of sunlight on chrome as they appeared round the corner, a sea of black leather and bronzed skin thundering towards us. The children were awed into silence by the deafening noise, polished metal flashing as the motorcycles sped past. I felt the longing rise up and wedge in my throat, as if I'd just accidentally bumped into someone with whom I'd once been deeply in love. Alfie climbed to his feet on top of the wall and was trying to say something over the din of the motorcycles. "What darling?" I asked, putting my arm out to steady him.

He put his hands on my cheeks and yelled into my ear. "They're so LOUD!"

He turned back around to watch the bikes and I put my chin on his shoulder, my arms around his waist, hugging him tight. The bikers drew to a halt in front of us as the lights turned red, full beards and thick forearms, meaty shoulders and muscular thighs. Amid the smell of exhaust fumes they turned to signal to each other or to check on their wives and girlfriends, occasionally revving their engines, the growl of the motors a soundtrack to the show.

I waited for the light to turn green, for the moment when they'd kick their bikes into gear and roar forward with a twist of the throttle, the rumble of the engines, and the smell of burning grease and oil pulling me back in time. I could still remember when that had been me: my legs clad in black leather, my torso hard and muscular like theirs, skin tanned, biceps tightening under a T-shirt, shoulders flat and wide, my motorbike taking the place of the only thing they possessed that I didn't. I was one of them, I was meant to be out there among them, a boy among men, nothing separating us except for a few inches of road. I could feel the spring coil of the throttle through the leather glove of my right hand, the fingers of my left hand resting lightly on the front brake, the heels of my boots wedged against the foot pegs, toes tensed under the gear, the vibration of the bike through my groin, the rev of the engine sending a secret code to the rest of the bikers: *I am with you, I am one of you, let's go, let's go, let's go . . .*

And suddenly we were all out on the road together, a symphony of men and muscle and machines. The heavy weight and throb of the engine between my legs as my thighs contracted on the chassis to maneuver the bike around the bends; chest down, shoulders back, neck tense, wind whistling through the gaps in my visor, the dull roar of the engine in my ears. And then the featherweight figure of a woman's body behind me, her helmeted head just behind my right shoulder, her fingers looped through my belt hooks, her knees lightly touching the sides of my thighs.

I sank deeper into the dream until it almost felt like a memory, the outside world disintegrating, the pieces of my life spinning in circles around me until I wasn't riding a motor-bike anymore, I was falling through the air. For a moment I panicked—my life flashing before my eyes—until I realized that I wasn't falling, I was floating, and as the world came back into focus, I could see exactly who I was: a man on a motorbike, in love with a woman.

For a moment it was as clear as the calm in the center of a storm. And then it was gone. The cyclone of my past moved off into the distance with the bikers, and my children reappeared on the stone wall in front of me. But the salience of the moment lingered, like a sharp, metallic tang in the air.

Chapter Three

The secret was contained in the car as I drove down Main Street towards Henry's a few days later. It was hovering around somewhere among the empty chip packets and crushed water bottles, over by a half-eaten Fruit Roll-Up that had melted onto the dashboard. I balanced my palms lightly on the steering wheel, trying to lessen the pain in my fingers. The secret drifted into my head and I let it float away like the meditation guide had instructed: *Fly away, little dark cloud.* A strand of hair released itself from my scalp and drifted slowly down the front of my sweater. *Two hundred and sixty-seven,* I counted as another strand sloughed off. *Two hundred and sixty-eight.*

Henry's building—the destination I half hoped I'd never reach—was only a couple of miles away. Henry had once told me a story about how he used a rock hidden below the surface of the water as his base when he went surfing; as long as he could swim back to the rock, he knew he was safe. I assumed he meant it as an allegory. I couldn't picture him in a wet suit, so instead I imagined him sitting on the rock in his armchair, his yellow legal pad on his knee, his wire-rimmed glasses balanced on his nose. Waves thrashing around him, a storm brewing in the sky, and Henry calmly taking notes.

A twinge of pain shot up my left leg, followed by the familiar prickling sensation in my scalp. I ran my fingers through my hair, glancing at the strands that fell out into my hand before shaking them onto the car floor. *Tension myositis syndrome*. At least now I had a diagnosis, even if I wasn't quite sure what to do with it. I'd thought I'd been suffering from some kind of nervous breakdown induced by the stress of looking after four kids under the age of seven, but it seemed to be getting worse, not better. Henry had prescribed medication for anxiety, but it didn't feel like anxiety to me, it felt like panic. In the middle of the night it felt like sheer bloody terror.

It was a year ago that the symptoms had started, an unexplained ache in my feet when I got out of bed in the morning that made it hard to stand upright. Then I noticed shooting pains in my thighs as I sat on a picnic blanket on the edge of a soccer field, watching Alfie career around in every direction except towards the ball. Finally it took over my hands, steadily increasing until I could barely hold a pen or a cup of tea. It was hard to tell whether it was in my muscles or my joints; sometimes it almost felt like it was in my bones. I mentioned it to Charles, and he said what he always said when he didn't know what else to say, "Let's wait, and see what happens." But when I started losing weight for no reason, I became more concerned. Over the previous six months I'd lost almost fifteen pounds and still the scales kept dropping, and now I was losing my hair too, handfuls of it falling out while I was in the shower, clumps of it appearing in my hairbrush every day. I'd stopped having baths because the sight of so much hair lying in the bottom of the tub after I let out the water was freaking me out. I went to see a dermatologist, who told me to count the hairs in my hairbrush each morning. "If there are over two hundred, we might have a problem," he said. I held up my bag of hair. "We might have a problem," he confirmed.

My doctor sent me off for a series of tests to check for everything from cancer to autoimmune disease to multiple sclerosis, but nobody found anything conclusive, until eventually a doctor at Greenwich Hospital suggested that the symptoms might stem from something psychological rather than physical.

"Tension myositis syndrome is when your body creates pain as a defense mechanism against unconscious mental stress," he told me. "Which is not to say the symptoms aren't real, just that they can't be treated medically. Do you have a therapist?"

I admitted that I did, although I'd been attending my monthly sessions with Henry in a somewhat desultory manner, sharing only as much information as I thought necessary for him to keep prescribing my meds.

"If you've been bottling something up, it might be a good idea to talk to your therapist about it," the doctor suggested.

I bought a book on the subject and took it with me to my next session, leaving it in my bag while I tried to explain to Henry that something was terribly wrong. I seemed to have developed some sort of agoraphobia-induced OCD, obsessively checking my keys, my cell phone battery, the gas level of the car every time I had to leave the house. Being out in public felt terrifying, although I couldn't explain why. I'd been bursting into tears randomly for no reason, crying uncontrollably at inopportune moments, and the insomnia that had first surfaced in my midtwenties returned. I could just about cope with the anxiety and hair loss, but I couldn't cope with the nights spent lying awake, my mind racing in uncontrollable loops. Eventually I pulled the book from my bag and asked Henry for his opinion on the diagnosis.

"I'm familiar with the syndrome," he said. "The body uses pain to divert the mind from repressed anger it's trying not to acknowledge."

I sat silently, waiting for Henry to fill in the blank space between us.

"So I've got one question," he said eventually.

"Which is?"

"What are you angry about?"

My cell phone buzzed just as I turned onto Henry's street. I clicked on the speakerphone. "Hello, Mum," I said.

"Your father's in France, darling. He's been looking at war graves."

"That's great, Mum. Nice for you to have some time off."

"Are you there?"

"I'm in the car."

"You sound echoey. I've got so much done while he's been away. Took down all the caging around the vegetable garden, it's been up for twenty years, remarkable how it's lasted. Can you hear me, darling?"

"I'm just parking," I said as I pulled into the small lot behind Henry's building.

"And I finished the latest Ian McEwan. Climate change, very topical. Have you picked up anything new?"

"No, old. Beckett. I just reread *The Unnamable*," I said.

"You're not . . . *indulging*, are you, darling? I don't want you to . . ."

"It's fine, Mum."

"I just worry that you're going to . . ."

"Mum, please. I'm at my therapist's, I must go."

"Good heavens," she responded. The use of the mild invective as a form of disapproval was so familiar I had to consciously prevent myself from apologizing. "I went to a therapist once," she said. "I was trying to get over the traumatic event of your father's retirement. Never went back. I worried he'd trick me into telling him something I didn't want him to know."

"Everyone has a therapist over here," I said. "It's like having a dentist."

"Nobody goes to the dentist over here either," she said. "What on earth do you find to talk to him about after all this time?"

"The brutality of the British boarding school system and the fact that you never hugged me as a child."

"Nonsense," she sniffed. "You had a perfectly happy childhood."

"I know, Mother. Your exuberant affection knew no bounds."

"Don't be facetious, darling. It doesn't suit you."

I clicked the telephone out of its holder. "Mum, I really do have to go."

I turned the engine off and leaned back. I didn't have to tell Henry what had happened at the motorcycle rally. I could talk and say nothing; that was a workable option. After all, I'd been doing it all my life. The inside of the car felt cold, like a holding room between one world and the next. I looked through the car window at Henry's building. It was nondescript, moss green, and didn't exactly inspire feelings of safety. The sign hanging over the optometrist store at the front was slightly crooked. Maybe I could spend the whole hour sitting in silence. Or perhaps I could just not go in, send an excuse by email, pretend I'd moved back to England, never see him again. I could hear the sound of my own breathing. The seat belt light flickered on the dash. I pushed open the door, wincing as a bolt of pain shot up my arm, and stepped out.

I sat in my usual armchair, my bag in my lap, my foot tapping anxiously. Henry rummaged through the drawer beside him, looking for my folder, while I thought about his question from our previous session. *What are you angry about?* I'd sat in silence for the rest of the session, not wanting to answer. Henry hadn't pushed. He was at ease with the sort of lengthy silences that would feel awkward in any other situation, and I was usually fine with this; sitting in silence with Henry was strangely comforting. He was the only person I'd ever met who was still interested in me when I said nothing—the only person who listened closely enough to hear what I wasn't saying—but now the pills weren't working, and my hair was falling out, and I weighed under a hundred pounds, and everything hurt, and the lack of sleep was beginning to make me feel like I was going quietly mad. If giving him an answer would solve all this, then I had to tell him the truth.

Henry looked up at me and smiled. His face was oval, soft-skinned, framed with short white hair like an actor I'd once seen playing Mr. Brownlow in a BBC adaptation of *Oliver Twist*. I'd been strangely envious of the orphan at the time, rescued and adopted by this kind, perspicacious father figure. Not that my own father wasn't kind, but he wasn't really the sort of person I could talk to. He had deeply entrenched opinions about what constituted acceptable moral behavior, whereas Henry seemed to have none.

Pain tightened in my wrist like carpal tunnel. I flexed instinctively, rotating my hand, trying to loosen my fingers.

"How are the limbs?"

"I'm finding it hard to sleep. I don't think the pills you gave me are strong enough."

Henry didn't respond. He'd already told me he wasn't going to increase my medication until we figured out what the problem was.

"Did you see the bike rally?" I asked.

"I didn't."

"I used to ride a motorcycle."

"What cc?"

"You know about motorbikes?"

"When I was younger."

I couldn't picture Henry on a motorbike any more than I could picture him in a wet suit, but then I knew very little about him beyond the fact that he was Jewish, married, and in his sixties. I'd always been careful not to ask intrusive questions about his personal life in case he started asking me intrusive questions back.

"It was the only time I ever really felt like myself," I said. "I wasn't responsible for anyone, I didn't have to be anything. It was such a powerful feeling. You know that feeling, right? Like you could outrun everything, just ride off the edge of the world?"

"What were you trying to outrun?"

I picked at the piping on the arm of my chair. Henry's eyes were pale blue behind his wire-rimmed glasses. I clenched my jaw, trying to force back the burning sensation that was growing halfway between the back of my eyes and my ears.

"It's like a jack-in-the-box: it keeps bursting out, and I keep trying to stuff it back in again."

"What keeps bursting out?"

I leaned forward, folding my arms around my stomach. "I just wanted to be back out there with the bikers. I wanted to be who I was back then. But I can't. It's too late. I'm in the wrong place now."

"Why are you in the wrong place?"

I closed my eyes. My body started to shudder, as if it were fighting to contain something. "Sometimes my friend Lola . . ." My voice cracked as I said her name. Dark shapes moved behind my eyelids, blood pounded in my ears. It was Lola I'd felt on the back of my bike. One morning, during a tube strike, I'd given her a lift into work. I eased the bike through the stationary London traffic while Lola flicked the cigarettes out of the car drivers' hands, laughing as we sped ahead, leaving them fuming behind us. I felt like I was king of the world.

"I think I might . . ." I pushed the heels of my hands into my eyes as the tears came. I didn't want to see his face as I said the words, I didn't want him to be able to see mine. "Henry," I said, "I think I might be gay."

For a while I could do nothing but cry. Henry sat in silence, waiting. Eventually I straightened up and pulled a handful of tissues out of the box. Henry sat quietly while I told him the story of what had happened at the motorcycle rally, the moment of revelation when I'd seen myself for the first time: the boy on the motorcycle with the girl on the back. There were two separate things going on here, obviously, but one of them wasn't something I was interested in looking at just yet, and anyway, the relief of having finally said the words "I'm gay" out loud to another human being was so great it almost overwhelmed the other thing. I focused my attention on Lola, the presence of Lola, my desire for Lola. *I want a girl on the back of my bike, therefore I must be gay.* The other thing would have to wait.

I felt it necessary to produce as much evidence as I could to corroborate this statement in case Henry didn't believe me. While I might have looked a bit like a baby dyke when I was in my twenties, I sure as hell didn't now, with my hair and my jewelry and my French manicure. Also, I'd never done anything remotely gay. I was forty years old, and I'd never even kissed a woman. But I'd been in love with dozens, so I went back through my history, naming all of them, starting with Georgia, whom I'd met at my first boarding school, and then Lola, whom I'd met while trying to get away from Georgia, and then the girl I had a crush on at art school, and the model I used to drop Ecstasy with, and the actress who once told me she like-liked me, and the musician I'd semi-stalked, and the school mom who'd made me forget how my limbs were supposed to work, and all the other women in between whom I'd pretended not to watch, or want, or wish for, or lie awake at night dreaming about. By the time I finished, I'd shredded an entire box of tissues into my lap.

"It's like a monster in the cellar," I said, taking the second box of tissues that Henry was passing me. "It keeps bursting up through the floorboards and yelling, *You're attracted to women and you don't like having sex with men*, and I just put my fingers in my ears and go *lalala* until it goes away. Because I cannot be gay."

"Why can't you be gay?"

"Jesus, Henry, I'm married with four children!"

Henry took off his glasses and started cleaning them with a cloth. I looked at the seascape hanging on the wall. It was probably meant to be soothing. I wanted to throw a brick at it.

"It might be different if I were a man, but I'm a woman," I said miserably. "I don't even know what the right type of gay *is* if you're a woman."

"The right type of gay?"

"Well, yes, because it's different for men, isn't it?"

"It is?"

"Because gay men can be kind of . . . glamorous, can't they?"

"And lesbians can't?"

I winced. "Well, no," I said. "I mean . . . no."

Admittedly, I hadn't actually met any lesbians recently, but I could clearly remember the expression on my father's face when he saw the pictures of the women at the Greenham Common peace camps back in the 1980s, lesbians with bad haircuts and shapeless clothes aggressively shaking the chain-link fence surrounding the nuclear military base while their boots sunk into the mud. Unfeminine women with left-wing ideologies were my father's worst nightmare, and somehow I seemed to have absorbed this fear without ever fully questioning it. I pulled another stack of tissues out of the box and blew my nose. My hands hurt so badly it felt as if my bones were splintering inside my muscles.

"Is this what's been causing the pain?" I asked.

"It sounds like you've been building yourself up in layers that don't belong to you," Henry said, gently. "Now you can start peeling them off again, find out what's underneath."

"What if I peel off all the layers and find there's nothing there? What if I just disappear in a little puff of smoke?"

"Why d'you think that would happen?"

"Because . . . because . . . I'm frightened I'm not *anything*!"

Henry looked at me patiently, waiting for me to explain, but I didn't know where to start.

"How am I going to explain any of this to Charles?" I asked instead.

"You don't need to talk to Charles just yet. Take some time to come to terms with your own identity first," Henry said.

"But I don't even know what that means! I don't know what my identity is! Who am I meant to be? Everyone's always saying, 'Just be yourself,' which would be great advice if I had the faintest fucking clue what they meant!"

"Did you have any gay friends when you were younger?"

"Of course not. I barely even knew 'gay' was a thing. It just wasn't something anyone talked about."

I'd asked my parents for their opinion on the subject once—obviously I didn't tell them I was asking for myself—and the response hadn't exactly been encouraging.

The Church of England doesn't stand for that sort of thing, my father said.

Why not? I asked.

My father frowned at me. *Ours is not to question why.*

Curiosity killed the cat, my mother added.

But aside from the fact that they believed homosexuality was a sin punishable by eternal damnation, the people who raised me were good people, and they'd never been anything other than kind to me. Coming out as a lesbian—or worse, whatever that other thing was—would be like taking a price-less family heirloom and hacking it to pieces. How could I do that to them? You don't take a sledgehammer to an antique; nobody's going to forgive you for that.

My body was beginning to shake, as if I were going into shock. Henry wrote something on his notepad and then looked at me, waiting for me to speak. I said nothing. What was there to say? We sat in silence while my body shuddered uncontrollably. The clock ticked through the minutes until we reached the end of the session. Henry slipped his legal pad back into its folder.

"What do you think you'll do now?" he asked, placing the folder on top of the pile on the table beside his chair.

"Now? Nothing! What can I do? I'm married with four children, for God's sake! I might have done things a bit dif-ferently if I'd figured all this out a bit earlier, but I can't do anything about it now, can I? It's too late!"

Henry looked at me with profound compassion. "What if I told you it's not too late?" he asked.

Chapter Four

I'd been bound by the rules and regulations of upper-class English society since the day I was born, although even now in my diasporic state it is excruciating to admit this. It should be an oxymoron to say one can be trapped by a condition of privilege, because the desire to escape from privilege is, in itself, a high-class problem. Complaining about having been born into generational wealth implies a willful ignorance of the hardships of generational poverty. The first rule one learns when one becomes aware of one's privilege—particularly if one is British—is to shut the fuck up about it. It becomes the entitled elephant in the corner of the room that nobody ever mentions. But not talking about it doesn't mean it doesn't exist, and trying to skirt the fact that I came from money would be both cowardly and disingenuous. I was born into privilege, but I had to find the courage to bite the hand that fed me before I could begin to live my life.

The first ten years of my childhood were idyllic. My parents came from old money, which meant everything we owned was old. We lived in an ancient farmhouse in a tiny hamlet buried deep in the heart of the English countryside, some part of which was always crumbing or in need of repair. Pipes rusted, heating systems clanked, windowsills rotted, paint flaked; we ate off cracked plates, sat on woodworm-infested antique furniture, and drove cars that were held together by bits of string and duct tape.

When it wasn't raining—which, since we were in England, it mostly was—I lived outside, playing make-believe in formal gardens that bled out into a landscape that was overgrown and wild. With my brother, Jack, I climbed trees and made camps in the shrubs, roamed the fields of sheep and cows that surrounded the house, picked blackberries from the hedgerows bordering the narrow country lanes, and rummaged for hazelnuts that hadn't been eaten by dormice or squirrels. When we grew tired of our adventures, we'd return home to a kitchen warmed by the hum of the Aga, where our mother would make us hot buttered toast and cups of tea served in chipped mugs.

It wasn't that we didn't have the money to buy new things, it was more that this wasn't how People Like Us spent our money. Flashy lifestyles and financial frivolity were the hallmarks of the nouveaux riches; inherited wealth was a gift, and to spend it all on oneself would have been considered gauche. Most of the excess money had disappeared by the time it got to my parents—eaten into by generations of women widowed by war or disease—but our status came from our history, not from multiple properties or overflowing bank accounts. We didn't need obvious wealth because we had breeding.

My father's oldest ancestor was a knight who came over from France with William the Conqueror in 1066 and settled somewhere in the north. His progeny developed a taste for hunting, shooting, and fishing, and by the mid-1800s my father's family owned a stately home near Edinburgh, a hunting lodge in Yorkshire, and a shooting estate in the Highlands. As landed gentry, they followed the blood sports around the country according to the season—salmon fishing in the summer, grouse shooting in the fall, foxhunting in the winter—sending the servants to each estate in advance before following a few days later.

Unlike the erudite branch of the upper classes—the liberal intellectuals who were propelled forward by international travel, sexual curiosity, and a love of good literature—the hunting, shooting, and fishing set were held in the past by a rigid adherence to history and tradition. One of the more arcane of those traditions involved sending their children to boarding school at a barbarically young age—the boys at eight and the girls at eleven—where they received a healthy dose of violent discipline along with their education. The system effectively severed the bond between a child and his family, which had been useful during the reign of the British Empire because it meant men could be sent out into the colonies unencumbered by the inconvenience of blood ties. My ancestors emerged from these brutal institutions with cauterized emotions, so it wasn't only wealth that was passed down through the generations; it was social dysfunction.

My father survived his childhood by making as many friends as possible, my mother by retreating into herself. They met shortly after leaving school, my father falling for my mother because she was pretty, my mother for my father because he was popular. They had little money to speak of, but their position as members of the ruling elite remained. They married and moved to a house in the Home Counties, where my father taught my mother how to make the right kind of friends and throw the right kind of parties: alfresco lunches in the garden in summer, cozy kitchen suppers in the autumn, dancing in the drawing room at Christmas. The guests at these parties were always the same people, as my parents tried to surround themselves with the impregnable sense of security they'd both lacked as children, sealing us off from strangers and strangeness as if we were living in an enchanted castle. I didn't know what lay beyond the castle walls, but I was told it was a scary place full of people less fortunate than us, and I should be grateful I'd never have to experience their suffering.

Everything in my parents' household was neatly ordered by gender: my father earned the living, my mother kept house; my father was forthright, my mother was deferential; my father was successful, my mother was beautiful. It was a comforting system that was easy to follow, particularly since feminism had entirely bypassed their small world, as if someone had marked an X on the door in blood and the feminist movement had just passed over. My father's love for pretty women was undisguised; the lengths to which women went in the pursuit of beauty should be appreciated, and he was a very appreciative audience. His admiring gaze went unchallenged by my mother, who understood it was simply her job to be prettier than all her friends. I learned from an early age that a woman's value was based on her beauty, and because my father—like many men of his generation—took very little notice of me when I was a child, I also learned that love was something I would have to earn.

But for the first decade of my life I was just a kid, doing my own thing in my brother's hand-me-down clothes, and none of this grown-up stuff applied to us. Our days were filled with apple blossoms and bumblebees and picnic teas on the lawn, with strawberries stolen from the garden and home-pressed elderflower cordial, and although I missed my brother terribly when he was sent off to boarding school, I had my books for company.

When I myself eventually arrived at boarding school at the tender age of eleven, I was perfectly certain I was on the cusp of a great adventure. The thirteen iron-framed beds that lined the dormitory to which I was assigned gave it the atmosphere of a wartime hospital ward, the cold linoleum floors and worn chenille bedspreads sufficiently fulfilling my expectations of poetic deprivation. I unpacked my trunk into my chest of drawers, fantasizing about being the young hero in *Oliver Twist*, stoically enduring the separation from my family by forming intimate bonds with all these other abandoned children. Within a matter of days, we'd all be best friends; we wouldn't need our parents because we'd have each other.

Unpacking her trunk onto the bed opposite mine was a blue-eyed, dark-haired girl with dimples; she glanced in my direction, and I grabbed my hairbrush, embarrassed to be caught staring at her. I started brushing my hair self-consciously while the dark-haired girl started a tour of the dormitory. I wished I had dark hair like hers; I hated my blonde hair because it came with blonde eyelashes and eyebrows, which left me looking slightly featureless, like a boiled egg with eyes. I watched surreptitiously as the girl introduced herself to each of the other girls in turn; perhaps we were destined, she was going to be my best friend, we'd become inseparable and ask to switch beds so that we could sleep next to each other, hold each other's hands after lights-out. My heartbeat sped up as she approached my bed. Determined to make a good impression, I frantically tried to rearrange my limbs to look as if I were exactly the sort of laid-back person she'd like to be friends with, leaning sideways with one hand on the bed while trying to position my other hand on my hip in a way that felt natural.

"Hi," she said, stopping at my bed. "I'm Georgia."

"I'm Nicky!" I said in a voice that sounded like a cat being strangled.

Georgia looked startled. "Uh, okay, so . . . good to meet you," she said, before moving swiftly on. Possibly this was not the best start.

Within a few weeks my fantasy of being the central character in a Dickens novel was beginning to fade. The dormitories were closed during the day, so the only place for us to hang out after school was in our classrooms, where the small desks and hard chairs didn't afford much privacy or comfort. Dressed in identical thick wool skirts and scratchy gray sweaters, we were allowed few personal possessions to remind us of home; none of the other girls had got the memo about the romantic bonding that we were supposed to be doing, nobody had anybody's back, and everybody seemed to be equally adrift. There was no dog to snuggle, no log fire to curl up in front of, nowhere to sit quietly and read a book, and most problematically, no mother making cups of tea and hot buttered toast in a nice, warm kitchen. I soon realized I'd made a terrible mistake and didn't want to be at boarding school at all.

"Please, *please* let me come home!" I sobbed to my mother during the first phone call we were allowed to make. "I hate it here! I miss you! I want to come home, Mummy! Please, Mummy, *please*!"

But my parents' allegiance to the system was rock-solid. Immune to the manipulative art of the weepy phone call, they always gave the same answer: *No, we're not going to come and pick you up.* Eventually I stopped asking, although I never gave up hope.

With no one else to turn to, I focused my attention on Georgia. Her desk in the classroom became the center of my field of gravity, my chair permanently turned towards the place between the windows where she held court, sucking her thumb and twirling her hair around a finger while she smiled at her audience. I didn't understand my feelings for her, I just knew I wanted her attention, and I figured the easiest way to get it would be to remake myself in her image. Suddenly, how I looked mattered, and my brother's hand-me-down clothes weren't going to cut it anymore.

Georgia became my mirror. Her style was feminine and girlish—flat-heeled pumps from Mr. Henry and pastel-colored cashmere cardigans from Benetton—so I saved up my pocket money and took the train up to the King's Road in London to purchase identical items. She wore Pink Shimmer by Rimmel, so that became my signature lipstick, and she smelled of Anais Anais perfume, which I begged my mother to buy for my birthday. She was into the Smiths, so I learned every lyric to every song, and when she said she liked Gustave Flaubert, I read *Madame Bovary* from cover to cover in a week. I even copied her handwriting, a beautiful curlicued script I spent hours perfecting.

Georgia's popularity gave her power, but she wasn't a mean person, and she indulged my infatuation with charitable grace. Still, I was under no illusion that I was anything more than a B-list friend. The handful of girls she surrounded herself with were way out of my league, their status elevated by varying degrees of physical beauty and social connection. My place on the periphery of this clique was unstable, and my desire to sustain it meant that I often neglected my other, more steadfast friends.

In our third year, when the attention of the other girls started turning to boys, my focus remained firmly stuck on Georgia. I was unclear what this meant, but I was pretty sure it wasn't good. As my feelings developed, so did my body. Early one morning I was standing in the communal bathroom, the fluorescent lights buzzing overhead while I held my cotton nightie flat over my budding breasts, trying to figure out why I disliked them so much. Were they too puffy? Were the nipples too big? I jumped as the door opened and my friend Natalie appeared. She walked to the far end of the bathroom and started brushing her teeth, squinting at her reflection in the mirror. Natalie had a boyfriend now. I'd overheard her talking about him the night before, comparing notes with her best friend about the boys they'd kissed during the school holidays, asking each other thrilling and terrifying questions about who'd done what with whom. *What does it mean if he . . . ? What does it feel like when you . . . ? Is it okay if you want to . . . ?*

I looked over at her reflection in the mirror. "Nats?" She peered back at me through eyes pinched with sleep. "D'you ever have dreams where you're kissing a girl?"

Natalie's eyes widened. "No, do you?"

"I just did, last night," I said without thinking.

The room went dead quiet, as if the lights had flickered and gone out. Natalie placed her toothbrush carefully into her cup, walked swiftly through the bathroom—recoiling slightly as she passed me—and stepped out into the safety of the corridor. Then she turned. "I strongly advise that you never tell that to another living soul for as long as you live," she said, and closed the door behind her.

The fear this piece of advice instilled in me was all the incentive I needed to get myself a boyfriend, which I did as quickly as possible, finding a just-about-attractive-enough boy I barely knew during the summer vacation. I endured the French kissing and was rewarded with a photograph and the requisite copper bangle—the British boarding school equivalent of the high school pin—and returned to school safely positioned on the right side of heterosexuality. Contact between my boyfriend and me was conveniently limited to writing letters, which were mostly filled with anecdotes designed to demonstrate to each other how cool we were. *Georgia got caught smoking behind the limekiln*, I wrote, as if even mentioning her name might raise my status. *My friends and I sneaked out to go to the pub*, my new boyfriend wrote back, precipitating an unsophisticated game of epistolary one-upmanship. I breathlessly shared his letters with Georgia, using them as physical evidence that I was becoming the sort of girl a boy would want to be with.

Occasionally I still woke from dreams about kissing girls—dreams in which, confusingly, I was often a boy—but I convinced myself that this dreamlike fluidity was something everyone experienced, and sensibly decided not to ask anyone for confirmation either way. I was terrified of making a false move, of doing or saying something that would reveal me to be different. Social exclusion at boarding school was a punishment like no other because there was no mother to run to, no bedroom in which to hide. I'd seen it happen to a scholarship kid who couldn't afford the right clothes. *She's probably a lesbian*, I heard one of the other girls whisper about her once. There was no respite, and I had no idea how the girl survived it.

Acting became my escape, my way of finding temporary relief from the constant vigilance of trying to behave like the other girls. It was also the one arena in which Georgia and I were on equal footing, and the two of us rose together, gaining more prominent roles in the school plays as the years progressed. I was mostly given male character roles that fit my diminutive physical stature: a sniveling martyr in *Androcles and the Lion*, a crippled lunatic in *The Roses of Eyam*. But the role I really wanted to play was Henry Higgins.

I had dreamed of this ever since the day I first snuck up onto the school stage. Hidden behind the safety of the velvet curtain, I slipped my thumbs into my hip pockets, imagining myself in the opening scene of *My Fair Lady*, dressed in a fedora, houndstooth suit, and brown wingtip brogues. I leaned back slightly and looked down at an imaginary girl sitting on a wooden crate with a bunch of flowers in her lap. *Woman, cease this detestable boo-hooing instantly or else seek the shelter of another place of worship! Heavens, what a sound!* I sniffed perfunctorily, imagining how I'd wow the audience in the next scene with my excellent rendition of *I'm an Ordinary Man*.

I wasn't aware of Henry's legendary misogyny, or perhaps it was so normalized in my world that it had become invisible. What I saw instead was a man held spellbound by the woman he loved. Henry didn't want Eliza's obedience; he wanted to be ruled by her, consumed by her, allowed to adore her unconditionally. And yet he couldn't, because subservience to a woman was not a suit society would allow him to wear. Something about this silent, melodramatic yearning for something unattainable felt familiar to me—plus I really wanted the wingtip brogues.

The play chosen for my fifth year at the school, however, was Arthur Miller's *The Crucible*. When the drama teacher handed out the scripts, I was fairly confident Georgia and I would both be given leading roles.

"You'll be playing Abigail," the drama teacher told me. "Georgia's playing John."

I should have seen this coming. Abigail was in love with John. Perhaps there was someone else I could play? The male character roles were all taken, but Mary Warren, a spine- less, impressionable girl who spent most of her time either screaming or sulking, was still available. I was good at playing character parts. You could do more with them. Lead roles were overrated. Who wanted to play the love interest anyway? Sure, there was a certain kudos to bagging the lead, but really, wouldn't it be more fun to play someone with a little more personality?

Impulsively, I asked the drama teacher if I could switch to Mary Warren instead. She looked taken aback. "Well, if you're sure . . . ," she said doubtfully.

"I'm sure," I said. "I think I could bring some strong dra- matic tension to the role, plus I'm really good at screaming." I ignored the pernicious little voice hissing *coward* in my ear. It wasn't cowardice, it was self-preservation. If I stood up onstage and told Georgia I loved her—directly, to her face, in front of the whole school—it wouldn't take them long to figure out the truth.

I couldn't stay at St. Mary's. It was too much of a risk. I was always on edge, could never relax—not even in my own body—and above all, I had to get away from Georgia. I persuaded my parents to let me transfer to a boys' school that accepted a small number of girls in the junior year, a practice that was relatively common at the time. My father agreed to let me move, because although St. Mary's was old, Charterhouse—founded by Carthusian monks in 1611—was even older, and in his eyes the older the institution, the better it was likely to be.

The year after I left, St. Mary's finally put on the production of *My Fair Lady* I'd dreamed about, with Georgia playing Eliza. The girls wrote to me, inviting me to the opening night, but I didn't go. I'd never have been offered the part of Henry Higgins if I'd stayed at the school—I was too small to carry off the physical dominance the role required—but the fact that someone else would be playing him felt like a punch in the gut. That was *my* role, that was *my* part.

Chapter Five

"**M**ummy, I've made up a new superhero!" Alfie yelled as he hurtled through the kitchen on his scooter. "He's called Mutzabeam, and he can fly ten miles and spit gum out of his mouth!"

"Useful superpowers," I said as he whizzed into the living room, following the racetrack his scooter wheels had ground into the hardwood floors. "But Mutzabeam still needs to have some breakfast."

It was the morning after my meeting with Henry. I'd spent the first hour of the day in much the same way as I always did: drawing curtains and kissing sleepy heads awake, wiping bottoms, flushing toilets, squeezing toothpaste onto toothbrushes, picking up discarded pajamas, helping small legs into knickers and tights, wriggling arms into shirts and sweaters, and finally shooing four small bodies downstairs into the kitchen. It was only when I turned on the coffee machine that I remembered that the afternoon before I'd told my therapist I was gay.

Lily was standing on her chair pouring Cheerios into her bowl. She put down the box and picked up the milk carton with the ineffable confidence of a three-year-old convinced that height improves accuracy. "I can do it!" she said as I removed the milk from her chubby hands.

"No, sweetie, best not." I might be gay, but I was also a parent who had to get their kids fed and ready for school on time.

"Here's what happened," Lily said to Rose as she sat down. "Mummy gave me a squeezy yoghurt and I absolutely spilled it." Lily was not going to lose face over a carton of milk. She'd already decided she was going to be either a NASA scientist or US president when she grew up, and she didn't want anyone to doubt her ability. Rose nodded solemnly, helping herself to a handful of Cheerios from her twin sister's bowl.

Alfie came whizzing back into the kitchen and I caught him round the waist, lifted him off his scooter, and plonked him onto his chair. Alfie's energy was relentless, as if he was determined to be the first kid who could demonstrably prove the theory of perpetual motion. He was also doggedly cheerful and didn't seem to mind the bumps and bruises that came with this ambition. He opened the lunch box I'd put beside his place and peered at the contents. "I'm doing much better with the cucumber," he said, "but it's not going so great with the eggs."

"Toast, no crusts," I said, putting his plate in front of him.

"When I get mad," Rose said to no one in particular, "I turn into a butterfly and then the caterpillars die with the letter *k*." Rose was dressed in a pair of pink cowboy boots and a striped top, which she'd accessorized with a pair of sunglasses, a terry cloth headband, and a feather boa. I made a mental note to try to get some pants on her before we left for school, although Rose knew her own mind and refused to wear anything she hadn't chosen herself, which meant the selection process could be frustratingly time-consuming and any attempt to intervene ran the risk of precipitating a stalemate, which would prolong the procedure indefinitely. Still, I was secretly impressed that she was so certain about her choices. The resulting outfits were often somewhat chaotic, but if you couldn't indulge in sartorial anarchy at the age of three, when could you?

While they ate their breakfast, I fed Biscuit, our golden retriever puppy, let her outside for a piddle, finished making sandwiches for the packed lunches, located Alfie's lost shoes, found Freddie's missing homework, packed up their book bags, pulled a hairbrush through four heads of tangled hair, rescued a half-chewed Barbie from the puppy, and finally wrestled the children into their coats. Not for the first time, I wondered what it would be like to have a slightly lower child-to-adult ratio, but since Charles always left for work before the kids got up, I'd never know.

On the way to school, Freddie set about re-explaining the plot of *Star Wars: Episode III* to his siblings in painstaking detail. Freddie was an earnest kid with an extensive vocabulary who found comfort in the procurement and distribution of knowledge, and both *Star Wars* and the Marvel Universe had given him a seemingly infinite amount of material to work with. No detail was too small to matter, no Easter egg too carefully hidden to be ferreted out and shared. As Freddie switched from plot to dialogue—*Once more the Sith will rule the galaxy and we shall have peace!*—I wondered how he'd failed to notice that our lives had just changed forever. How could this sensitive little kid, who was so finely attuned to my moods, not notice the anxiety rising like steam off my shoulders? How could we all be acting like this was just another normal day, when nothing would ever be normal again?

After dropping the children at school, I came back to my empty house, wondering what to do next. I wanted to call Elisabeth, my best friend from childhood who now lived in New York, but what would I say? *Elisabeth, I know we've known each other our whole lives and you think you know everything about me, but there's something I need to tell you . . .* I had no idea how to frame this conversation. Also, I needed Elisabeth, and however radical her lifestyle, my being gay might be too much for our friendship to survive.

I considered the internet, but my adolescence had pre-dated computers, so the internet was not somewhere I felt either comfortable or safe. I was old-school, I preferred to get my information from books. I turned to my bookshelves and started skimming the spines, looking for gay authors. I had Auden, Baldwin, Berendt, Cunningham, Ginsberg, Hollinghurst, Isherwood, Maugham, the entire collection of Armistead Maupin, Tóibín, Whitman, and Waugh. With this much gayness in my library, how had I managed to stay in denial for so long? Maybe I'd been living my life vicariously through them, safely enjoying the experience of being gay without having to be gay myself. But then, I wasn't technically gay, was I? I was a lesbian. Where were all the lesbian writers?

I went to my desk and turned on my computer. I couldn't walk into my local bookstore and ask them whether they had any lesbian nonfiction; the women who worked there knew me. My only option was Amazon. I started searching for memoirs by women who'd come out later in life; finding nothing, I selected Self-Help under the list of categories and typed *married lesbian* into the search bar. I stared at the list of books, trying to take in the volume of work that had been written on the subject. I purchased the top three titles and then sat back, relieved that the whole exercise had been relatively painless The website returned me to a confirmation page. I leaned forward, my heart lurching into my mouth as I read the list of recommended titles, each one more explicitly lesbian than the last. I shot up out of my chair. I'd forgotten that Charles sometimes used this account. Would his next email from Amazon contain a list of recommended lesbian erotica? I sat back down, trying to engage my brain through the waves of panic. Perhaps if I ordered enough books on another subject, I could persuade Amazon's algorithms to change their recommendations. I started searching for all the children's books I'd been meaning to buy over the last few months, piled them into my cart, pressed Place Your Order, and sat back, shaking. The confirmation screen showed a new list of recommendations. Thankfully, it had changed genre.

I spent the rest of the week worrying that the books would arrive while I was out, and Charles would open the box and see what I'd sent myself. Luckily the package didn't arrive until after the children had gone to school the following Monday, so I took it into my bedroom, despite being alone in the house. I sat down on the bed and pulled *Late Bloomers: Awakening to Lesbianism After Forty* out of the box. I winced briefly at the pastel-colored, soft-focus petals on the cover—I wasn't a huge fan of self-help books—and then started reading. It was hard to identify with most of the women in the stories, but I did relate to many of the reasons they gave for putting up with decades of bad sex. I'd always blamed my lack of interest in sex on my first sexual encounter, a shitty one-night stand with a drunk and careless boy when I was sixteen, but if one bad sexual experience with a man made you a lesbian, there'd be no straight women left. I put the book back in the box, pushed the box underneath the bed, and went to pick up the girls from preschool.

Lily led the way up the back stairs from the garage later that morning, toppling under an eight-pack of toilet paper, which she was determined to carry by herself. Suddenly she halted, blocking our way into the living room.

"Lily, darling, don't stop there."

"But Mummy," she said, putting down the loo rolls. "Look."

I peered over her head. There were bits of paper everywhere, all over the living room floor, through the kitchen, and out into the hallway beyond. Large scraps of torn pages littered the carpet, chunks of what looked like mangled book spines. It was a snowfall of shredded paper, as if a library had sneezed all over the inside of the house. Sitting in the middle of the scene of devastation—with a half-chewed book still in her mouth—was our golden retriever puppy, her head bent sheepishly, her tail wagging furiously.

"Biscuit, what have you done?" How many books had she chewed up? And where had she got them from? All my books were on the bookshelves, out of the reach of sticky fingers and chewing puppies. I picked up a scrap of paper: *Her lips seemed to fit into mine so easily, so perfectly. There was nothing odd about it. God, I thought, a lesbian is kissing me . . .* My heart started hammering as I picked up the next piece: *One night I asked her if she'd ever done it with a woman. She said she'd had her pussy eaten by a woman once. She said it had been a blast . . .* "No, no, no, no, no!" I wailed, rescuing a gnawed book cover with the remains of a pink-and-mauve soft-focus petal on it from Biscuit's mouth.

"What is it, Mummy?" Rose asked as I followed the paper trail down the hall to my bedroom and the half-eaten Amazon box that Biscuit had pulled out from under my bed. A wave of nausea rolled up from my stomach.

"Okay, girls," I said, crouching down in front of them. "We're going to play a game. I'm going to give each of you a bag, and we're going to see how much of this paper we can pick up before Daddy gets home."

"Is it a race?" Rose asked hopefully.

"Yes, yes, it is," I replied.

"I'm gonna win!" Lily squealed.

I went back to the kitchen and pulled a handful of plastic bags out from under the sink. I handed one to each girl and we set off round the house, picking up masticated dust covers and torn pages and chewed book spines and cramming them into our bags. I pushed aside the curtain by the window seat, looking for pieces of paper hiding underneath, but I knew the whole exercise was futile. My secret was out now, I couldn't stuff it in a bag and hide it in the garbage. I sat down on the window seat, searching for something about myself I could hold on to—I was a woman, a wife, a sister, a daughter—but none of these identities felt stable anymore. Motherhood was the only thing I had. My children. They couldn't take away my children.

I was still feeling disorientated the following Friday evening as I stood inside my walk-in closet, trying to remember whose life I was living and what I should be wearing to the party we were going to. I wished I could stay home with the children, curl up in my pajamas with them, and watch a Disney movie.

Alone with the kids was the only situation in which I felt safe these days.

I pulled myself together. It was only a party, nobody knew my secret, and the hostess, Bianca, was one of my closest friends. Bianca and I had met shortly after our children started preschool together, and she was living proof that you shouldn't judge a book by its cover. The first time I saw her she was maneuvering her way through the playground towards me as if she were networking at a corporate event, stopping to kiss and greet as she went. "Are you Alfie's mom?" she asked when she reached me. "I think our sons have become friends." I took in her dark-blonde hair, blow-dried into a news-anchor wave; her pastel-colored cotton shift dress; and her jeweled sandals, and decided she was the last person I wanted to be friends with. But I accepted her invitation to coffee, and after one morning in her company I changed my mind. Her spotless exterior concealed the scars of a rough childhood. Raised in a roach-infested apartment in Fort Lauderdale by a single mother who'd survived on food stamps and cash gifts from her mafioso boyfriend, Bianca learned from a young age that she'd get only what she fought for. She graduated from high school despite being abandoned by her mother in her freshman year, worked her way through college, paid her way through business school, covered the cost of her own surgical enhancement, married and divorced a Wall Street gambler, and now worked in corporate finance managing portfolios for wealthy investors. I'd never met anyone so resolutely sure of herself, so singularly dedicated to making a success of her life.

And here was I, forty years old, born with a silver spoon in my mouth, and without the faintest clue who or what I wanted to be. Beyond motherhood, my life had no purpose.

It was almost a relief that parenting my children occupied my every waking hour, because the rest of the time I felt like an empty vessel.

I looked at the clothes hanging in the closet. Nobody needed this many clothes. It was ridiculous. The only ones I really wore were my jeans and T-shirts; the rest just hung there, gathering dust. And yet I kept buying them, as if somehow I might find the one item of clothing that would make me feel good about myself. I turned to the side of my closet where my collection of jackets hung, suddenly missing the simplicity of my old closet—a few pairs of jeans, a handful of T-shirts, my biker boots, and my beloved leather jacket. I didn't care how they looked, they were just clothes that would survive oil stains, tough enough to offer a bit of protection on the bike. If only life were still so easy. I started sifting through tailcoats and frock coats, casual denim jackets and smart bouclé opera jackets, big men's blazers and tight little riding coats, tweed jackets and military jackets, long wool coats and cropped fake furs. No wonder I had no idea who I was; there was no coherence here at all.

Lily tottered into the closet, grasping onto the skirt of one of my dresses for balance as she carefully placed a chubby leg inside an ostrich-skin boot. "I can do it!" she said, fending me off before I could help her. Rose appeared in the doorway. "I don't want to talk to Lily because Lily is too talkerly and nice," she announced. Pushing past her twin, she headed towards the high heels at the back of the closet, pulling them off the rack one by one until she'd made a giant pile of designer leather on the wardrobe floor.

I slipped on a pair of black jeans and a Foo Fighters tour shirt, pulled a large men's blazer off the rack, rolled up the sleeves, and looked at myself in the full-length mirror. I pulled out my hair tie and let my hair fall over my shoulders, wondering whether I should add some lipstick and jewelry. I missed the simplicity of my tomboy days, but I'd have to be careful not to slip too far back into old habits. I knew my value here in Connecticut was partly based on my nationality—both the British vernacular and the dry sense of humor seemed to delight my American friends—but it was also based on my looks. Staying slim was crucial, obviously, but my blonde hair mattered too. If I wanted to retain my status when I finally came out, I would need to keep it long.

I heard the bedroom door open behind me. "Daddy, shoes!" Rose wriggled her toes to show off the pair of high-heeled sandals she'd pulled on over her stripy socks.

"Hello, naughty," Charles said amiably. I turned to look at him; he was rooting around in the chest of drawers for something. "When are we leaving?" he asked.

"Half an hour," I said.

He pulled a tie out of the drawer and then looked over at me. An almost imperceptible frown crossed his face. "Is that what you're wearing?"

"Yes?"

"It's not very . . ."

"Very what?"

"The Bensons are going to be there."

"So?"

"David's invited me to the Yale Club next week. And you're . . ."

There was a pause while I waited for him to finish. "I'm what, Charles?"

"You're making friends with his wife, right?"

"Yes, but—"

"How about that dress you wore to your fortieth? You looked great in that."

"Pretty Mummy!" Lily said.

"Exactly," Charles replied, swinging her up into the air. "Mummy looked so pretty, the whole restaurant stopped to look at her."

"But I feel more comfortable in jeans," I said. "Maybe if I add some heels?"

Charles shrugged. "I like you in skirts."

He deposited Lily onto the bed and disappeared into the bathroom. Once I heard the shower running, I stripped off my clothes and stood in front of the mirror in my underwear. My relationship with mirrors had grown increasingly problematic over the last few years; I hated looking at myself and yet was repeatedly drawn back to my reflection, hoping to find the answer to my discomfort by obsessing over my appearance. It felt a bit like my relationship with alcohol—an unhealthy preoccupation I knew I needed to quit—but there seemed to be no solution other than to break all the mirrors in the house.

I turned sideways, trying to look at myself objectively. I was on the small side, but everything seemed to be in proportion, a bit skinny because of recent weight loss, but nothing about me looked hideous. Nice shoulders. A bit ribby around the chest. Hips sticking out a little too much, but at least my stomach was flat. Bad thighs. Funny knees. Men's knees. I put my hand over my eyes, shutting out the image. The problem was that I didn't know what the problem was. Mostly I seemed to have a problem with my breasts: they always seemed extraneous, as if my body would look so much neater if they weren't there.

Charles reappeared in the doorway. "Are there any clean towels?"

"In the airing cupboard," I said, grabbing a robe to cover my body.

Charles disappeared again. I dropped the robe, pulled on a skirt, and zipped up the waistband. There it was, the strange wave of nausea I felt every time I did this, as if my waist were too small, my hips too wide, my ass too round. I looked at myself in the mirror, feeling my mood sink, all my confidence draining away. I added a silk top and a pair of six-inch heels, but it only made me feel worse. I'd always assumed this was what all women felt about their bodies—which was why we were all so intent on starving ourselves—but after what had happened at the motorcycle rally it was beginning to feel a bit more sinister. I angled the mirror so it cut off my head. Now the woman in the mirror looked perfectly attractive. But the minute I moved the mirror to reattach my head, I felt grotesque again. *The problem is, that's not the body I want*, I thought. *The body I want is . . .* I turned away and picked up my clutch, not wanting to follow this thought to its conclusion. Maybe I should just avoid mirrors altogether for a while.

I rang the doorbell of Bianca's house, my feet already aching in my heels, while Charles stood beside me holding a bottle of Moët. Bianca opened the door and quickly ushered us in as if there might be paparazzi waiting outside.

"Jesus, is that Hervé Léger you're wearing?" I asked.

"It's a rip-off," she said in a stage whisper, taking the bottle of champagne from Charles. She clutched me by the arm as we headed through the hall, diamond rings encrusting her fingers like a knuckle-duster. As she led us into the oak-paneled library I stiffened, subconsciously preparing myself for the appraisal, watching carefully for that brief eye flicker from the men signaling their approval, clocking the compliments from the women about my figure or my outfit, the subtle messages that would tell me whether I'd failed or succeeded.

Charles got me a seltzer and I hovered on the edge of a small group of women who were discussing the merits of Nantucket over Cape Cod. I picked at my cuticles, feeling ridiculous in my stupid, tight skirt. With nothing useful to contribute to the conversation, I resorted to throwing in bons mots for entertainment, using humor to hide my anxiety. It was a tried and tested technique. I'd worked hard to find the perfect level of self-deprecating wit that could disarm the most uptight Connecticut housewife, and I used it indiscriminately. But now it felt cheap, like showing too much leg. I glanced over at Charles, who was chatting with the men on the other side of the room: broad shoulders in expensive blazers, large-knuckled hands holding cut-glass tumblers, starched shirts and signet rings, they exuded the sort of masculine self-possession one might find in a commercial for expensive wristwatches.

All at once I felt suffocated by the smell of face powder and expensive perfume, overwhelmed by the glitter of silk and lipstick and jewelry. I swayed on my heels, the blood draining from my head as the room around me shimmered and glitched. I was an interloper, a spy; I was here under false pretenses. I didn't belong with the women because I didn't feel like a woman, but I didn't want to switch camps and join the men—even if that were possible—because these weren't the kind of men I wanted to be.

Chapter Six

When I left St. Mary's to move to Charterhouse, the boys' school that was to become my home for the next two years, I traded in my Madonna-inspired beaded crucifixes and lace gloves and settled on a look that fell somewhere between Judd Nelson from *The Breakfast Club* and Morrissey from the Smiths. If I was going to hang with the boys, I was going to dress like the boys. My parents found my sartorial choices mildly amusing—as if I were going through a phase we would one day chuckle about together—but I didn't care about their opinions. Five years of seeing my parents only during school vacations had made me secretive, and I had no interest in trying to explain why I didn't feel comfortable in skirts, or how much I wanted the boys to accept me as one of them.

What I hadn't understood, however, was that this wasn't the role I'd been selected to play. While the girls' schools had been teaching their charges to serve, the boys' schools had been teaching theirs to govern. They were trained to enter the work force as members of the ruling elite, and having survived the first few years of their initiation, they were emerging as the men they were designed to be, with a strong sense of entitlement to the lifestyles they'd been promised. The handful of girls delivered to them in their junior year were the final part of this training. We weren't their equals; we were their practice.

The boys moved quickly, sizing us up and selecting the best. Overwhelmed by the attention and flattered by their suddenly elevated value, most of the girls succumbed to the temporary high of being a sought-after prize, allowing themselves to be won, and tossed aside, and fought over and won again. I stood watching from the safety of the sidelines, mostly because I didn't have the faintest clue how to participate. The girls were the center of attention, the boys rippling in concentric circles around them, hovering around their chosen prey with body language that swung from nonchalantly cool to shamelessly blatant. What I didn't understand was how to do what the girls were doing. How did one stand in the middle of all this attention being funny, charming, and cute? How did one affect this appearance of being coolly disinterested and seductively alluring at the same time?

Lola was my role model, since Lola seemed to attract attention merely by breathing. We met on the first day of school, when she bounced up to me, a blur of brown hair, tanned limbs, and smoky laugh. She was dressed in jeans and a sweater, slim-hipped and gamine, her hair tied back in a ponytail. My reaction to her was instantaneous, the infatuation I'd felt for Georgia immediately transferring to this new person, this tomboyish girl who seemed to be doing life bigger and bolder and better than anyone else. Lola chose me as her friend and I felt lit up, almost holy with the honor. Autumn had never felt more romantic, the wind blowing Lola's hair across her face as we walked to class together. I imagined myself carrying her books for her, sick with love and guilt and confusion and shame as I tried to work out the secret to her effortless confidence, her magnetic charisma.

It was during a field trip to the British Museum that I was rudely woken from my childish dream. Lola and I were walking through the Egyptian sculpture hall when we passed the museum coffee shop. "D'you fancy a coffee?" I asked.

"Nah, I'm all right," she replied. Five minutes later—after we'd been separated by the exhibits—I saw her walk into the coffee shop surrounded by a group of boys. I felt a sickening sensation in the pit of my stomach. Was I indignant that she'd passed me over for male company, envious that she was more popular than I was, or just straight-up jealous of the boys? Either way, my place in the pecking order was clear: I was back to B-list status.

Fortunately, there was one boy at the school who wasn't like the others. Daniel was a scholarship kid—the first person I'd met who came from a different background—and he was small, lean, and olive-skinned, with a lock of black hair that fell over his forehead. I hung back, waiting until the mating-frenzy died down before I approached him, and when we finally kissed, I felt the relief of normality. He hadn't grown up in a family that had prepped him to inherit the world, so he possessed none of the arrogance displayed by the other boys, and he didn't see me as a conquest or a prize. Instead, he became my first real friend, someone I could trust.

My relationship with Daniel was a revelation. He treated me less like a lover and more like his best friend. He taught me how to play snooker and smoke pot, introduced me to the music of Joy Division and Bauhaus, lent me the books of the Angry Young Men. I even started to dress like him—in muscle tees and leather jackets—although I stopped short at cutting off my hair, because I knew Lola preferred it long. *It's your best feature*, she'd tell me occasionally, tugging out my hair tie and letting it tumble down my back.

Everyone assumed that when I left school I would study fine art, because other than creative writing and drama, it was the only thing I was any good at. Obviously I wasn't going to become an actor—because how did that even happen?—and my dreams of becoming a writer only served to further confuse my already bewildered parents, who didn't understand that a writer was something one could actually be. Art school should have been the place I found my people, but I didn't realize until I got there how much of an outsider I would feel. My accent immediately identified me as posh, someone who couldn't be taken seriously, and I wasn't confident enough to try to break into any of the cliques that quickly formed. I missed Daniel, who'd broken up with me when he left school, but I missed Lola even more.

Lola had gone up to Oxford to major in politics, and occasionally I'd drive up to visit her. We'd go out and get drunk and eat kebabs on the street and then stumble home to the house she shared with a bunch of other students. One night we walked into the living room to find a group of boys watching porn. A man was fucking a woman from behind, the camera up close on his cock as it moved rhythmically in and out of her vagina. I felt myself materialize inside the body of the man, something stiffening between my legs as my eyes focused on the woman's buttocks. "Jesus, boys, could you actually not?" Lola complained, laughing as she pivoted out of the room. I snapped out of the fantasy. Flushed with shame, I followed Lola into the kitchen, resolving to hide the experience in a deep corner of my mind and never look at it again. Porn was now officially off-limits.

Down in London I got a part-time job pulling pints at a pub in a dodgy part of town, hoping to gain enough real-life experience for my art school friends to start treating me like a human. That was where I met Sid. Sid had everything I was looking for: an attitude, a history of delinquent behavior, and a BSA Road Rocket. I was hooked on his stories of life as a London punk. I begged him to tell me as much as he could remember so I could relive the eighties vicariously through him, and he willingly obliged.

The problem with dating Sid was that I also had to have sex with him, a vaguely unpleasant experience I learned to just about tolerate if I was very drunk. Like Daniel before him, Sid treated me like I was one of the lads, but now that I wasn't at boarding school—where sex was against the rules—I had little excuse not to sleep with him. Eventually I figured out that if I propped my head up a bit so I could look down at his cock pumping in and out of me, or angled the mirror so I could see our reflection and then removed myself from the experience entirely and approached it as if I were watching Sid having sex with someone else, I could persuade myself to find the whole exercise vaguely exciting. This required a colossal degree of concentration—trying to remain active enough to avoid arousing suspicion while remaining passive enough to disengage from my body—but it was usually just about achievable if I'd had a few drinks first.

I refused to acknowledge that my lack of interest in sex with men might somehow be related to my feelings for women. If I'd been brave enough to befriend the handful of lesbians at my art school, things might have been different, but I wasn't.

I'd been brought up to believe it was impolite to ask questions, and since I knew nothing about being a South London lesbian, there didn't seem to be a way in. It was different with the bikers, because we could talk about bikes, but I couldn't talk about being a lesbian with the lesbians because I wasn't a lesbian. My logic in this regard was flawless: I could absolutely not be gay, because if I was gay that would mean I was in love with Lola, and I could absolutely not be in love with Lola, because Lola was not gay. The only way to continue my friendship with her—a friendship I was entirely unwilling to give up—was by being straight. So that was the end of it. But Lola had got herself a new roommate, which somehow made everything exponentially worse. Polly was tall, beautiful, and charismatic, knew all the most interesting people, and got invited to all the best parties. I had no idea what I could offer Lola that could possibly compete with this, but I kept trying.

Sid and I broke up after eighteen months together, but I continued to hang with him and his buddies for the next few years. I graduated from art school and got myself a job working for a photographers' agent. From that moment on I refused all financial help from my parents. I earned my own money, rode my own motorbike, bought my own drinks, paid for my own drugs, held my own opinions, answered to no one, and let nobody tell me what to do. But my independence came at a cost. I rode with the bikers by day, but in the evenings they all went home to their wives and girlfriends, while I mostly went home alone. I started to worry that they'd never see me as one of them, that I was only their mascot, the token posh chick along for the ride.

And then the Britpop band Pulp released the single "Common People" and I knew my time was up. The song ridiculed a rich girl who thought she could get in with a working-class crowd at art school, and it was so on the nose it would have been funny if it hadn't been so devastating. I wasn't sure how Jarvis Cocker had found out about me, but somehow he had, and his horrible song played on repeat everywhere I went—in the pubs, in the cafés, in the garages where we fixed our bikes—shaming me with its awful truth. I'd been exposed for what I was: a class tourist, slumming it because I thought "poor was cool." There is nothing the English despise more than a fake—you are what you're born, and that's what you stay—and it had been stupid of me to think I could just walk away from my background. Jarvis was right: I didn't know what it was like to have no choices, and I hadn't earned the right to be here, because however self-sufficient I was, I knew my father would always bail me out if I needed rescuing.

I became suspicious of the bikers, convinced they were laughing at me behind my back. I worried they tolerated me only because I was attractive, so I made the bold move of cutting off all my hair, hoping it would stop them from wanting to sleep with me. In this it was successful. Overnight I became invisible—worthless, even—which only increased my paranoia that I'd been nothing more than a blonde trinket. I wanted to be treated like one of the boys, but instead I was simply treated like less of a girl.

By this time Lola and Polly had both moved down to London. Lola's social life now revolved around Polly and her friends, but periodically she'd come round to my flat to lie on my sofa and smoke joints if there was nothing better going on. Inevitably at some point in the evening I'd have to escape into the bathroom and stand in front of the mirror, silently repeating my mantra: *Just remember, don't try to kiss her.*

Whatever you do, don't try to kiss her. If Lola ever considered being with a woman, she wouldn't choose me, she'd choose someone like Polly. And if she wanted to be with a man, well, I wasn't a man, was I?

The turning point came one New Year's Eve when Lola, Polly, and I took the ferry over to Paris with a group of boys to go to a rave that was being held in some ancient historic building. Technically Lola hadn't really invited me—I was just in the room when the plans were being made and was automatically included—but I figured this was the perfect opportunity to prove I was as cool as Polly. All I had to do was turn up, take a shit ton of drugs, and demonstrate my infinite capacity for fun. It was my last shot, ride or die.

Unfortunately, I hadn't factored in the strength of the Ecstasy Lola brought with her. By midnight the room was heaving, the crowd pressing in around us, the colors beginning to brighten as the drug seeped into our bloodstreams. Soon we were all convulsing together, melting into the frequency, shattering into a thousand tiny waves of sound. Lola was radiating light, a direct conduit from the heavens, and the light was the music and the music was the beat and the beat was a sensory manifestation of pure love. The sensation started to crescendo until I imploded into the universe, momentarily ceasing to exist as an individual and becoming one with everyone, until suddenly my gut reacted to the strength of the drug and I vomited onto the floor.

"Fuck, Nicky." Lola grabbed me by the arm and pulled me through the crowd towards a small door at the side. "Breathe," she said as she sat me down at the bottom of a stone staircase. "You're rushing too fast." She was trying to be kind, but she clearly didn't want to be out here babysitting me. *I'm fine,*

I'm fine, I gestured, waving her away. She opened the door to the dance hall, and I caught a glimpse of her and Polly disappearing into the crowd together before the door swung closed behind them.

I was left in a tiny stone anteroom containing a spiral staircase that disappeared up into a turret. To my right was a glass exit door, through which I could see a quad of trees covered in Christmas lights. For a long while—I have no idea how long—I watched God dance through the lights in the trees, the branches shimmering as if they were alive. I wanted to break myself open to let the beauty in. I started laughing, and then realized I was beginning to rush again, and closed my eyes.

When I opened them, Georgia was standing in front of me. For a moment I thought I was hallucinating.

"Georgia?"

"*Nicky?*" Georgia looked almost as shocked as I was. "Is that you?"

"I think so?" I managed to say, but I was rushing so badly I could barely get the words out. I also couldn't make anything about this picture fit. I hadn't seen Georgia in almost ten years. What was she doing here? Where had she come from? Was she real? Georgia sat down next to me on the step and was trying to say something, but I was too high to respond. When I opened my mouth a wave of nausea washed over me, and I realized I was going to vomit again. I got up quickly, pushed open the exit door, which mercifully was unlocked, stumbled outside, and threw up in a flower bed.

I stayed in the quad for a while, pressing my cheek against the cold stone of the outside wall, wondering whether Georgia had seen me being sick. There didn't seem to be much chance that she hadn't—which was mortifying—but perhaps if I went back inside and told her how incredibly happy and successful my life now was, I could mitigate the damage a little. The stairwell, however, was empty. Georgia had disappeared back into the throng, and given that there must have been over two thousand bodies in there, I knew I'd never find her.

I stayed sitting on the steps for the rest of the night. My despair filled the stairwell as I started to come down from the drugs, the mind-altering effects of the MDMA leaving me with a clarity of perspective I hadn't asked for and didn't want. I'd blown it. My humiliation was complete. I had spectacularly failed to prove to anyone that I was a fun person to party with and instead had spent the entire evening sitting in a fucking stairwell by myself.

I took the ferry back to England with Lola and Polly, who fell asleep on each other's shoulders while I stayed awake, wondering whether life could get any worse. I was too young and naive to understand that I'd externalized my identity. I didn't know that Georgia and Lola weren't the only girls I'd ever fall in love with, or that I didn't need a bike to be a boy. All I knew was I couldn't be a boy, because the bikers wouldn't have me, and I couldn't love girls, because girls like Georgia and Lola would never love me back. This didn't just mark the end of everything I wanted, it marked the end of everything I was. It was the end of *me*.

I went back home to my flat and refused to leave my bedroom for a week. It was the first time I wanted to kill myself, and I only didn't because I couldn't figure out what to write in the suicide note. It was only one stupid night, and nobody else knew, let alone cared, how catastrophic it had felt for me. They were all just getting on with their lives as usual. No doubt within a few days Lola would call, and she'd come round and smoke joints on my sofa again, and I'd go out for a ride with the bikers, and everything would go back to normal.

Unless I didn't want that to be my normal anymore.

Chapter Seven

Shortly after Bianca's party I got a call from my best friend Elisabeth, asking me whether I could bring the car down to New York to help her move to a new apartment. Charles agreed to let me go if I organized a babysitter and got home in time to put the children to bed, which would leave me only a brief window of time in Manhattan, but I figured I could risk being slightly late for the bedtime stories if it meant I could spend a few hours with the only person who might be able to restore me to sanity.

Elisabeth and I had known each other since childhood— our mothers were also best friends—and we were cut from the same spiritual cloth. She'd been as restless as I'd been as a teenager, although her restlessness was driven by a creative urge that had carried her across the Atlantic on the skirt-tails of a septuagenarian performance artist she'd met at an artist's salon in London. Stumbling into a poetry reading at CBGB shortly after she arrived in New York, she discovered Patti Smith sitting on a stool reading Rilke, and she knew she'd found her people. She ended up marrying a friend of Patti's, a charismatic musician who resembled a slightly drunk Johnny Depp. The marriage lasted only a couple of years, but

Elisabeth stayed in Manhattan after it ended, and had been scraping together a living in the world of underground theater and counterculture performance art ever since.

When Elisabeth's mother heard Charles's firm was relocating us to New York, she was thrilled, sensing an opportunity to rescue her daughter from the grips of the East Village punk scene.

"You could be a very stabilizing influence on her," Lady Fitz-Waterford said to me over tea and cake in my mother's garden. "Darling Elisabeth, sweet child, she's really chosen a very unusual life. I'm not sure it's been a *great success*. I do worry."

"Such a shame," my mother sighed, passing Lady Fitz-Waterford another scone. "She looked so lovely at the wedding."

But Lady Fitz-Waterford's dream that her daughter might fall in love with the suburbs—and a nice man to whom Charles would introduce her—turned out to be a little optimistic. Instead of coming up to Connecticut to be seduced by our bourgeois lifestyle, Elisabeth suggested we meet in a coffee shop in the East Village, and the minute she walked through the door I realized that out of the two of us, it was not she who needed rescuing. As she described the poetry readings she wanted to take me to, the plays she knew I'd love, the people she wanted me to meet, I noticed she still spoke with the Received Pronunciation that was the trademark of the British upper classes. But when I asked her whether she'd struggled to be accepted by the artists and musicians who'd become her friends, she waved off my concern, reassuring me that over here her accent signified nothing more than that she was English. "New York is where people who don't fit anywhere else come to feel like they belong," she told me, and I wondered what my life might have been like if I'd known this sooner. Elisabeth was single and childless. She owned nothing more than she could squeeze into a few suitcases, rarely had any idea where the next paycheck was coming from, and had no clue what her future held, and yet she seemed to be the most emotionally fulfilled person I'd ever met.

I rang the bell of her building and she buzzed me in. "Nicky!" she said, appearing through her apartment doorway. "Oh my God, how are you?" She enveloped me in a hug, and I briefly relaxed into her arms before I remembered I was here to move boxes, not to be rescued. "Hey, are you okay?" she asked, pulling back to look at me.

"Yes, yes, honestly, I'm fine," I replied. "Just . . . glad to be out of Connecticut."

Elisabeth was wearing an unlikely outfit for moving boxes: a huge black fake-fur coat over a bright-yellow seventies shirt, a tiny pair of black velvet shorts over opaque tights with a run down one leg, peeling purple nail polish, and hair that looked suspiciously like it had been cut with nail scissors. She chattered away as we taped boxes and filled the car, and it felt good not to have to think about myself for a few hours. Every time we emerged onto the street with another box, Elisabeth bumped into someone she knew: an older woman with frizzy hair whose three small dogs kept getting tangled up in their leashes; a tall, thin, bearded poet, sweet and slightly vague and apparently wandering in search of inspiration; a journalist named Maeve who offered to help us pack.

Maeve smiled at me as she talked with Elisabeth, holding back the dark hair that kept blowing across her face, pale-skinned and slightly wild-looking, as if she'd be more suited to standing on the edge of a cliff on the Galway coast than on a sidewalk in New York. I dropped my eyes and focused hard on the box I was holding. If I looked at her, she might think I was attracted to her. But what if I was attracted to her? She was a New Yorker, perhaps she wouldn't mind. I peeked back up at her; she glanced at me and I quickly dropped my eyes again, then felt stupid, painfully aware that I was coming across as unfriendly. Was this what I'd been doing with women all my life? Putting up so many boundaries I couldn't even make eye contact?

When the car was full, we drove to First Avenue and pulled into a parking space opposite the Hells Angels headquarters. Elisabeth unlocked a large wrought-iron gate in front of a tenement building, and I followed her up a flight of stairs, through a door, and into a small, high-ceilinged studio apartment with a bed in one corner, two large sash windows, and a fireplace set in a brick wall. It was tiny, but gorgeous.

"This is fabulous, Elisabeth!" I breathed enviously. I pushed up the window and looked out over a large cemetery. "Look at your view, it's so peaceful."

"It is if you don't mind dead people," Elisabeth said, shrugging off her fur coat and pulling on a sweater. We started to unpack while Elisabeth told me about a friend of hers who'd written a screenplay about an Englishwoman living in New York; she'd be perfect for the part if they could only get the movie financed. Lady Fitz-Waterford worried endlessly about Elisabeth's lack of employment, but I envied her ability to pick up and discard opportunities at will, her refusal to allow her artistic pursuits to be compromised by such pedestrian concerns as financial security, even though she lived a hand-to-mouth existence and refused all financial aid from her parents. There was something about the way Elisabeth moved through life that reminded me of myself back in my biking days, a freedom that wasn't fought for but simply followed. I wondered if I could go back to living this way if Charles and I divorced—with the satisfaction of being self-sufficient, of not having to ask for support from either husband or parents—but then I remembered I had four children to raise.

"Nicky, are you okay?" Elisabeth asked again, plugging a kettle into a socket. "You're very quiet today."

I opened one of the boxes and pulled out a handful of books. "Yeah. I mean, no, not really . . . kind of. Just dealing with a bit of shit at the moment."

Elisabeth leaned against the fireplace. "What sort of shit?"

"Oh, you know, just marriage shit. Charles and me, that sort of stuff," I said evasively. I turned one of her books over in my hands. Wasn't E. M. Forster gay?

"Is everything all right?"

"Yes, well, sort of . . . I can't really explain. I'm just . . ." I trailed off. I squeezed the book in between Jodorowsky and Houellebecq on the bookshelf, trying not to notice that Elisabeth was looking at me closely.

"Can I ask you something?" she said.

"Sure."

Elisabeth was still leaning against the fireplace, watching me through narrowed eyes. "Have you fallen in love with someone?"

I froze. "No . . . it's not . . ."

"So then . . ." She paused as if trying to find the right words. "Are you . . . do you think you might be questioning your sexuality?"

I turned and stared at her, my heart pulsing in my ears. "Actually," I managed to stammer, "I'm kind of . . ."

"So you're . . ."

"I think I . . ."

"You might be . . ."

"Gay?"

We looked at each other in amazement. It was unbelievable. I hadn't even had to tell her; she'd just asked, and now there it was, out in the open among all the half-unpacked boxes. "Oh my God, I feel sick," I said, sitting down on the bed.

"Nicky!" Elisabeth sat down on a trunk in front of me. "What's going on?" There was a roar from outside, the revving of a motorbike; the boxes around me lifted and rolled like waves and I clutched the bed to stop myself from pitching forward onto the floor. Elisabeth put her hand on my arm to steady me until the vertigo subsided.

"Nicky?"

I looked down at her, trying to find my voice through the surge of nausea. "Why did you . . . How did you know?"

"There's something about the whole 'wife' thing that's not quite right," she replied.

I shook my head. "You could tell?"

"I'm surrounded by gay people. I know what it looks like."

I stared at her, trying to see myself through her eyes. "Am I what 'gay' looks like?"

"There's a bit of digging to get to it, but it's there."

Warmth spread through my body, like Pinocchio turning into flesh and blood. "You can see it?"

"I can see *you*," she said. "Tell me what's been going on."

Haltingly, I told Elisabeth everything while she sat on the trunk, playing with the sleeves of her sweater. My body started to tremble with involuntary shakes. However progressive Elisabeth was, this would be too much, I'd be breaking a code of conduct, violating the unspoken rule that we should be free from the oppression of sexual desire when alone with our female friends. But Elisabeth appeared unalarmed by the news that I liked women, as if the whole conversation were perfectly normal. She even admitted she'd slept with a few women herself when she was younger and was astonished when I told her I'd never even kissed a girl. I wondered how she and I could have come from such similar backgrounds and yet have led such different lives. Where had Elisabeth found the audacity?

Elisabeth stood up and flipped up the catches on the trunk she'd been sitting on. She scooped out an armful of clothes, carried them over to the closet, and started hanging them up. "What about all your boyfriends? I mean, what about the sex?" she asked.

"Jesus, Elisabeth."

"No, seriously . . . I want to know."

Suddenly I felt like crying. How could I say out loud something I'd hardly even admitted to myself? I wrapped my arms around my legs, resting my chin on my knees. "I never liked it. I did try. I thought perhaps it was something you had to get used to, like listening to Dvořák or liking the taste of olives. But I couldn't get my body to respond properly. I thought it was my fault, like there was something wrong with me."

I couldn't share with anyone how I felt during sex, not even Elisabeth, because the only words I could find to describe it sounded too loaded. I didn't know how to explain how wrong it felt to have someone's penis inside me, how it had started to feel like a violation. I couldn't turn it around like I used to in my early twenties; the only way to get through sex now was to dissociate completely, and God forbid Charles should go anywhere near my breasts, which were so sensitive it felt like I was being tasered if they were even touched. Fortunately, we had sex only a couple of times a year, which I conveniently managed to blame on exhaustion.

"And Charles?" Elisabeth asked, as if reading my mind. "Do you love him?"

I sighed. I thought I loved him, once, but it had always felt practical, slightly mechanical, like something I had to wind up every morning. It didn't flow the way I'd expected love to flow, driven by some deep force within me.

"I'd pretty much given up on love by the time I met Charles," I admitted. "I never felt anything close to what the poets wrote about, so . . . I don't know . . . I guess I just began to question the authenticity of their descriptions. I assumed the whole notion of romantic love must be nonsense peddled by mentally unstable creative people to make the rest of us feel inadequate. Like it was the equivalent of fashion magazines promoting unattainable body images to teenagers. I didn't want to succumb to the romantic equivalent of an eating disorder."

Elisabeth was rattling the closet door on its broken hinge. She pushed a vacuum cleaner that was blocking it with her foot and slid the door closed before the ironing board fell out.

"What am I going to do?" I asked. "I'm trapped in the wrong life, but I have four children and it's their life too. I can't just drag them out of it, can I?"

Elisabeth stood still for a moment, as if she were weighing her words. "Your life . . . I know you think it's the only one, but it really isn't. I found something different. You do have choices."

"But I put myself here. I can't just walk away now; the whole thing will fall apart if I pull out. We're like parts of a machine, we all need to work together or the system won't operate. Broken homes are called broken for a reason."

I looked around at the mess of clothes spilling out of the suitcases onto the floor. I didn't want to leave this little room with all its books and its unpacked boxes. I wanted to stay here with Elisabeth forever.

Chapter Eight

When I finally surfaced from my flat a week after the Paris rave, I realized it was time to make some changes. I was approaching thirty and needed to start acting like an adult, which meant all the things I'd done for the benefit of the bikers—or my own self-indulgent conceit— now had to be undone. To start with I should never have cut my hair. If I wanted to have a normal life and a normal relationship with a normal man, I would need to start looking a bit more attractive. The masculine clothes would have to go too, as would my obsession with staying emotionally and financially independent.

But the process of reversing my masculinity turned out to be harder than expected, and instead of relieving my depression, it seemed only to make it worse. I grew my hair out, invested in some skirts and dresses, and taught myself to walk in high heels, but it all felt uncommonly difficult. My long hair felt weird and uncomfortable unless I tied it back, which rather defeated the point of having long hair in the first place. And every time I put on a skirt, my breasts became problematic, as if there were some kind of sartorial domino effect going on that always ended up with me hating my entire chest area.

The movie *Single White Female* gave me the final push I needed to start letting go of my friendship with Lola. The lack of identity, the miserable, melancholic longing—it was all too close to the bone. But I found it hard to process my grief at the loss of our relationship because I couldn't directly name it. I quit my job and took on an apprenticeship at a landscaping firm, hoping nature might offer me some relief. Instead, my depression got worse. I stopped sleeping and started having panic attacks, began to self-medicate with escalating amounts of weed and alcohol.

For three years the loneliness untethered me. I belonged nowhere, to nobody, to nothing, and the clock was ticking. More than anything I wanted children, but that would require a husband, and I was failing to muster anything beyond lackluster indifference for any of the boys I dated. I had fantasies about marrying someone who impregnated me and then immediately died of some terrible disease so I could justify not being married for the rest of my life, but this was not an easy scenario to manufacture without it somehow involving homicide, unless I married someone who was already suffering from a terrible disease, which would be weird and also complicate the impregnation part of it. And consciously chosen single motherhood? Just traipsing off to a sperm bank and coming back with a fertilized embryo? Well, that wasn't something people did in those days. Or at least not anyone I knew.

My relationships with everyone in my life became so complicated that I started to remove myself from people as much as possible. I escaped into the countryside, finding solace in the smell of the earth and the silence of the plants. I was a functioning alcoholic, but only just. My hangovers lasted longer in the morning, and my drinking started earlier in the afternoon, and the brief window of time in which I was capable of constructive work was getting shorter by the day. While I could hide my ill-health from the clients under the disguise of the disheveled gardener, I knew that sooner or later the men who ran the landscaping company were going to start asking questions. The obvious solution was to start my own company, which would leave me answerable to nobody except my clients. I committed to two years of study, earned a couple of diplomas from the English Gardening School and the Royal Horticultural Society, and launched my own business. My income was meager, but it was enough to pay for the drugs and alcohol, and now that I was my own boss I could solve the problem of my hangovers by self-medicating with vodka first thing in the morning.

I met Charles the year I turned thirty. I couldn't remember much about the New Year's Eve party where we met—I may have blacked out shortly before midnight—but I must have given someone my phone number, because a strange man called to ask me out a few days later. He invited me to fly to Amsterdam, where he was living at the time, which immediately set him apart. He rented a couple of bicycles, and we spent the afternoon browsing secondhand bookstores and drinking hot chocolate. He took me to the Van Gogh Museum and then to the floating flower market, where he bought a large bunch of sunflowers. He looked sweetly comical as he bicycled through the cobbled streets with the flowers tucked under one arm, wobbling furiously as he turned back to grin at me, his shirttails flapping in the breeze.

Over dinner in a dimly lit restaurant he entertained me with stories of his travels, his political views, his vast knowledge of current affairs, while I wondered what it would feel like to fall in love with someone who could love me back. After dinner we walked back to his apartment along the Prinsengracht. Charles seemed relaxed and confident, and it was a relief to let someone else take the lead for once. He asked me little about myself during the evening, but I didn't mind; I didn't know who I was anyway, and I didn't much want to tell him about the person I'd been. As we crossed a bridge over the canal it started to snow, and I wondered whether it was a sign. The date couldn't have been more romantic, and if I wasn't feeling it, then there must be something wrong with me. Maybe it just wasn't my destiny to feel that all-consuming fire, maybe I'd been born without the necessary pilot light. If I was looking for stability, then Charles fit the bill. I should give him a chance.

A month later Charles moved back to London, and we started spending more time together. My friends and family adored him. He was a good-looking man, tall and broad-shouldered with bright blue eyes, and his overt masculinity and massive stature made me feel petite and feminine by comparison. When I wore dresses and high heels, his eyes lit up, as if I were truly beautiful, and when he showed me off to his friends, he did so with pride. He invited me as his date to an ex-girlfriend's wedding in the South of France, and I understood the assignment. I took great care in choosing my outfit, dieting myself down to a size zero, getting expensive highlights to bring out the once-natural blonde in my hair. The wedding reception was held at the couple's property perched on the hillsides of Provence, and as we walked through the arbor of flowers that led to the garden, I heard someone whisper, "Who's *she*?" Charles heard it too, and we both knew I'd passed the test.

I started getting to know Charles's quirks and habits. He read only biographies or history books, and his newspaper of choice was the *Financial Times*. He felt most confident at dinner parties talking about politics, and he was ambitious in his career, driven by a deep-seated urge to impress his father. He enjoyed watching rugby at the pub with the boys, but he wasn't a big drinker; he loved the countryside and was delighted by my newly launched career as a landscape designer; but most of all, he seemed to appreciate the fact that I could cook.

His apparent emotional stability, however, was offset by a lack of practicality that might have been alarming if it hadn't brought out my best qualities. He was forgetful and could rarely get anywhere on time; he was constantly losing his keys, his wallet, or his phone; and he seemed to be so completely incapable of running a household that I was amazed he'd survived for so long on his own. One evening while I was in his flat cooking for a dinner party, the gas got shut off because he'd forgotten to pay the gas bill, so I had to carry the entire meal back to my flat, finish cooking it in my own oven, and then rush it all back to his place before the guests started arriving. It was clear he needed looking after, and I was more than capable of rising to the challenge.

Soon Charles started to talk about owning a house in the country, somewhere we could have a bigger kitchen, throw better parties, plant our own garden. We never argued because I never disagreed with anything he said. If I felt doubt, I kept it to myself. Charles didn't like people with messy emotions—I could tell from the way he talked about his exes—so I was careful not to let him see how much I was drinking. I glossed over the more complicated aspects of my past, hid the fact that I was still chronically depressed, and made sure he never picked up on my weird feelings about women. Charles wanted a calm, harmonious relationship, so that's what I gave him.

It was less than a year before Charles proposed, although in truth it wasn't even a real proposal. We were drunk after a party one night—a rare occurrence for Charles, if not for me—and he said, "So d'you want to get married then?" I said, "Yeah, all right," and when we woke up the next morning we were both hungover and engaged. Charles went off to work while I lay in bed wondering what was supposed to happen now. Wasn't I meant to be feeling more than this? I tried to picture the future Charles had painted for us: a house in the country surrounded by a beautiful garden, a large kitchen full of children, a dog curled up in front of a crackling log fire. It was so warm, so familiar and nostalgic. Who wouldn't choose this life? Then I tried to overlay the image with another picture, any picture of any other future, but I couldn't do it. There was no other future I could see.

What I did see, a few weeks later, was *Kissing Jessica Stein,* a movie about an annoying straight, white girl who tried to become a lesbian because she was fed up with dating shitty men. She went through the whole rigmarole of coming out to her family before discovering that she didn't actually like lesbian sex, and then had to go through the excruciating process of retracting her publicly declared lesbianism before going back to her nice straight life. The movie's message was crystal clear.

We started planning the wedding, but the whole ordeal of having to try on wedding dresses and look permanently happy proved more stressful than I'd anticipated. Charles seemed to be taking it in stride—partly because he was leaving all the arrangements to me—while my drinking got progressively worse. During our engagement party, when I found myself snorting lines of coke in a toilet stall with a complete stranger, it began to occur to me that my accelerating drug use might be a bit of a problem after we got married. Bags of weed and coke were harder to explain away than empty bottles of vodka, even if they were easier to hide. Eventually I woke one morning to find myself lying on the floor, surrounded by empty bottles of wine and overflowing ashtrays. Beside me was my journal, which was filled with page after page of desperate scrawl, the writing growing increasingly illegible as I'd got more incoherently drunk. There was something wrong with me, something possibly genetic I might pass down to my children, something related to a recurring nightmare I'd started having about doing something unspeakable to myself with a gun. *I can't marry him*, I wrote, the writing smudged as if I'd been crying. *I can't, I can't.*

In retrospect that was probably the moment when I should have asked for help, but there was no one to ask. Everyone was invested in the wedding. And what would I have said? *There's something terribly wrong but I don't know what it is?* You need a pretty good reason to call off an engagement. Charles was a good man; everyone loved him, especially my parents. "Don't fuck this one up," my mother said the first time I brought him home, neatly echoing everyone's opinion that fucking things up was a thing I tended to do.

Instead of talking to Charles about any of this, I decided to write a list of reasons why I should get married:

1. I am unhappy and I don't know why
2. My parents are happy in their life
3. Before I went to boarding school, I was also happy in that life
4. Everyone agrees it was a very nice life for which I should be grateful
5. Because I cannot find the cause of my unhappiness, the problem must be me
6. If I'm the problem, I should focus on making everyone else happy
7. Which I can do by marrying Charles, whom everybody loves
8. Hopefully if everyone else is happy, I will be happy
9. This is a gamble, but the alternative is to kill myself

The fact that I wasn't in therapy and was an active alcoholic might have been a contributing factor in how wildly misguided this thinking turned out to be, but at least it helped me recognize that my drinking had become a bit of a problem, because my drinking *had* become a bit of a problem. So, I joined a twelve-step program and gave up alcohol—along with my motorbike, my leathers, my homegrown weed, and my outstanding commitment to my coke dealer—and went ahead with the marriage.

Charles took to our new life like a duck to water. Shortly after we married, he got a promotion, so he bought a rambling old house in the country, which I set about decorating. I planted the garden and improved my cooking skills and tried to make friends with all the other upper-middle-class housewives who lived in the area, while my career in landscaping was slowly relegated to the status of a respectable hobby. Charles was thrilled when I finally got pregnant, and although the preeclampsia I developed was a mild worry for him—he was a little alarmed by all the blood when I hemorrhaged after the birth—when the baby and I both survived he returned to work, secure in the knowledge that he wouldn't have to change nappies or wake in the night for bottle feeds, because I respected his need to remain well rested. The arrival of a second baby eighteen months later came a little sooner than he planned, but I seemed to be managing okay, and it gave him a sense of deep joy to come home on the weekends to the family he'd always dreamed of. Usually I'd organize a house party, or we'd be invited to dinner by one of our new friends, but if it was just us, Charles would put Freddie in a backpack and take him out for a long walk with the dog in the morning, stopping occasionally to pick blackberries or let Freddie jump in puddles, while I stayed home with Alfie, cooking the Sunday roast. After lunch, Charles would settle down with a newspaper in front of the fire while I did the clearing up, Charles usually falling asleep in front of the television while I got the kids ready for bed. It was exactly the life Charles had expected when he married me. He never knew I was unhappy, because I never told him. Anyway, there was nothing for me to be unhappy about. He provided me with everything I needed.

I didn't know why I was unhappy either. My main problem still seemed to lie with my enduring inability to feel like the sort of woman I was pretending to be. I couldn't figure out what I was doing wrong. I loved parenthood—alone with my children was the only time I felt like myself—but marriage had reduced me to the roles of wife and mother, and the harder I tried to adapt to these roles, the more I seemed to fail. I wasn't witty, sweet, or charming enough, my house wasn't perfect enough, my parties weren't glamorous enough, my heels weren't high enough, my body wasn't thin enough.

Sometimes I'd remember how simple everything had been when I was just one of the boys, but I knew there was deception in nostalgia. I was remembering how I'd wished things had been, not how they actually were. I'd never had the authority of a real man, as I'd been reminded one day at the hardware store when all the men behind the counter ignored me because I wasn't one of them, although I was clad in my biker gear. When I'd gone back to the same hardware store as a feminine woman, the men had climbed all over each other to serve me. There was power in femininity—even if that power depended on the male gaze—and since all the women around me seemed to enjoy the male gaze, the problem, yet again, must lie with me.

And then Charles got offered a job in New York, which was obviously my chance to escape. I imagined us raising our children in Brooklyn. We wouldn't need a big house because we'd find friends who cared about each other more than they cared about wealth or social status. We wouldn't need a large garden because we'd have bookstores and coffee shops and parks to play in. I wouldn't need to keep up with these impossible standards of rich, white womanhood because I'd be surrounded by people who tested boundaries, and broke rules, and refused to conform. Starting over in Brook-lyn, I might finally be able to be the sort of person I wanted to be.

Except that Charles didn't want to live in Brooklyn, of course. He wanted to live in Connecticut. And Charles earned the money, so he had the final say.

Chapter Nine

It was a Sunday evening a month or so after the motorcycle rally, and I'd just finished putting the children to bed. Charles had been out walking the dog during the bath time–story time–bedtime routine, and I came downstairs to find him in the kitchen, standing by the fridge, eating cold chicken salad out of a container.

"TV?" he asked, walking over to the sofa and picking up the remote.

"I think I'll do some writing," I said. I wondered whether he'd comment on my reluctance to join him, but he just switched on the television and started channel surfing. I wandered into my office, sat down in front of my computer, and opened my journal. I paused briefly to hear whether anyone was stirring in the house, but the children's bedrooms were silent. Writing about being a lesbian felt like a small act of rebellion, a way to reclaim something that belonged only to me. *I want to be with a woman*, I wrote. *I want to touch a woman, I want to kiss a woman, I want to fall in love with a woman*. I stopped and looked at the words, feeling like someone had cut a hole in my heart. *I want it, I want it, I want it.*

But what would I have to sacrifice to get it? If I divorced Charles, then what? Where was I supposed to find the time to work? There was nobody else waking up for crying babies in the middle of the night, or staying home if the children were sick, or clearing up vomit, or breaking up fights, or listening to problems, or helping with homework, or doing any of the actual parenting. It was just me. As Charles often reminded me, if he didn't get enough rest, he'd either lose his job or die of a heart attack. So if I had no way of earning money, and Charles didn't have the skills to parent the kids, how could we possibly split?

I pictured the kids upstairs, snuggled safely under their comforters. Freddie was the one I worried about the most. He already suffered from anxiety and was prone to panic attacks; how would he survive the disruption if his father and I separated? And yet how would I survive if we didn't? The quiet sounds of the house seemed to grow around me, as if I could hear the individual heartbeats of my sleeping children, the gentle snore of the puppy in the kitchen, my husband nodding off in front of the television. I bent forward over my keypad, choked by a paralyzing feeling of loss. Somewhere deep inside me I must have always known that this wasn't my life. None of it belonged to me. I was going to have to give it all back.

The phone rang and I lurched back into the present. "You haven't signed up yet!" It was Bianca.

"Signed up?" I looked at my computer, realizing with panic that my journal was still open. Could she see it? No, of course she couldn't, she was on the phone. I clicked on Print so I could store a hardcopy of the pages I'd written before closing the document.

"The volunteer spot at the bookfair. You promised."

The last page appeared out of the printer smeared with ink. The Low Ink light flashed on the screen. "Oh God, I forgot. Okay, I'll do it now." I stopped the printer, replaced the cartridge, scrunched up the piece of paper that hadn't printed properly, and threw it into the wastepaper basket.

"What's going on?" Bianca sounded irritated, as if she could tell I wasn't giving her my full attention. "People have been asking about you. It's like you've dropped off the face of the earth."

"Sorry, I've just been a bit overwhelmed recently. I'll sign up right now, I promise."

I hung up the phone, reprinted the last page, pulled the sheets of paper out of the printer, carried them through to my bedroom, and hid them away carefully in a box high up on the top shelf of my wardrobe. Then I sat down on the bed, waiting for the knot in my gut to loosen.

I was brushing my teeth the following morning when Charles appeared in the bathroom doorway.

"Nicky," he said, leaning heavily against the doorjamb. I spat out my toothpaste and looked up at him in the mirror. He'd nicked himself slightly with his razor just beneath his chin, and the shaving rash on his neck was vivid against the starched white collar of his shirt.

"I was sitting at the kitchen table having breakfast." His voice sounded measured, as if he was trying to keep it steady. What was he doing in my bathroom? He never disturbed me during my morning routine. And why hadn't he left for work yet? Had he missed his train? I blinked expectantly as I pulled the hand towel off the rail. Should I reach up and wipe off the drop of blood on his neck before it stained his shirt? He ran his hand over his head; he was shaking slightly.

"I was sitting at the breakfast table eating my toast," Charles repeated, as if this piece of information were somehow vital. His voice sounded thick with effort. "Biscuit came up to me. She had something in her mouth." I looked down at his other hand. He was holding a crumpled sheet of paper. "I didn't take it," he said, sounding almost apologetic. "She just put it in my lap." It was the last page from my journal, the one I'd thrown in the trash. The words were still legible beneath a smear of printer ink and puppy saliva. "I'm not sure if I should have read it," Charles continued. "I'm not sure whether it was the right thing to do." He put the piece of paper on the counter and we both stared at it, as if a movie camera had zoomed in, close focus. It was so quiet I could hear the drip of the shower faucet. "I think it's a page from your journal. It says . . ." I watched his lips form the words, as if he were speaking in slow motion. "It says that you think you're gay."

I put my hand on the side of the basin to steady myself.

"Is it true?" He was looking directly at me. "Nicky, is it true?"

I opened my mouth but nothing came out. *We can't do this now, not here in the bathroom, what if we wake the children?* But it was too late, we were already doing it. I fought the urge to blurt out, *It's not my fault!* How could I possibly explain? I hadn't even had a cup of coffee yet. Comprehension dawned on his face as my silence answered his question. I had a sudden urge to laugh. "I've been wanting to talk to you," I said. "I didn't know how."

Charles frowned, as if struggling with some kind of revelation. I stood motionless, waiting for the explosion, but before I realized what was happening he pulled me towards him, hugging me into his chest. He didn't speak, just held his big arms around me, my face muffled against his shirt. I breathed in the smell of the fabric softener I used on the children's clothes. Mountain Spring. It didn't smell anything like a mountain in the spring. I pulled away and looked up at him.

"Are you okay?" he asked.

I shook my head. "Are *you* okay?"

He rubbed his forehead. "I think we have a lot to talk about."

"Yes, maybe tonight we can . . ."

"This hasn't come as a huge surprise."

"It . . . Wait, what?"

"I'm not sure I'd have come up with this by myself, but it does make sense."

"It does?"

"I've seen how you react to certain women."

"You have?"

"I know you get crushes on women. I could probably name most of them."

I couldn't fathom why he was being so calm, given the magnitude of what he'd just learned about me. Where was the disbelief, the rage? He smoothed out the piece of paper still sitting on the counter. "You wrote . . . It says here that you're not having an affair, you haven't been unfaithful to me. Is that true?"

"Yes, it is."

"Well that makes a difference. If you'd slept with someone else, that would have changed things, but you haven't."

"There's no one else involved."

"Okay, well, I think that's important." He straightened his jacket and tucked his shirt into his trousers, organizing himself. "I have to go to work now, but we can talk about it tonight." And he turned and walked out of the bathroom.

The minute I heard his car leave, I called Elisabeth. "Elisabeth, I just got outed by the dog!"

"Outed by the who . . . by what?" Elisabeth's voice was muffled with sleep.

"The dog, Elisabeth! Biscuit outed me to Charles! I wouldn't believe it myself if it hadn't just happened!"

I heard Elisabeth surface from under her duvet. "Oh my God, tell me everything!" I started to feel slightly euphoric. Perhaps he'd seen it coming, Elisabeth suggested when I told her about Charles's reaction. Maybe he was as relieved as I was that we could finally talk about it. Perhaps it wasn't so far-fetched to believe we could redefine our relationship, figure out a way to co-parent amicably. "You could move to Brooklyn!" Elisabeth said, and I allowed myself to be swept up in the idea. If we rented a couple of apartments next to each other, the kids would be able to run freely between the two homes. It would be unconventional, but as long as the children knew they had the love of both parents, surely they'd be fine. Charles would be free to start having sex again after the long drought of our marriage, and I could go back to being the person I was when I was hanging with the bikers. I could run my own household, make my own decisions, earn my own money, hold my own opinions. I'd be me again. The thought made me almost giddy with excitement. Maybe I'd even buy another motorbike.

I went upstairs to wake the children. "Mummy, why are you dancing?" Lily asked as I drew the curtains. I picked her up by the armpits and swung her out of her toddler bed "Because now you get to be anything you want to be when you grow up!"

"Anything?"

"Yes, anything!"

"Even a penguin?"

"Even a penguin!" I bent her over, as if we were doing the tango, and then swung her back up again, pirouetting around the room. "I'm coming out," I sang. "I want the world to know, I want to let it show . . ."

Charles's arrival back home that evening was announced by the grinding of the coffee machine in the kitchen. I shut the door to Freddie's bedroom and tiptoed downstairs to find him waiting for me on the sofa. He was balancing his coffee cup on his knee with one hand, the other arm spread out across the top of the sofa cushions.

"Hey," I said, sitting down on the coffee table. "How are you doing?"

He shrugged. "Well, it's not every day you find out your wife thinks she's a lesbian, but . . ." He trailed off. This sounded like typical British reserve. It must have come as a shock to him, regardless of his suspicions, and Charles wasn't a man who liked to be taken unawares. And yet his face betrayed no trace of the kind of emotion I had expected to see in someone who was about to address the end of his marriage. This level of self-control was disconcerting, and it made me nervous.

"I'm sorry, Charles, I really am. I wanted to tell you, I was trying to find a way." I searched his face for any glimpse of distress. "Are you angry?"

"No, I'm glad it's out in the open," he replied, crossing his legs.

"Me too," I agreed.

"Does anyone else know?"

"Only Elisabeth."

"You told her?"

"She kind of asked." I hunched over my knees, curling my toes as if I could make myself smaller. "It was unavoidable."

"Well, at least she's in New York and doesn't know anyone up here. No one else knows?"

"No."

"Good. Okay. Well, that's something. And you really haven't slept with anyone else?"

"No, it's just been theoretical up until this point."

"Okay, then this can be contained." He leaned forward and put his coffee cup down on the coffee table. "I know you're going to need to talk about it," he said, leaning back again. "But you've got me and Elisabeth, so that should be enough."

I squinted at him. "Okay, I understand that for now, but at some stage I might want to talk to my parents, or—"

"Why would you need to talk to them?"

"Because this changes things."

"How?"

"Because I'm gay."

"Right. I know that, and you know that, but nobody else needs to know that."

I began to wonder whether we were talking at cross-purposes. "Charles, this attraction to women isn't like wanting a side order of fries. I'm not bisexual, I'm gay, I'm *only* attracted to women. I'm not attracted to men at all." Charles looked at me blankly, as if he didn't understand the significance.

"Which means at some stage we're going to have to start discussing ways in which we can reformat the family to accommodate this."

"What do you mean?" Charles frowned. "We're not going to reformat the family. We can accommodate this by me knowing you're gay, and you having me to talk to about it. That's as far as it needs to go."

"But we need to start talking about the possible implications of all this. Like how at some stage, I'm probably going to want to be with a woman."

Charles looked at me as if he had no idea what I was talking about. "But that's not possible. We're married."

"Yes, I know . . ."

"And you said you hadn't slept with anyone."

"I haven't yet, but in the future—"

Charles's jaw tightened. "In the future what?"

"I mean, at some point, separation is something we're going to have to—"

"Separation? Why are we talking about separation?"

"Well . . . aren't we?" Now I was confused. "Isn't that usually the first step before divorce?"

My words seemed to hit him with physical force. He rocked forward slightly. I almost put out my hands to catch him, this giant of a man, but he steadied himself, putting both hands on his knees.

"Are you okay?" I asked. Charles didn't reply. He seemed to be struggling to breathe. "Charles, I didn't mean to . . . I don't . . ."

"Why would you want to divorce me?" he managed to say.

I was at a loss. "I thought *you* would want to divorce *me*. I thought you'd be angry. I thought you'd throw me out."

"Why would I do that?"

"What else do you do when you discover your wife's a lesbian?"

"We've been in this marriage for ten years, Nicky. I've always been here for you."

This was true. Charles saw himself as my rock, my savior, the stabilizing force that kept me centered when I lost sight of who I was supposed to be. Suddenly I understood why Charles had reacted to my alleged lesbianism with such complacency: he must have thought it was just another quirk that with careful management could be absorbed by the marriage, just as all the others had been.

"This is different, Charles," I said. "This isn't about us; it's about me. It's not something you can help me with. I need to figure this out on my own, which means I don't think we can stay married."

The room went quiet as my words sunk in. Then the blood started to rise in Charles's face. Too late, I realized my mistake. This was an ambush. He was completely unprepared. He'd never known the person I'd been when I was with the bikers, the person who had complete autonomy over herself and her life, because I'd never shown her to him. And now here I was, the recipient of ten years of his benevolence, inexplicably telling him I didn't want to be saved anymore.

Charles heaved himself up off the sofa as if fighting some huge force and walked over to the window seat. I turned to face him, but he was standing with his back to me. I tried to soften my voice, make myself sound a little more feminine, hoping it might appease him.

"It's not like we need to make any changes in a hurry. But, for example, in the long term, if we moved to Brooklyn maybe we could live in two apartments near each other . . . We could possibly do it here, too, if we found a house with a guest cottage . . . I mean, I'm not saying you'd have to live in the guest cottage . . . but it would probably be better in Brooklyn because it's a little more progressive . . . My point is, if we were in the same building but different apartments then we'd have some space from each other, and you'd be able to . . . And I'd be able to . . ."

He turned. My words dried up as I saw the expression on his face. "We made a commitment when we started this family. I have not invested all this time and money into this marriage just to see it go to waste."

"Yes, but—"

"*But?*" he shot back.

I didn't know what to say. I groped around in my head for another suggestion to offer him, but I had nothing. Divorce was all I had. Divorce was all I wanted.

"This is our *life*, Nicky. We have responsibilities. Isn't your first obligation towards your children?"

"Yes, of course it is, but I also need to . . ."

"We're not going to just up sticks and relocate to Brooklyn on a whim. Don't you think the welfare of our family is a little more important than some sudden desire to go off and find yourself?"

"*Find myself?* I'm not talking about backpacking around India!"

"You might as well be. You're acting like it!"

I took a breath, trying to stem the adrenaline that was now flooding my body. "I need to accept that I'm a lesbian," I said, speaking as slowly as possible. "And you and I need to start talking about how that might impact our family."

"This will *not* impact our family!" Sweat was beginning to break out on Charles's forehead. "If people find out you're a lesbian we'll all be fucked. Have you stopped to consider what it would do to the kids? They won't get asked on playdates anymore, they'll get bullied at school. Not to mention the trauma they'll suffer if we separate. Do you have any idea what divorce does to children? How much damage it causes? If anyone finds out you're gay it will fuck up our children's lives forever. Do you really want that on your conscience?"

I was momentarily speechless. "Then what do you suggest I do?"

"I suggest you . . . I don't know . . . watch some lesbian porn and get over it!"

"I've tried my whole life to get over it; it hasn't worked!"

"Then we'll have to get you some more help, increase your sessions with Henry. We probably need to check your medication too."

"Wait, you think there's a *pill* for this?"

"Oh, for God's sake, be reasonable. How would you even meet anyone anyway? You're a forty-year-old married house-wife raising four children in the suburbs, and all the lesbians live in Brooklyn."

"I know. That's why I suggested . . ."

"So you want to uproot our entire family just so you can go hook up with some random woman in a bar? Come on, Nicky, it's not exactly like you've had great judgment before. I mean, look at your history—your alcoholism, your anxiety, your breakdown—it's not like you're a very stable person, is it?"

I felt the breath leave my body. Had his opinion of me always been this low? If he thought so poorly of me, why did he want to stay married to me? Or more to the point, if he'd been aware of how much I'd been struggling, why hadn't he tried to talk to me about it? Why hadn't he tried to help?

"Please, Charles, I've been so unhappy . . ."

"Then learn how to hide it!"

"*Hide* it?"

"Yes, hide it! I will not have your unhappiness damaging our children."

"How do you expect me to do that?"

"If I can do it, you can. Do you think I'm happy about you being gay? About having to make the choice between resigning myself to a sexless marriage or fucking up our children's lives? There's no good outcome for me, is there?"

"So we're just going to lie to everyone? Pretend nothing's changed?"

"Exactly," he said.

"This is madness, I can't do it!"

"Well, you'd better start practicing," Charles replied acidly. "Because you're going to be doing it a lot from now on."

Chapter Ten

The following morning Charles showered and dressed for work while I prepared breakfast for the children. I held my breath when he came into the kitchen, but he just walked over to the coffee maker and started spooning in fresh grounds, leaning against the counter and talking to me about his work schedule as if the previous night had never happened. There was nothing aggressive about his body language, no trace of anger in his face. Today was just another day, as would tomorrow be, and the day after that, and so on for the next forty years until we were both dead. I watched his car disappear up the drive with a sense of dread. Silence was the tool our people used to shut down any attempt at rebellion. If an insurgence was neither acknowledged nor discussed, it held no legitimacy.

I tried to access some hidden well of compassion for my husband—given that I'd just torn his life apart—but during the morning all my attempts at empathy were drowned under a rising tide of fury. I'd seen him like this before, on the phone with clients: the forceful manipulation of the opposing party into a corner, the hardness in his voice as he reached the end of the transaction, his determination to leave no room for negotiation. I just never thought he'd use these tactics on me.

I sat in the car in the school parking lot at lunchtime, waiting for the girls to be let out of preschool. Charles hadn't asked me a single question before he shut me down. Maybe he didn't want to know what I'd been going through. Maybe he didn't care. Or maybe he thought I was making the whole thing up. If that were the case, he wouldn't want to validate my feelings with displays of curiosity or compassion; he'd want to make absolutely sure no one found out, to frighten me into silence until I came to my senses. I wound down the window but still felt like I was suffocating.

"Nicky? Are you okay?"

I looked up to see Bianca peering through the car window at me. "Yes. I mean, no. I mean, oh Jesus, Bianca . . ."

"What is it, Nicky? What's going on?"

"I don't . . . I can't talk about it yet . . ."

"Okay," she said. She looked disturbed, almost frightened. "But I'm here for you. Any time you need me, whenever you're ready to talk, I'm here. Promise you'll call if you need me?"

"I promise."

I gathered up Lily and Rose from the playground when the teacher let them out of their classroom, the storm still churning inside me. I strapped the girls into their car seats, turned up the music, and headed for the store, hoping I could get through the grocery shopping before I split apart at the seams. The car in front of me slowed down and I jammed on my brake. The stoplight turned green and I leaned on my horn. The car in front of me started to move again and I lurched forward. Did Charles really think I was going to spend the rest of my life playacting happy? But of course. Misery was a socially unacceptable emotion, always had been, ever since I was a kid. Nobody ever bothered to question why I was unhappy or suggested that it might be a good idea to find out. They just told me to stop, and if I couldn't stop, at least not show it. That's why I'd got myself into this mess in the first place. I'd been conditioned to hide everything, trained to shut down any part of myself that made other people uncomfortable. So obviously this was Charles's go-to solution for the problem. That's what people like us did. We were experts at it.

But something had opened up at that motorcycle rally, and now forty years of pent-up rage was spewing out. Pure, unbridled fury at anyone who'd prevented me from asking the most basic questions about myself. Was this what had been trapped inside me for forty years? No wonder my body had started to break down under the pressure.

At the store, the patience I usually employed with the girls was entirely beyond my reach. Rose climbed on and off the side of the cart, making it impossible for me to move, while Lily disappeared down an aisle and had already opened two boxes of cereal and emptied them onto the floor by the time I found her. Rose filled my cart with things we didn't need, and while I stuffed them all back on a random shelf, Lily vanished again. I stormed around the store shouting her name, got her back to the cart, pushed it towards the checkout, and was trying to get all the food onto the belt as quickly as I could when Rose broke free and started running towards the exit door.

"Rose! Get back here!" I yelled, charging after her. I could see the automatic door start to open as she reached it, and I lunged forward and grabbed her by the wrist. "You never,

ever leave the store without Mummy! There are cars out there! You will get run over!" I yanked her back into the store and she flipped round like a rubber chicken, letting out a high-pitched shriek.

"Ow, Mummy! Ow!" she cried, her face dissolving in shock. I let go of her wrist and she hugged her arm to her chest, cradling her elbow with her hand. "You hurt my arm, Mummy!"

I scooped her up onto my hip and carried her, sobbing, back to the till, aware that we were attracting the attention of the people around us. I thrust the bags into the cart, Rose howling on my hip, and wheeled it quickly towards the exit, desperate to escape the accusatory stares of the other shoppers.

Rose started screaming again as soon as I tried to put her inside the car, as if any movement was causing her excruciating pain. Once she was strapped into her car seat, she went dead quiet.

"Does it hurt if you keep it still?" I asked, dread rising. She shook her head, staring at me wide-eyed. I touched her elbow and she started crying again. Dear God, what had I done? I put Lily into her seat and climbed blindly into the front of the car. "I'm going to take you to a doctor, poppet," I said, watching Rose's terrified face in the rearview mirror as I backed out of the parking space. "We're going to the doctor right now. Mummy's sorry. It's going to be okay, poppet. We'll go to the doctor right now."

In the exam room at the ER, I held Rose on my lap, while Lily sat on the floor with a picture book. Rose closed her eyes and leaned back against me, her arm lying still in her lap. I felt her breathing slow as she started to fall asleep. The room was quiet, apart from the small shuffling sounds of Lily turning the pages of her book. I rested my cheek on top of Rose's head, breathing in the smell of her hair. Only the night before I'd been defiant in the face of Charles's suggestion that I try to regulate my emotions, but now that very lack of regulation had resulted in one of my children being hurt. What sort of person had I become? Charles was right: I wasn't a pioneer, I was an immature little fool, and this selfish journey towards self-fulfillment wasn't just narcissistic and idealistic, it was dangerous.

There was a knock at the door and the doctor came in. "Let's have a look, shall we?" he said softly, feeling Rose's elbow. He woke her gently, and she sat up, blinking as she tried to remember where she was.

"It's all right, poppet, the doctor's here, he's going to make you better again," I whispered.

The doctor repositioned her on my lap. "Hold her tight," he said to me. He placed one hand on her shoulder, took her tiny forearm in the other hand, and twisted her elbow back into its socket. Rose let out an earsplitting scream and spasmed with the pain, turning rigid in my arms. I buried my face in her hair. "Mummy's here, Mummy's here," I whispered until I felt her relax back against me.

"All done," the doctor said. "She'll be fine now."

Rose turned and put her arms around my neck, clinging to me, as a social worker arrived with a pamphlet on nursemaid's elbow. She explained that she was obliged to let me know it was something the child protection services were trained to keep an eye out for. My mind raced to criminal records; divorce courts; custody battles; Charles standing in front of a judge citing my alcoholism and unstable mental health, claiming I was an unfit mother.

"Can you tell me what happened?" the social worker asked.

"She . . . she was holding on to the side of the shopping cart and she tripped. She must have twisted her arm when she fell." I glanced down at Lily, willing her not to say anything. Rose buried her face in my shoulder, and the social worker smiled at me reassuringly. *But of course*, her expression said. *You're clearly such a kind and loving mother, I didn't for a minute think that you'd hurt your own child.*

That evening I gave Lily and Rose their baths while Freddie and Alfie ran up and down the hallway in their pajamas, fighting each other with plastic lightsabers. By the time the girls had finished trying to wash each other's hair, the bathroom was flooded with bubbles. I lifted them out of the soapy water, wrapped them in warm towels, and cuddled them until they dried. Then I let them somersault across their bedroom floor until they'd worn themselves out, helped them into their nighties, and curled up with them on the beanbag to read a bedtime story. This was usually my favorite part of the day, their warm little bodies relaxed against mine, their heartbeats slowing as they slipped into sleep, but tonight I was full of apprehension and fear.

I tucked them into their toddler beds and turned on the night-light, then went through to Alfie's room. He sat beside me on the bed, playing with the rough skin on my elbow while he told me about a minor brush with authority he'd had earlier that afternoon when his kindergarten teacher caught him dancing on his desk to "Party Rock Anthem" by LMFAO. She seemed to have taken particular exception to the hip-swinging move Alfie had copied from the music video, so we had a little chat about how this kind of self-expression might best be confined to his weekly breakdancing lessons and about the dangers of too much YouTube, and then I tucked him into bed and gave him his goodnight kiss.

"I love you all the grains of sand on the beach," he said sleepily.

"And I love you all the drops of water in the sea."

Freddie was already in bed, reading a *Star Wars* book to himself, when I went through to his room. I climbed in next to him and helped him finish the story. Freddie had been suffering from bad dreams recently, so when it was time to turn out his light I sat on the floor by his door, waiting for him to fall asleep. I'd been doing this more frequently recently, which meant his anxiety level had been rising. Sometimes I'd have to sit here for a couple of hours, but I didn't mind. I wanted to be there for my children; I wanted to answer every question, listen to every story, acknowledge every slight or upset, validate every feeling. I needed them to know that it was okay to be human, that they didn't always have to be happy to be loved.

There were times when that felt impossibly hard. When they were younger, I often woke in the night to find more than two of them crying at once. Those were the moments when I wondered if I had it in me to meet even the basic expectations of motherhood. I was so exhausted I was almost hallucinating; I could carry only two children at a time, and my inability to soothe whichever one I couldn't hold made me frantic with anxiety. But this was how my children had made an adult of me. Nobody else was going to step in and help me in the middle of the night, nobody else was going to comfort my children if I couldn't. All I could do was give them my best and hope it would be enough.

When I was certain Freddie was asleep, I went back through to the girls' room. I was too tired to think, too tired to cry, too tired to feel anything except a bone-aching fear for my children. I watched the gentle rise and fall of Rose's chest, soothing myself with the rhythm of her breathing until eventually I fell asleep on the beanbag. I woke to hear Charles clunking around in the kitchen. I smoothed the hair away from Rose's face; her long eyelashes were curled against her soft, pink cheeks, her expression peaceful, as if the accident had never happened. But it *had* happened. And to make matters worse, I'd lied at the hospital, using my obvious wealth and the whiteness of my skin to buy my innocence.

I came downstairs to find Charles standing by the fridge, stirring sugar into a cup of coffee. "Charles," I said, "something happened today. Something bad."

Charles looked at me. The teaspoon froze in his hand when he saw the expression on my face.

The tears came before I could stop them. "I'm so sorry, I didn't mean to hurt her."

I pulled up a chair at the kitchen table and told him what I'd done. Charles's face softened as he sat down opposite me. He almost seemed relieved. "I'm glad you told me about it," he said.

"How could I not tell you? She's your daughter too." I gazed miserably at a small vase of flowers that Lily had picked earlier that week, now sitting forlornly beside a box of crayons and one of Rose's hair ties in the middle of the table. "I don't want to hurt our children," I said, wiping my eyes with the back of my hand. "It just hadn't occurred to me that you might want to stay married to me once you found out I was gay."

"Maybe we're lucky this happened now, before it got any more out of hand."

Perhaps he was right. What if I really did have terrible judgment? What if the exhilarating freedom I'd briefly felt the day before when I'd thought our marriage was over was simply part of some greater midlife crisis? I'd always dreamed of escape, but I should have left such asinine fantasies behind me when I sold my motorbike. Escape meant leaving my children, which I'd never do.

"Nicky, if you stay with me, I'll give you everything you've ever wanted." Charles's face was a picture of compassion. "You know that my love for you is unconditional, right? I understand if you don't want to have sex with me anymore. It's not like we have sex much anyway. I'll willingly sacrifice that part of our life."

"How can you be okay with that?"

There was a beat, and then Charles said, "Because the kids come first."

I winced as the image of little Rose appeared in my mind, the terrible confusion of need and love and fear on her face. Charles's commitment to the family didn't make much sense given how little he was at home, but I was too exhausted to question it. If Charles was willing to give up sex for the sake of the kids, then obviously I could too. Surely it was best just to take the path of least resistance. I couldn't do this by myself. Who else did I have except Charles? The world was set up for heterosexual people, fighting it was too much hard work, so much easier to just let it go and not have to think about it anymore. It was only sex. How much could it matter? What was I dreaming of anyway, the love of a perfect woman?

"Nicky, we can do this. I know I can make you happy." Charles leaned forward, hope written all over his face. "I promise you we can do this together."

Maybe all of this had happened because we didn't spend enough time together. Maybe I didn't have enough support and I was finally cracking under the strain. Maybe I was just terribly tired. Maybe I was clinically depressed.

"Okay," I said. "If you really want to stay married, maybe we can find a way."

I lasted about a week before I broke. I wanted to choose my husband, to fight for my marriage, but it felt like trying to turn my brain around inside my skull. Nothing felt real. Nothing made sense. Did Charles really believe he loved me? There was no substance to our relationship, it was an empty structure built on the rituals of working and parenting and entertaining. As a father he was there only for the good parts—as soon as the arguing or crying began he always left the house—so why was he putting the children first now, when he never had before?

I woke at midnight from a recurring nightmare about shooting myself in the groin with a gun. Rolling away from my husband, I curled as close to the edge of the bed as I could get, wishing I could scrape the dream out of my mind. From my fetal position I could hear the ticking of the grandfather clock in the hallway turning the seconds of my life into minutes, hours, days, years—time that I'd never get back—and with every tick the voice in my head got louder, until it was drowning out every other thought: *You never get to be with a woman, ever. You never get to be with a woman, ever.* The fear of being alone had propelled me into this marriage, but the isolation I was now facing made that misery feel tame by comparison. *Tomorrow, and tomorrow, and tomorrow.* It would be sixteen years before the girls left home. How could I fake being something I wasn't for another sixteen years?

But Charles had stuck his knife into my most vulnerable spot. A vicious divorce would ruin the children's lives forever. I couldn't do it to them—why should they have to suffer for my mistakes? Better that I should take the hit, stay in the marriage until it became intolerable for Charles, tough it out until he himself realized the relationship wasn't worth saving. I could find other ways to explore my identity while I was waiting—read books, spend more time in New York, perhaps actually meet some other gay people. It wouldn't take forever. Nobody could live like this indefinitely, not even Charles.

Chapter Eleven

I spent the rest of the next week trying to mentally prepare myself for what I thought would be a difficult conversation—negotiating the new terms of our marriage— but when Charles and I finally sat down to talk the following Friday evening he seemed perfectly at ease. Confident, even.

"Look," he said. "You made the decision not to drink, right? This is basically the same thing, and I'll be here to support you."

However absurd it was to suggest that my sexual orientation was something I could give up—like alcohol—at least Charles seemed to be safely back in the driver's seat. Now that I'd witnessed what could happen if the balance of power in our relationship was destabilized, I knew it would be better if he felt he was in control. The safest course of action would be to reveal myself slowly, in stages. Negotiate the changes in bite-size pieces. After ten years of marriage, this was the least I could do.

"I'd like to tell Bianca," I said. "I need someone here in Connecticut to confide in."

"Okay," he agreed. "But only Bianca."

"And I want to be able to go to New York and—"

"Meet other gay people?" Charles finished. Clearly, he'd been giving this some thought himself. "Okay, here's the deal. You can go and meet people in New York, but you have to keep it separate from our life up here. You *must* keep this a secret. I want your word on that. And we need to put some rules into place."

"What kind of rules?"

"About what happens if you meet people who have an agenda."

"What sort of agenda?"

"The gay agenda. To persuade you to come out. People who don't understand your incentive for keeping it all under wraps." I didn't want to point out that the incentive for keeping it under wraps wasn't exactly coming from me. "And what if you meet someone you're attracted to? If I let you go down to New York to meet other women, you must promise it won't go any further than that."

"Further than what?"

"You know what I mean. Coffee. Just talking."

"Okay, I promise."

"So, we're good?" Charles asked, getting up from the table. He seemed satisfied that everything was in order, confident that once again he'd got it all back under control.

"Yes," I said. "We're good."

The next morning I called Bianca, who was working from home. "Bianca, I need to talk to you," I said, offering no explanation. "Are you free?"

"Rachel, I have to cancel!" I heard her call to someone in the background. "No, it's an emergency! I'll text you to reschedule!" She came back to the phone. "Nicky? I'll be there in ten."

I went to the window overlooking the front yard to watch for Bianca's car. At the end of the long gravel drive, behind the row of trees that shielded the house from the road, cars were slowing down as they approached the bend. It had only been thirty seconds since I'd hung up the phone, this was silly, she wouldn't be here yet. I crossed to the window seat that overlooked the large lawn leading down to the lake on the other side of the house and started rearranging the cushions on it. Where would Bianca sit? On the sofa, she always sat on the sofa. Should I sit next to her, or would that make her uncomfortable? I went back and perched on the window seat. Would it look odd if I sat over here? Perhaps I should stand. But would that seem threatening? I returned to the front window and peered up the drive; a car slowed down on the road but sped up again as it passed the gate. Cars always slowed down on that bend; it was misleading. I decided to go to the bathroom to use up some time.

"Nicky?" I heard Bianca call from the kitchen. I hurried back through to find her making herself comfortable on the sofa, two soy lattes on the coffee table. She was dressed in expensive yoga clothes, a pair of fur-lined suede boots on the floor beside her.

"Thanks so much for coming," I said, foolishly formal. I stopped between the window seat and the sofa, unsure whether to sit or stand.

Bianca was looking at me with a disconcertingly sympathetic expression, her head tilted slightly to one side. "Oh Nicky, you're losing all your beautiful hair!"

I touched my hair. Was it that noticeable?

"You should have told me," she continued. "I could have helped. Organized a meal schedule or something."

A meal schedule? Had she been worrying about my weight loss?

She patted the sofa, inviting me to sit down. "When did you start treatment? You're so brave. Charles must be so worried."

"Charles only just . . . I mean, I only told him . . ." Wait, what did she think Charles was worried about?

"How long have you known?"

"Bianca, I'm not . . ."

"Have you told the children?"

"No, I mean, it isn't . . ."

"Sometimes it's better if you—"

"Bianca!" I interrupted. "I don't have cancer!"

Bianca froze. "You don't?"

"I'm not *dying*, for goodness' sake. I'm gay!"

Bianca's body jerked backwards, her jaw dropping with an almost audible click. She stared at me in astonishment.

"Jesus, I'm sorry." I looked around, my hands wafting through the air as if I could conjure up something to sit on. "I really just threw that at you, didn't I?"

I managed to get my legs to move and sat down at the other end of the sofa. Bianca was still staring at me in disbelief. "I don't understand," she said. "I thought you were sick."

"I have been, but I think it was the strain of trying to hold it all together."

"So, you're a . . . what, a . . . lesbian?" I could see myself fragmenting in Bianca's eyes, as if she were watching me disintegrate and trying to put me back together into something that was still vaguely recognizable. "When did this happen?"

"When I was born?" I said with a small laugh. Okay, maybe it was too soon for jokes. Biscuit climbed onto the sofa beside me and put her head in my lap, and I stroked her ears while I told Bianca everything that had happened. "Back in England it just seemed impossible," I explained. "I just stopped seeing it, pretended it wasn't there. Every time I felt it, I pushed it down, like sitting on top of a suitcase."

"Jesus, Nicky. This takes denial to a whole new level."

"I just wanted to be normal like everyone else."

"Define 'normal.'"

"I don't know. Not set apart. But also not weird or scary or creepy. Not *Single White Female*."

"Wait, you thought *Single White Female* was about a lesbian?"

"Didn't you?"

"No! Jesus, Nicky, it was about a psychopath with borderline personality disorder! Why did you think she was gay?"

My brain fogged with panic. Didn't everyone assume that women who crushed that hard on other women were lesbians? And therefore lesbians must be deranged serial killers who should be locked up for everyone else's safety? Or was it just me?

"I'm scared I'm going to lose all my friends."

"I don't think that's going to happen," Bianca said flatly.

"But look at you, Bianca. People are constantly not inviting you to things just because you don't have a husband. It's insane. If they can't fit a divorced single mom into the picture, how are they going to fit a lesbian?"

"Yes, but look at *you*, Nicky. Just because you're a lesbian doesn't mean you're going to lose any of your charm. You're still gorgeous."

Reflexively I touched my hair. Bianca was right: if I wanted to maintain my status, I'd have to maintain my looks. This wasn't the time to tell her I felt more comfortable wearing men's clothes, or that once upon a time I'd wished I were a boy.

Bianca picked up her coffee cup and wiped the lipstick mark off the rim with a perfectly manicured finger. "What about Charles? Are you filing for divorce?"

"I don't think it's going to be that easy. He threatened to destroy me if I tried, and he's got the money to do it."

Bianca rolled her eyes. "This isn't the 1950s, Nicky. You're not going to lose custody of your children just because you're gay."

"I don't want to put them through an acrimonious divorce, though," I said, pushing Biscuit off my lap and brushing ineffectually at the hairs she left all over my jeans. "What would that say to them about my sexuality? That it's okay for their own father to try to ruin me because of it? And even if we did divorce, what then?"

"You meet a woman, fall in love, and live happily ever after?"

"But how? Where am I going to find her? I understood the narrative when I was trying to find a husband, but how am I supposed to go about being gay? There is literally no story where the hero ends up as a happy lesbian living in the suburbs. Where is that story, Bianca? *Where?*"

Bianca looked at me silently.

"Exactly," I said.

Chapter Twelve

U nable to picture life as a suburban lesbian, I decided it might be prudent to take my first steps in New York. I needed to find somewhere in the city where gay people went, somewhere safe and anonymous where I could sit invisibly in a corner and soak up the atmosphere. Somewhere like the Bluestockings bookstore.

The following Friday afternoon I took the train down to New York. Surfacing out of the subway on East Houston I picked my way across the rubble of the roadwork and turned down a side street, passed a small bodega and a closed cell phone shop with shutters covered in graffiti, until finally I came to a wooden bench sitting in front of a warmly lit window. I pushed open the door and went in, trying to look as inconspicuous as possible. The table at the front of the store was covered with books laid out for browsing, so I picked one up and flicked through the pages while I tried to orient myself. Behind the counter an orange-haired woman wearing a fifties prom dress was chatting with a bearded man. A handful of people were drinking coffee at the tables by the window, and a few more were browsing the bookshelves. So far nobody seemed to have noticed me.

I looked down at the book in my hands: *Best Lesbian Erotica*. I dropped it quickly and moved away from the table, edging my way through the shelves and wondering how the books in counterculture bookstores were categorized. A girl holding an armful of books was standing in front of a section labeled Queer, trying to stuff the books back onto an already crammed shelf. She had a pixie face and short brown hair tucked under a beanie, combat pants and a baggy T-shirt. She didn't look remotely threatening.

"Can I help you?" she said, turning to me and smiling.

I blushed, embarrassed to have been caught staring. "Um, well, yes, actually you might." I bit my lip and motioned to the sign above the bookcase, my curiosity overcoming my embarrassment. "Why is this section called Queer? I thought 'queer' was pejorative."

"We reclaimed it," she said amiably. "Now it covers everything that isn't straight or cisgender."

"Sis-what?"

"Cisgender. Identifying with the gender you were assigned at birth."

"Oh, okay." Perhaps if I could get a better grasp on all this I'd be able to figure out why I mostly didn't feel like anything at all, why my identity still felt like an empty void I'd been trying to cover up with clothes. "D'you have anything on lesbian identities?" I asked.

"How about this?" she suggested, pulling a paperback off the shelf. "It's the history of lesbian feminism in America. Are you doing research?"

"Nnnn . . . Well, not really . . . I mean, yes, a bit . . . but not academic. I've just come out of the closet."

"Oh, well then we'd better get you some more help," she said, smiling warmly. She waved over to the couple behind the counter. I tensed preemptively as they approached, certain they'd identify me as a hostile intruder the minute they heard my accent.

"Hey, what's up?" the orange-haired woman said in a remarkably friendly voice.

"I'm looking for . . . I don't suppose you have . . . something by someone who's come out later in life," I mumbled, holding my fingers in front of my mouth as if I could somehow disguise my voice.

"I can't think of anything," she replied apologetically.

"Then something on lesbian identities, perhaps?" I suggested, feeling a little bolder.

"Sure, let me see if I can find *Butch and Femme* for you," she said, disappearing around the other side of the bookcase.

"How about some memoir?" suggested the man.

"And you definitely need some pulp fiction," the girl in the beanie added, leading me towards a section in the corner. I tried not to look embarrassingly grateful as they shared their recommendations with me, but the impulse to hug everyone was overwhelming.

"*Stone Butch Blues*," the man with the beard announced as he placed the final book on top of the pile by the cash register. "Leslie Feinberg's one of the trailblazers."

I glanced at the photo on the cover. This was the sort of lesbian my father had described coming across once when he and my mother were looking for a taxi in the wrong part of London. The group of women had hurled insults at them, and my mother had been terrified. My father had made the women out to be almost subhuman, his mockery of their masculinity not quite masking his fear.

"You should visit the Leslie-Lohman Museum," the girl with the beanie said as she rung up the purchases. "It's walking distance from here."

"I'll give you the address for the Lesbian Herstory Archives in Brooklyn," the man with the beard added, scribbling something down on a notepad. "And Dixon Place does a lot of queer theater."

I left the bookstore and headed down Rivington to meet Elisabeth, who'd promised to take me to a lesbian bar called Cubbyhole. I hugged my bag of books to my chest as I walked, trying to prevent myself from smiling like a fool at everyone I passed. An old man in a deerstalker hat leaning against a wall smoking a roll-up: beautiful. A group of Middle Eastern men making noisy conversation outside a deli: beautiful. A thin woman with rolled-up jeans and a fedora walking a small dog on a leash: beautiful. The autumn leaves lying in the puddles with the discarded coffee cartons and cigarette butts: beautiful, beautiful, beautiful!

Elisabeth was waiting for me on the corner of Prince and Crosby, wearing a frayed houndstooth wool coat belted over a voluminous black skirt. The early evening sun silhouetted her with a golden halo. "God, look at you, you look amazing," I said, hugging her tightly. We walked through SoHo arm in arm while I told her about my adventure at the bookstore. "They were so friendly, so . . . *nice*."

"You sound surprised."

"I am surprised." We stopped at a crosswalk, and I pulled *Stone Butch Blues* out of my bag. "This is what I was expecting:

politically radical, aggressive-looking lesbians who'd never tolerate someone like me."

Elisabeth took the book out of my hands and looked at the picture on the cover. "You can't seriously tell me this is what you thought all lesbians looked like. Come on, you're a cultured, intelligent, well-read woman. I don't believe it."

"But where were all the other lesbians when we were growing up?" I asked. "Nowhere. Not in the media, not on television, not in film or magazines—they were completely invisible."

"What about more recently?"

I shrugged. "I've been too busy having babies." I'd moved from the upper-class bubble of the English countryside to an equally secluded life in Connecticut, where every minute of my day was devoted to my children. I had no time for watching television or reading newspapers. I could barely get through one chapter of a book each evening before passing out from exhaustion. The growing visibility of the gay rights movement had completely passed me by, leaving me with views that I'd inherited from my father, which he in turn had picked up in his own childhood. I was living in the 1950s.

I took the book back from Elisabeth, feeling myself tense reflexively at the author's defiant expression, the uncompromising provocation of her shaved head. But looking closer I realized it wasn't hostility in her expression. It was something else, something that felt eerily familiar. She almost looked vulnerable. I felt a rush of shame; women like this had fought for the freedom I was trying to enjoy, at God knows what cost.

By the time we turned onto a cobbled side street it was almost dark. Ahead of us a series of bars and restaurants were throwing warm light onto the uneven pavement; outside one of them a woman was sitting on the edge of a planter smoking a cigarette. She was older, with smudged lipstick and wild hair, the sort of bohemian style that always caught my attention.

"We're here," Elisabeth said, pulling out her ID for the doorman. I looked down at the woman; she was gay? Before I could register my surprise, Elisabeth pushed the door open and pulled me inside.

I understood immediately why it was called Cubbyhole: it was tiny, the bar took up the whole of one side of the room, and the bartenders were the only people who had any space to move. Elisabeth elbowed her way through the crowd, dragging me by the hand. She reached the bar and waved to get the bartender's attention. A woman in aviator shades and a transparent T-shirt was sitting to our left, deep in conversation with a muscled woman with black spiky hair; to our right a girl with bony shoulders in a loose white tank top was whispering in the ear of a skinny rock-chick in leather jeans. A large girl with an asymmetrical haircut, a button-down shirt, and red suspenders was shouting something over my shoulder at the bartender; a tall girl with a shaved head holding the hand of an Asian girl in a beanie pushed past me, while two Black girls with their arms around each other shoved me from the other side, dancing together to the deafening music. I could just make out a group of white girls who looked like sorority sisters taking up the seats in the corner, all shiny hair and lip gloss and flashing white teeth, and next to them, a girl in a pair of low-slung jeans was grinding her girlfriend up against the wall. There were tall girls and fat girls and butch girls and pretty girls and drunk girls and dancing girls and cool girls and laughing girls and fierce girls and stylish girls and beautiful girls. Every possible category I'd ever imagined and a whole lot more I hadn't. How this many people could fit into such a tiny space was anybody's guess. It seemed to defy the laws of physics.

Elisabeth turned to me with our drinks. "You can close your mouth now, Nicky."

We pushed through the crowds and found a spot at the far end of the bar. The noise level made it almost impossible to talk but I didn't care; all I wanted to do was watch. The woman I'd seen smoking outside came in through the door at the other end of the room. I could have put my head on my arms and wept. I nudged Elisabeth and nodded towards her.

Elisabeth followed my eyes. "D'you want to go and talk to her?"

I shook my head. The music was too loud for conversation, and anyway, she was just a projection of my fantasies. I lived near a city where women like this existed; for now, that was all I needed to know.

Chapter Thirteen

Women and sex, women and sex, women and sex. All I could think about was women and sex. I thought about women and sex in the car while driving the kids to school, I thought about women and sex while I was walking the dog, I thought about women and sex while I was doing the laundry, I thought about women and sex while I was cooking dinner. Any time my brain went into autopilot my mind would become engulfed by sexual fantasies, my complete lack of experience apparently no impediment to my ability to imagine every possible way in which I could make love to a woman.

The one benefit of Charles working such long hours was a little time to myself in bed before he came home at night, time I now spent trying to figure out what my body wanted. Confusingly, however, my internal sexual orientation dial seemed to be stuck on heterosexual; I was finally allowing myself to fantasize about making love to a woman, but I always ended up taking the part of the man. I assumed it must have something to do with how deeply society had embedded its heteronormative stereotypes into me. I'd been reading a bit about compulsory heterosexuality recently, so I understood the concept of lesbian erasure. I just hadn't realized that I'd internalized the patriarchal system so much that I was now incapable of excluding men even from my own private fantasies. Maybe I should buy some lesbian erotica from Bluestockings; perhaps with a bit of time and practice I could rewire my brain into accepting that it was okay for a woman to make love to a woman.

It was over a month before I found time to go down to New York again, late November and icy cold. Salt caked the sidewalks, slush lay in dirty puddles beside the curbs, steam rose from the manhole covers in the road. I took the subway down to the Lower East Side, pulling my scarf up around my ears and hunching my shoulders against the cold. The irony of wanting to spend time in a bookstore with Occupy Wall Street posters all over the walls when my husband worked on Wall Street was not lost on me. Charles had adjusted to our new situation by escaping into politics. He'd been cutting out articles on gay rights from the *Wall Street Journal* and leaving them on the kitchen table for me, going to great lengths to update me on the legal issues surrounding Proposition 8 and DOMA. I appreciated the effort he was making, but I wasn't sure I wanted the queer rights movement mansplained to me by my husband.

I pushed the door of Bluestockings open and stood looking at the list of fair-trade coffees and vegan muffins beside the coffee machine, bouncing slightly on my toes to get warm. In my peripheral vision I saw a woman approach from the other side of the counter.

"Can I get a cup of coffee?" I asked, my eyes on the list of muffins, my voice hushed with cold.

She leaned forward, her elbows on the counter. "Why are we whispering?" she whispered.

I looked up to see a pair of pale-blue eyes framed by arched eyebrows.

"I don't know," I whispered back.

She moved in a little closer. "Would you like a large coffee or a small coffee?"

"A small one, please." I glanced up at her again and had time to register a long aquiline nose set above a full, wide mouth, before she stood up and turned round to put the cup under the coffee maker.

She turned back to me, leaned on the counter, and gazed at me with an intensity that was unbalancing. "That's a very nice scarf," she said, reaching out to touch it.

"Thank you," I said. "It's very cozy."

"It's important to be cozy in a bookshop."

"It is." I managed a smile.

"And I like your tweed coat. You look like the Artful Dodger." She peered over the counter at it. "It has tails, it's a tailcoat."

"It does, it is," I agreed. She had red hair falling over her shoulders and smooth, white skin. She passed me my cup of coffee and I picked up the sugar shaker, feeling her eyes burn into me as I tried to pour the sugar into the teaspoon. My hand started shaking and I dropped the spoon into the coffee cup, splashing coffee and sugar all over the counter. Flustered, I looked for a napkin to clear it up. She was still watching me, her face so close I could almost smell her. I picked up the coffee cup, trying to stop it from rattling in its saucer. "Is it okay if I borrow a book?"

"Of course it is," she said, resting her chin on her hand and looking at me with a sleepy smile. "Read any book you like."

I pulled a book off the display behind me, hurried around the end of the counter, and hid at a little table behind the coffee machine where she couldn't see me. I sat for a minute trying to slow my breathing down. I was trembling so hard I didn't trust myself to pick up the coffee cup without spilling it, so instead I opened the book—a manifesto on lesbian feminism—to give myself something to do until my heart resumed its normal pattern. Elisabeth would be here soon. I pushed up my sleeve to check my watch and my eyes caught the diamonds flashing on my engagement ring. Suddenly it seemed horribly ostentatious. I pulled off the engagement ring and then tried to tug off my wedding ring, but it was too tight. I glanced around to see if anyone was looking, then put my finger in my mouth and sucked, hoping the saliva would help ease it off. I managed to wrestle the gold band over the joint but then couldn't figure out what to do with it. I couldn't just put the rings loose in my bag, I might lose them, and my wallet didn't have a zip compartment. What would Charles say if I came home with no wedding or engagement ring? I looked at my left hand; the rings had left an indentation in my ring finger that was almost as conspicuous as the ring itself. Suddenly I felt stupid and thought I'd better put them both back on again, but my finger was swollen from all the tugging, and I couldn't get them back over the knuckle.

The door swung open, and Elisabeth walked in, unwrapping her scarf from around her neck. "What are you doing?" she asked as she dumped her bag on the seat.

"I've got myself into a pickle with my wedding ring," I whispered. "I took it off and now I can't get it back on again."

"Why did you take it off?" she asked, sitting down next to me.

"Because I didn't want the girl behind the counter to see it."

"Which girl?"

I gave up with the rings and put them loose into my handbag. "Don't look now, but there's a girl with long red hair behind the counter who was flirting with me when I came in. Try to look when she can't see you. It's hard to see her from here."

"Holy shit, someone was flirting with you?" Elisabeth craned around in her chair to see.

"Don't be so obvious!" I hissed.

"The one with the pale skin?" Elisabeth was still craning. "Christ, she's beautiful! And you were flirting with her?"

"I wasn't flirting with her, she was flirting with me. Well, I may have been a bit flirting with her."

"I want to see it! I want to see you flirting with her!"

"This isn't a spectator sport, Elisabeth."

"I know, but my God! You've just broken your lesbian-flirtation virginity!"

"D'you think she's gay?" I asked.

"If she's working in a gay bookstore and she flirted with you, I think we can safely assume she's gay," Elisabeth said dryly. "What's this?" She nudged the lesbian manifesto.

"I was reading it while I was waiting for you. I haven't bought it." A thought occurred to me. "Jesus, if she sees you, she'll probably think you're my girlfriend."

"Then I'll have to do something very heterosexual in front of her. Let's go and speak to her; I want to see her flirt with you." She picked up the book. "I'll buy this, you chat to her while I'm paying." Before I could stop her, she stood up and headed towards the cash register. The redhead was lounging behind the counter with her back against the wall. I took a deep breath, caught her eye, and took the book from Elisabeth.

"Have you read this?" I asked her.

"I'm afraid not," she said, moving towards me.

Elisabeth took the book back from me. "I'm buying it for her birthday," she said.

The redhead's eyes didn't move from mine. "Are you a Sagittarius?" she asked.

"No, my birthday was last April, but she keeps forgetting to buy me a present."

"If she waits any longer, she'll have to buy you two." She leaned across the counter and took my hand. "I'm Rebecca," she said.

"I'm Nicky." I looked down at Rebecca's fingers, long and smooth with perfectly manicured nails.

"Are you visiting?" she asked.

"No, I live in Connecticut." I thought for a second and then added, "Not the best place for a gay woman to live."

"I live on Long Island. That's not the best place for a gay woman to live either."

I smiled at her, relieved that we'd managed to clarify the situation. "You come all the way from Long Island every day?"

"We're volunteers, we set our own schedules."

"What a great thing to be able to do," I said, enviously.

"You could too, if you liked."

"I wish I could, but I have kids."

She tipped her head to one side. "Oh, I'm sorry."

"Me too. I mean, I'm not sorry about the kids."

Elisabeth walked back over and gave me the book. Rebecca ignored her, her eyes fixed on mine. "Here you go," Elisabeth said pointedly. "Happy birthday, from me and my husband."

I felt the corners of my mouth twitch. "I have to go," I said to Rebecca.

"What a shame." She leaned her elbows on the counter. "Come back soon."

It was dark out on the street. I turned and looked back; through the window I could see Rebecca still leaning on the counter, watching us walk away. When we were out of sight I turned to Elisabeth. "Holy Mother of God, did that just actually happen?" I asked, hiccupping ecstatically. "Did you see it? Did you *see* it?"

"I didn't have to see it. The heat coming off the two of you was radioactive."

"I can hardly walk! I don't know whether I'm walking or floating, I feel like a teenager!"

"Why don't you go back and ask for her number?"

The pavement reappeared beneath the soles of my feet. I told Elisabeth about the agreement I'd made with Charles; flirting with a woman in a bookstore wasn't breaking the terms of that agreement; asking for her phone number definitely would be. Suddenly I felt like a dog chained to a stake. It had been only a couple of months, but already I was starting to regret the promises I'd made.

When I got home Charles was in the shower. I got into bed, trying to transition out of my fantasy world where Rebecca was my girlfriend and into the real world where I still shared a bed with my husband. Charles came out of the bathroom with a towel wrapped round his waist. I watched him as he pulled on his pajama pants.

"How's Elisabeth?" he asked.

"She's good. We had dinner at a little Sicilian restaurant. We met at the bookstore first."

"The gay one?"

"It's not gay, it's counterculture."

"But gay people work there." Charles sat down on the edge of the bed with his back to me. Drops of water were sitting on the great mass of his neck below his hairline; his back was huge, covered in hair and moles. I thought of Rebecca's slim, marble-white fingers.

"There was this girl at the bookstore . . ."

Charles pulled on his pajama top, the bed creaking under his weight like a boat that had landed an enormous fish.

"She flirted with me. It's the first time it's happened."

He tilted his head slightly. "Were you attracted to her?"

"Yes, I was."

Charles started to button up his pajama top, waiting for me to go on.

"We talked for a little bit, and then Elisabeth arrived."

Charles climbed into bed and turned onto his side, facing me. "Was she beautiful?"

"Yes, she was." Now that we were having this conversation face-to-face, Charles suddenly seemed much more vulnerable than I'd expected him to be. "I'm sorry. I did promise I'd tell you."

"Do you want to go back and see her again?"

I let the question hang in the air for a moment. "Yes, I do." The expression on Charles's face didn't change. Suddenly I felt horrible. Was I inhuman? Charles didn't deserve this. Nobody deserved this. "Are you okay?" I asked.

"I'm fine."

"Are you sure?"

He turned onto his back and stared at the ceiling. He was lying so still it was hard to tell whether he was even breathing. "I don't want you to go back there," he said eventually.

"Okay," I said. I tried to think of something else to say, but I knew there was nothing that would make it any better. "I wish you had someone to talk to."

"I've got you to talk to."

"That's not what I mean. I wish you had a friend, or a therapist, or something."

"I don't need a therapist." There was another long pause, then, "We're never going to have sex again, are we?"

"No," I said quietly. "I don't think we are."

Charles lay still for a long time, staring at the ceiling. Then he rolled over onto his side, turning his back to me. "I'll move into the guest room after Christmas," he said.

Chapter Fourteen

I tried to sideline thoughts of Rebecca as Christmas approached, afraid that if I spent too much time dreaming about her it would show on my face, betray me for the liar I'd become. The gulf between life inside our home and the facade Charles and I were presenting to the outside world was growing wider by the day. Whatever his personal feelings were about my attraction to Rebecca—and how definitively it had sealed the end of our relationship—he kept them to himself. Charles was a proud man and emotional vulnerability was not part of his playbook. I tried to respect that what mattered to him most right now was not to lose face. If he had to battle with his emotions then at least he should be allowed to do so in private, and that meant making sure nobody cottoned on to the fact that there was anything amiss.

For his sake I agreed to go to all the Christmas parties with him, tottering on my high heels while trying to act like the charmingly supportive wife I was supposed to be, but I felt like I was trapped inside some perfumed and painted woman, operating her machinery according to the owner's manual. My limbs—mostly now pain-free when I was home alone with the kids—started to ache the minute I put on a skirt, while my fingers frantically picked and tore at my cuticles as I nodded and smiled my way through the evenings.

As if that wasn't enough to contend with, my mother and father were due to arrive shortly before Christmas. Being around my parents always made me feel like I was being stretched to the snapping point, but now the wires of my anxiety had tightened to a whole new pitch. The snowplow had left a mountain of ice at the end of the drive over which the kids were climbing when the taxi pulled in. I peered out the window to see my mother and father disembark from the cab like the Queen and Prince Philip arriving at Balmoral, all tweeds and headscarves and quilted jackets. The children scrambled down the ice and launched themselves at their grandparents, jumping up and down for hugs and kisses. I walked down the steps to join them, busying myself by paying the taxi and taking their suitcases, hoping in all the pandemonium they wouldn't notice my anxiety.

The rest of the afternoon was a mess of early Christmas presents and unpacking and jostling for attention, until by early evening the children had worn themselves out. When I came downstairs from putting them to bed, my mother had set the table for supper, creating the sort of warm ambience I knew would make Charles feel homesick for the kind of life he'd thought we were going to have. The tablecloth had been ironed, the silver had been polished, candles were burning in the candlesticks, and Charles was sitting at the table wearing an expression of relief that there were still women in the world who understood how a household was meant to be run. I ached to point out to him that he might enjoy meals with his family, however chaotic, if he got home early enough. Only the previous evening the children and I had had a long and important conversation over dinner about whether narwals were real, and how to catch a Squirtle that hadn't yet evolved, and why one should never hold hands with a lobster, but he'd missed it because yet again he'd got back too late.

During dinner Charles and my father discussed the prime minister's veto on the European Union treaty, the continuing strength of British nationalism under the Tory party, and the success of the single currency. My father leaned back in his chair, nursing a large glass of claret, the light from the candles reflecting in his half-moon spectacles. I'd learned to pick and choose my battles with my father, so I stayed out of the conversation. My mother, who'd developed a finely tuned instinct for the exact moment at which a conversation was veering towards dangerous territory and should be brought to a swift close, was sitting upright at the table, scooping tiny bites of brandy butter out of the bowl with a teaspoon. The pearls around her neck complimented the streaks of white highlighting her blonde hair, and I noticed how her aging skin was beginning to soften the bone structure that had once made her incredibly beautiful.

After supper Charles excused himself to go do some work, at which point my parents turned their attention to me. "So darling, when are you moving back to England?" my mother asked.

"Ah, well, I was going to talk to you about that . . ." I got up, poured some dish soap into the sink, and ran the tap. My father crossed his legs and looked at me expectantly. He was wearing the same mustard-colored corduroys he'd had for decades. I had no idea how he managed to make his clothes last so long. "Charles has been offered another promotion, but it would mean staying in this country." I plunged a plate into the water and looked over at my mother. She was concentrating fiercely on the silver bowl that contained the brandy butter, trying not to betray her emotions. "The kids are settled, and . . . I don't know, the American lifestyle just seems to suit us better."

"I thought the plan was to stay for three years," my mother said carefully.

"It was," I said, "but . . ."

My father looked up at me. "But what?"

"Alfie's just started breakdancing classes, and we'd have to do the whole boarding school thing, and then there's the British class system . . ."

"There is no class system anymore," my father said stoutly. "It's a meritocracy, isn't it? That's what they're calling it now."

"Dad, you're living proof that the class system is still fully functional."

"Me?" He raised his eyebrows in surprise.

"Your group of friends isn't exactly diverse, is it?"

My mother was sitting completely still, her back straight, the teaspoon poised in midair. I could tell by the frozen expression on her face that I needed to rein myself in.

"Anyway," I said, changing the subject, "we'll be back in England for the summer."

"For a whole month?" my mother asked hopefully.

"Probably. I may take the kids down to Cornwall." I picked up a saucepan from the draining board and started to dry it.

"Cornwall's been all over the British press," my father said, swirling his claret around his wine glass. "A scandal in a guesthouse near Penzance."

"Two men got asked to leave by the owners," my mother explained. "It was a lifestyle issue."

"Homosexuals," my father harrumphed. "They created a frightful scene and then took the owners to court. Just being bloody-minded, if you ask me."

"It's not like it was a hotel," my mother explained. "It was their actual home."

"And if you're generous enough to open up your house to strangers, you should have a say in how they behave," my father agreed.

"Perhaps they should have checked first?" my mother suggested. "Then they could have avoided all the legal expenses. It doesn't take much to ask, does it?"

"They should never have won. There's no respect for people's religious beliefs anymore. Churches are going to start closing if we're not careful."

"It's so hard to keep a small country church going," my mother sighed. "And baptisms are down, which doesn't help."

"Nobody believes in original sin, that's the problem."

I froze. "Original sin?"

"I know it sounds extreme, darling, but it's a valid Christian belief," my mother said in a mollifying tone.

I turned to my father. "Dad?"

"You can't call yourself a Christian if you're not prepared to be cleansed of sin. Either you're in or you're out; you don't get to cherry-pick your beliefs."

I put the saucepan down and walked out of the kitchen. I locked the bathroom door behind me and leaned forward, resting my forehead against the mirror. Is this what was going to be expected of me in the future? That I'd have to check in advance to see whether people would be willing to open their doors to me? Ask them politely whether my existence might be offensive to them? I'd been subtly calling my father out on his homophobia for decades, cautiously intervening whenever he dropped antigay remarks into the conversation, and I thought I'd made some progress. *Dripping water hollows out stone*, my mother always said, but maybe my drips had been too gentle. Maybe he needed a hailstorm.

"Darling?" My mother's voice through the door.

"Just a sec, Mum."

"Are you okay?"

"I'm fine, Mum. I'll be out in a sec."

I turned on the faucet and held my hands under it. The water ran over my wrists, turning the veins blue. I couldn't wash this sin off my skin, it was inside me. It was in my blood, running through my arteries, pumped around my body by my own heart.

Within a couple of days, the pressure of having to act normally became almost intolerable. The calm way my mother tidied the house around me betrayed the judgment lurking beneath the surface, her offer to clean out the filter in the washing machine clearly an unspoken accusation that I wasn't staying on top of the household chores.

"Mum . . . ," I said, wishing she'd stop fussing.

"It's fine, darling! Just trying to help," she assured me, disappearing down the hall with an armful of the children's clothes.

Charles got up from the sofa. "Okay, I'm off out. Drinks with the boys."

I stood by the kitchen window and watched his car disappear down the drive. My mother came into the kitchen and looked pointedly at the plate of baked beans and scrambled eggs I was holding, which Freddie, who was aggressively swinging his legs under the table, was refusing to eat.

"You let them have too many snacks," she remarked, picking toys up off the floor and putting them back into the toy basket. "In my generation—"

"Mum, please don't."

"They need a more balanced diet, proper meals—"

"I cook them proper meals."

"More variety, so their taste buds develop—"

"I'm on survival mode here, for goodness' sake. If I can get them to eat anything, I consider it an achievement!"

My mother raised her hands in defense. "I'm only suggesting . . ."

I glanced over at the children, who were not sitting around the table in quiet obedience like my brother and I had done at their age. Rose was squirting tomato ketchup over her cutlery, Lily was standing on her chair with her fork and spoon clutched in her fists, and Alfie was crying because Freddie was kicking him in the leg. My mother, overwhelmed by the chaos, disappeared to get a fresh tea towel from the laundry basket.

"Orange juice!" Lily yelled from her standing position on the chair.

"There is no orange juice," I told her.

"Orange juice!"

"I can get you a glass of milk, Lily, but we're out of orange juice."

"Orange juice!"

I opened the fridge door with my free hand to show her. "There is no orange juice. I can't give you any orange juice because there isn't any. *We have no orange juice!*"

"ORANGE JUICE!" Lily bellowed.

"*I can't do this anymore!*" I roared back and hurled the plate of baked beans across the room. It smashed into the corner underneath the window. Lily froze on her chair, Freddie's legs stopped midkick. We all watched the congealing glops of food drip down the wall, puddling in the shards of broken china on the floor. I turned to see my mother standing, ghostlike, in the doorway.

The next morning I took the phone outside while I was taking out the trash so I could call Elisabeth. "I'm a terrible parent!" I sobbed after I told her what happened. "And I'm trying so hard to be happy and nice for everyone, but every time Charles comes anywhere near me, I just frost him out. I can't seem to help it. I'm a horrible person, Elisabeth, I don't like myself like this! And I can't take how vigilant I have to be all the time. It's like I've forgotten how a normal woman is supposed to behave, so I keep having to double-check everything I do and say in case I do or say something I shouldn't. I don't think I can keep this up much longer!"

I wanted to peel the flesh off my bones, to climb out of my skin and escape. I was beginning to lose all sense of myself. I could barely even recognize my own reflection anymore—every time I looked in the mirror all I could see was a man in drag staring back at me. But worse than this was the constant crawling sensation under my skin, as if my clothes had been tumble-dried with shards of glass, my cosmetics poisoned with traces of acid.

"Wouldn't it be better if you just told them?" Elisabeth suggested.

"No, no, I can't. Not yet!"

"Do you have any idea how they'd take it?"

"Oh God, Elisabeth, it's going to be awful! I'm going to wreck their lives! But I'm not being deliberately cruel, I'm just being truthful, right? I can't hold myself responsible if their hearts get broken, can I? If Dad thinks homosexuality is a sin, that's his problem, not mine! I'm not committing any crime! I'm just trying to be myself!" My voice seemed to have gone up an octave. "Jesus, Elisabeth, I've never wanted a drink so badly in my life."

After my parents returned to England, Charles and I divided our possessions into two bedrooms at either end of the house. The children didn't notice that anything had changed. They were too busy playing with—or breaking, or fighting over—the presents they'd been given for Christmas. I hadn't planned on giving them gendered toys, but the boys wanted to be Super Mario Bros., and the girls wanted to be Disney Princesses, and I wasn't able to dissuade them. I tried to compensate by talking to them about resisting societal pressure to conform to gendered roles and not succumbing to unattainable expectations of power or beauty, but I couldn't get them to pay attention for more than half a second. Rose stole Lily's tiara, so Lily started crying, Freddie's mustache kept falling off and needing to be glued back on, and then Alfie got stuck inside one of the kitchen cabinets, and by the time we extracted him, Rose had torn her tutu. Eventually I gave up. These kinds of conversations would have to wait for when they were a little bit older.

Months passed. Winter started to turn into spring. I looked after the kids, ran the house, tried to avoid Charles as much as possible. Although I was willing to honor his request that

I not return to Bluestockings, there was nothing to stop me from reading all the books I'd already bought, so I started devouring them one by one. All except Leslie Feinberg's *Stone Butch Blues*, which still sat unopened on my bookshelf. Occasionally I'd pull it out, look at the photo on the cover, and then put it back again. I wasn't sure where my reluctance came from, I just knew something inside me didn't want to connect with whatever was in that book.

Early in April, Charles asked me to go with him to a work event, dinner with a client and his wife. It was a duty call, he said, but reassured me that the restaurant had a Michelin star and the food would be delicious. The client was pompous, his wife was boring, and the pretense now felt unbearable. I choked my way through a plate of lightly smoked trout with celery root puree, food which felt like sawdust in my mouth, wishing the night would end. Back at home I paid the babysitter, pulled off my high heels, and headed out of the kitchen towards my bedroom without saying a word to Charles.

"Nicky?"

I stopped, my back to him.

"You were very quiet tonight."

I dug my fingernails into the palms of my hands. "I didn't really have much to say."

"Are you okay?"

"I'm fine."

"Nicky, we have to maintain some level of . . ."

I turned. "Of what?"

"Why are you so angry all the time?"

I waved my arms around me. "I can't go on faking this."

"What are you faking? You haven't even started being gay yet!"

"What?"

"You haven't . . . *done* anything yet."

I stared at him in disbelief. "Is that what you think? That I don't start being gay until I've slept with a woman?"

"Well, yes. I mean, you're not, are you?"

I didn't know where to start. I wanted to say I felt more like him—a man—than this wife-person he wanted me to be, but this wasn't true. I didn't feel like him at all. I knew how Charles felt about women, and God forbid I should ever feel that way myself.

"Being gay isn't something I can put on and take off," I said. "It's me, it's my whole identity. I can't separate myself from it like you want me to." I could see from the expression on Charles's face that he had no idea what I meant. He'd never had to question his identity, so it was completely beyond him why anyone else might need to question theirs. "When people see me as a straight, married woman, they're not seeing me. I'm walking through the world completely invisible. I need to be honest about who I am."

"You have been honest."

"With you, yes, but it's not enough. I need to be seen."

"By whom?" Charles stared at me as if I were a petulant teenager. "The cleaning lady? The babysitter? The grocery store clerk? What d'you want, a megaphone?"

"For God's sake, Charles, I'm telling you I can't do this for much longer!"

"But you've done it for so long already, why can't you keep doing it until the children leave home?"

"I can't, I just can't. I don't know how to explain how hard it is now." I wasn't sure exactly what was happening to me, but I did know that some part of me was trying to return to that boyish person I'd been in my twenties, and that wasn't someone who could share a house with Charles.

"What if I said it was okay for you to contact Rebecca?"

I startled, taken aback by the sudden change in direction. "You mean open up the marriage?"

"If that's what you call it."

"Are you sure you're ready for that?"

Charles shrugged. "I always knew you'd have sex with a woman eventually. Maybe you just need to get it out of your system."

Chapter Fifteen

I figured I'd approach Rebecca the old-fashioned way, by writing her a letter. It had been over three months since our encounter at the bookstore; was this a crazy thing to be doing? But when I voiced my fears to Bianca, she quickly dismissed them.

"You can't keep hiding in books," she said firmly. "Reading isn't a substitute for living. At some stage you're going to have to find the balls to get out there and live your life, and if you want to be taken seriously as a lesbian, having sex with a woman might be a good place to start."

After rewriting the letter half a dozen times, I mailed it to Elisabeth and asked her to drop it off for me next time she was passing Bluestockings.

Two days later I got a text from Rebecca: *I was wondering when I'd hear from you.*

I stared at it, half surprised she wasn't just a figment of my imagination. I called her later that night, swallowing several times as the phone rang, afraid I might choke and be unable to get the words out. When she answered, she also sounded nervous, her voice high-pitched and staccato. We stumbled through the pleasantries for a few minutes until I decided that perhaps it would be easier if I got straight to the point.

"Would you like to meet up for coffee sometime?" I asked.

She didn't reply immediately, and then said, "Yes, I'd like that." She paused, then said in a strained voice, "I can't talk for long. I have to go to work."

"At the bookstore? Is it open at this time of night?"

"No, I mean my real job."

"What d'you do?" I asked.

There was another pause, lengthier this time, and then she said, "I'm an escort."

I obviously hadn't heard her correctly. Either that or the job description meant something different in this country. "Which means you . . . ?" I prompted.

". . . have sex with men for money."

I almost dropped the phone.

"It's a bit like being a masseuse," she added, "only I mostly work at night."

I tried to put the pieces of my brain back together while she waited silently on the other end of the line. What the hell should I do now? I couldn't just back out; what kind of a hypocrite would that make me? Sex workers, lesbians—it was all just blind discrimination, and I wasn't buying into that shit anymore. Anyway, if I really wanted to learn about real life, maybe I should start by spending more time with the real people who were out there living it.

"Okay," I said. "So how about that coffee?"

I arranged to meet Rebecca at a French café in the Meatpacking District, and then spent every waking hour for the next few days trying not to panic. I had no idea how to go on a date with a woman. Who was I meant to be? How was I meant to behave? I wanted to take the masculine role, but I wasn't sure how that translated into an actual identity. "Butch lesbian" didn't feel right; it felt *too* masculine somehow, incompatible with the boyish style I was drawn to. But butch couldn't be the only option for a masculine-presenting lesbian, could it? I asked Bianca for advice, explaining that I wanted to take the role of the man without mentioning the somewhat blurred boundary between acting like a man and being a man.

"I can tell you exactly what a woman wants," she said. "Assertiveness. Power. Confidence. Make her feel like you're totally in control. Don't show any weakness. When I'm with a man, I want him to take over completely."

That figured. She was currently dating a Navy Seal, and I knew she used her relationships as a way of finding relief from the relentless pressure of life as a single parent. But I wasn't sure this was the kind of man I wanted to be, and anyway, how could I pretend to be in control when I had no idea what I was doing?

Next came the problem of what I should wear. Trying to act like a man and dress like a woman felt unnecessarily complicated, but I was worried that if I dressed too much like a man, I'd lose all the qualities that made me attractive in the first place. I pulled a purple velvet smoking jacket out of my closet, tailored and classically chic enough to be sexy, and yet manly enough to let Rebecca know I wanted to take the lead. I fretted over my hair, whether to tie it back or leave it loose. If Rebecca was attracted to women, she would probably want me to look like one, so in the end I left it down.

I arrived at the café early and found a table beneath a large gilt mirror from where I had a good view of the room. A handful of waiters were polishing glasses behind the bar, one or two tables were occupied by couples having afternoon tea, a man was mopping the black-and-white tile floor. I wondered whether I should have chosen somewhere a little smaller and darker for us to meet; there didn't seem to be much privacy here.

I ordered a pot of Earl Grey and opened a book I'd brought in case I was early, *Queer* by William Burroughs. Could anyone see what I was reading? Should I have chosen something less obvious? The door swung open and I looked up to see a man in an overcoat enter with his wife. I was about to hide my book under my napkin when I saw a red-haired figure slip into the café behind them, wearing a wrap dress and high-heeled boots. She walked towards me, her head to one side, smiling coquettishly. I stood up and kissed her on the cheek, and she looked down at the teapot.

"What are we having?" she asked.

"I got us a pot of Earl Grey," I replied, stuffing my book into my bag to cover my self-consciousness. Rebecca sat down opposite me, rested her chin on her hands, and smiled at me. Her lips were painted with coral lipstick, her eyebrows shaped into immaculate arches as if she'd combed each hair individually into position. "Would you like a cup of tea?" I asked. "We could order some cake." I picked up the teapot, remembering too late my shaking hands and the disaster with the sugar at the bookstore. Pouring the tea into her cup with the concentration of a neurosurgeon, I asked her to tell me about herself.

Rebecca took the cue and launched into a series of stories about her childhood on Long Island, her college years at Cornell, her love of baroque music and classical literature. She talked in an uninterrupted flow as if the speech had been pre-rehearsed, and referred to the Ivy League degree several times, as if we were in a job interview and she was the prospective employee trying to prove her suitability. I was tempted to point out that if anyone was trying to sell themselves it should probably be me, but she was on a roll. Now she was telling me she loved German poetry, which she preferred to read in its original language, a claim she corroborated by pulling a book of poetry by Bertolt Brecht out of her bag. I started to feel mildly incidental to the whole conversation.

"So how did you . . . end up doing what you do now?" I asked, wondering whether the subject of her current profession was something we should address head-on or avoid mentioning at all costs.

She told me she'd been volunteering at a rape crisis center when she realized she wanted to train as a social worker, but this meant getting a second degree, which she couldn't afford. "A friend suggested I could make a lot of money as an escort, because my Ivy League degree would make me more attractive to the sort of man who wants intelligent conversation over dinner."

I wondered what kind of friend suggested sex work as a solution to potential college debt, although perhaps it was more enterprising than asking Daddy for a loan, particularly if that option wasn't available. Rebecca explained that they had a website—professional photographs, well-written bios, everything done through referrals. Her clients bought her clothes, jewelry, gifts. She dined in Manhattan's most expensive restaurants, attended the opera regularly, and every morning she woke up two thousand dollars richer. It occurred to me that Rebecca wasn't the only one performing sex she didn't like with men she didn't love in return for some kind of payment. Admittedly I hadn't married Charles for his money, but I'd certainly married for security, which was a far less noble cause than the one that had led Rebecca into sex work. She wanted to be a social worker, whereas I'd merely wanted to be socially acceptable; her sex work paid for her independence, whereas mine had tied me to a life of indentured servitude. Which of us had really sold themselves out?

Rebecca reached out and touched my hand across the table. "And what about you? What's your story?"

I bit my lip, hesitating for a moment before I confessed. As I explained my situation, I realized it wasn't so much the fact that I was married that was making me so uncomfortable, it was the fact that I was married to a man. Being married to a man meant I was a woman, and I didn't want to be a woman. Suddenly I felt confused; was it my womanhood or my wifehood that felt so wrong? Perhaps it was a bit of both. It was impossible to exude the kind of confidence I wanted to display while simultaneously admitting I still had to defer to a superior patriarchal authority. I wanted to be the boss, and I couldn't be the boss while Charles was still in the picture.

Rebecca stirred the tea leaves in the bottom of her cup while I talked—apparently unaware of my rapidly deflating ego—until I concluded my explanation by telling her that as far as women were concerned, I was still very much a virgin, since there didn't seem to be any point in pretending I had any credibility.

"I'd be your first?" Rebecca asked, seemingly unconcerned by my self-professed innocence.

"Well, you would be, if . . ." I trailed off, holding her eyes. She gazed back at me, her face an unmistakable invitation.

I checked my heartbeat, but it didn't seem to be responding appropriately to what was clearly a proposition. Where was the pulse-fluttering excitement I'd felt back in the bookstore?

Rebecca lowered her eyes and played with her teaspoon, smoothing the inside of the curve with a fingertip. "So, you're not available for a real relationship? The kind I'm looking for?"

"Probably not, no," I said. For a moment the question of whether I was actually gay was the only thing in my mind. I tried to focus on her mouth, wondering what it would be like to kiss her. As if reading my thoughts, she suddenly leaned across the table and kissed me on the lips.

A tornado swept through the room.

She pulled away and I glanced around quickly. The waiters were still polishing their glasses behind the counter, the couples at the other tables were still engaged in conversation with each other, nobody was looking at us. But two women had just kissed *right in front of them*! Hadn't they been blown apart by the blast?

Rebecca picked up my hand and held it in hers. She started to stroke my palm with her fingers, telling me how she'd just had her heart broken and didn't want to go through the experience again. The way she elongated her vowels made her voice sound almost hypnotic, but even as I wondered whether turning general conversation into a seduction routine was a habit she'd fallen into because of her profession, I realized it was working. I could see her mouth moving but I couldn't hear her words because all I could think was *Please kiss me again, please kiss me again.*

Rebecca sat gazing at me wistfully. "What are we going to do?" she asked, as if we'd reached a critical point in our relationship. I'd read of U-Haul lesbians who went from first date to living together within the space of a week, but we seemed to have bypassed all that and were into the devastating make-up-or-break-up scene after just one kiss.

"I don't know," I replied, not knowing what else to say.

"I know what I should do," she continued. "I should get up and walk away."

"I don't think I can give you what you want," I said.

She leaned forward and put her mouth on mine again, and this time I kissed her back, conscious only of the softness of her lips, the warmth spreading through my body.

She pulled away. "I'm probably making a terrible mistake," she said.

"Probably," I replied, still feeling the imprint of her lips on mine.

"I should leave," she said, not looking like she meant it.

"Yes, you should," I replied, not meaning it either.

We sat in silence for a moment, contemplating our options.

"Book a hotel for Friday?" Rebecca said.

"Done," I replied.

"Is that what you're wearing?" Charles asked as I walked into the kitchen. After my date with Rebecca, he seemed to have switched tactics. Now, rather than acting like my lesbianism was something we should both pretend wasn't real, he was acting like it was something we could share between us. I wasn't sure which was worse. It was almost as if he were indulging the whims of a crazy person, although why he wanted to remain married to someone he considered crazy was beyond me. He never quite said so directly, but I was worried he believed if he waited patiently for long enough, eventually I'd get bored of it all, and we'd return to the relationship we used to have before this all started. He'd been so relieved when I told him that Rebecca was a sex worker he'd almost laughed. It was inconceivable to him now that she could pose any threat to our family.

I looked down at my outfit. "What's wrong with it?"

"It's not very sexy."

I was wearing a black vintage frock coat I'd bought back in the eighties, and I'd slipped my grandfather's gold fob watch round my neck. I felt like a buccaneer.

"Perhaps a dress? What about that purple one you wore to the school gala? You don't want her to think you haven't made an effort." I flinched inwardly. He sounded like an insecure parent not wanting to get left out as his child got ready for prom. "Or a pair of heels? You look great in heels."

"I'm not wearing heels, Charles." I checked my bag for my keys, wallet, and phone, and pulled up the handle of my small suitcase. Now probably wasn't the time to tell him I might never wear a pair of high heels again.

I could feel Charles's eyes on me as I opened the door to the playroom, where the children were watching *Dora the Explorer*. Freddie took one look at my suitcase and immediately started howling.

"Mummy, don't go! Please don't go!" He ran to me, fell dramatically to his knees and clutched at my leg, shaking with sobs.

"It's only for one night, sweetheart."

"But I can't live without you!"

I knelt down to hug him. "I'll be back tomorrow, I promise. You'll be fine with Daddy."

"We don't want Daddy!" Alfie joined in, infected by Freddie's distress. "Mummy, stay!"

I'd read somewhere that this was what happened to parents who rarely went out, that children needed to learn that a parent who left would come back as promised, that it was a valuable lesson in independence and trust. It didn't make it any easier. Lily and Rose were sitting on the sofa in their pajamas with their sippy cups, their eyes wide at all the drama. I needed to go before they started crying too.

"I love you, poppets. I'll be back tomorrow," I said, showering them with kisses then tugging away from them towards the door. Down in the garage I sat in the car for a moment before I started the engine. I was abandoning my children to go on a date with a lesbian sex worker. What kind of mother did this?

The outside of the bar where Rebecca had arranged for us to meet was unimposing, a small dark window set in a bare brick wall, the only indication that this was one of the oldest gay venues in New York being the pink neon sign that spelled out its name: THE STONEWALL INN. I pushed open the heavy oak door and stepped into a room that closely resembled an English pub, complete with wood paneling, a pool table, and the smell of beer-soaked floorboards. Rebecca was at the bar, posing on a stool in a black dress like a model in a commercial for an expensive alcoholic drink. She smiled as I approached, and I kissed her on the lips, feeling more confident now that I was protected by the dark safety of the bar. Rebecca put her arms around my neck and pulled me closer, and I felt a flood of familiarity and belonging.

"Do you know the history of this place?" she asked as I pulled up a stool. When I admitted I was hazy on the details, she started filling me in on the gay liberation riots that had exploded out of the room in the late sixties, describing the brutality of the police with the sort of specificity that suggested personal experience. While my adolescence had been spent in the safe shelter of an exclusive boarding school, here in America queer people and sex workers had been fighting for their lives. My whining complaint that my class had excluded me from the gay community now looked like the petty grievance of a spoiled child; it wasn't my class that separated me from these people, it was my complete lack of empathy. I remembered the Pulp song from the nineties; I didn't want to be a class tourist anymore, I wanted to belong, but inclusion in this community was something I'd have to earn.

The obvious first step would be to connect emotionally with Rebecca, but the feeling that we were talking at each other rather than with each other was hard to shift. My gaze kept straying to two men who were deep in conversation on Rebecca's other side. One had his hand on the other's shoulder, his mouth close to his boyfriend's cheek as he whispered in his ear. His torso—barely covered by a white tank top—looked as if it had been carved out of marble, the muscles on his arms shining leanly through his smooth skin. I felt a pang of envy; no amount of time in the gym could give me a body like that, and my skin was too pale and soft to glow with such a sleek, polished shine. His partner laughed at something he said and turned his face to kiss him; their lips met briefly and then parted, their eyes extending the gesture of affection. My envy shifted from their bodies to their relationship; this was the kind of intimacy I wanted, and my hope that it might magically appear between Rebecca and me just because we were both lesbians was possibly unfounded.

But then I remembered that I was the newbie here, and if we weren't connecting, it was probably my fault, not hers. Rebecca knew who she was—an intelligent, determined, queer woman who had to work harder than most to achieve her ambitions—and she was comfortable in her identity as a femme lesbian. Whereas I still had no idea who I wanted to be, or how to manifest my masculinity in a way that felt right.

We left the Inn and started walking down Christopher Street, heading for the restaurant I'd booked. Away from the safety of the bar I started to feel anxious and agoraphobic. I realized I was shaking.

"Can we stop for a minute?" I asked. We sat on a stoop while I tried to regain my composure. Rebecca stroked the hair away from my neck and kissed me, the warmth of her breath and the softness of her skin calming my racing heart.

"I'm sorry," I said. "This is very new to me."

"Not as confident as you seem, huh?" Rebecca smiled.

"Not so much," I admitted.

On the other side of the road, a mother and daughter were standing nervously on the sidewalk. The mother was wearing a Chanel bouclé jacket and heavy emerald earrings, and the daughter was in a tailored silk shift dress with a pashmina wrapped around her shoulders. They looked odd and out of place, as if they rarely ventured out of the Upper East Side and had no idea where they were or how they'd got here. For a moment I felt like I was having an out-of-body experience, unable to place myself in the picture. Only a short while ago I'd have aligned myself with these women, but now they seemed like aliens; and while Rebecca's life was completely foreign to me, sitting here on the stoop with her I almost felt safe.

We arrived back at the hotel around midnight. I kissed Rebecca in the elevator going up to our room, hoping it might steady my nerves. I was about to get naked with a woman for the first time; how would I know what to do? Rebecca politely ignored my fumbling fingers as I unlocked the door to our room; she moved to the bed and lay back on the pillows, watching me silently as I hung my jacket in the closet, turned off my phone, and lowered the lights, buying myself time until my heartbeat slowed. Finally, I sat down on the bed beside her and stroked the hair away from her temples. To be on this side of the equation—to be the desirer, not the desired—felt both liberating and strangely familiar, as if for the first time I was in the right place.

"Are you okay?" I whispered.

"Yes, I am," she replied. I leaned in and kissed her. Her skin smelled faintly of apricots. I could feel the soft hairs on her upper lip, taste the peppermint she'd sucked in the taxi. She wriggled her dress over her head, leaving me to remove her underwear. I moved slowly, discovering that everything about her was soft—her lips, her tongue, her smooth skin, the curves of her flesh, the warmth between her legs. I pulled off my clothes, wondering whether I'd retreat into my head, where I usually went during sex, but as I moved back over her, she arched beneath me, wrapping her legs around my hips and running her hands over my back. I closed my eyes, allowing her touch to send waves of heat through my flesh, feeling myself bloom into my body. I bent my head and kissed her mouth, and then traveled slowly down, until all I knew was the warmth and the smell and the taste of her, all I could hear was the sound of her breathing.

Hours later we lay among the mess of sheets, my body spooned around hers, one arm under her head, the other draped across her waist. I breathed in the salty sweat of her skin, watching the soft stripes that the moonlight painted across her hips. I wished I could stop the moon's journey across the sky so I'd never have to leave this bed, never have to peel myself away from her body. I'd become a different person while we'd been making love, present in my body in a way I'd never experienced before. She coaxed my masculinity to the surface so comprehensively that my body had morphed into a new shape, one that fit perfectly into hers. Was this what all lesbians felt during sex? Why hadn't anyone told me about this before? I pressed my mouth against the base of her neck as I felt the craving rise inside me again, thinking that perhaps if I kept my lips against her skin it would start to fill the void inside me.

"Will you be able to go to sleep with me holding you like this?" I asked. I'd never been able to sleep while touching another person, but nothing on earth would have induced me to let her go.

"I'll try," Rebecca purred.

"You're amazing," I whispered.

"I think that was the best sex I've ever had," she replied. "You're a natural."

I smiled into her hair. It didn't matter that the comment might be disingenuous—or that she probably said it to everyone she slept with—because she was right. This came as naturally to me as breathing.

Chapter Sixteen

Once Charles realized that I had no intention of sharing any details about my new relationship with him, we largely stopped communicating. The only time we spent together now was when we were with the children, each of us in our own way committed to trying to keep things as normal for them as possible. In one sense little had materially changed. Charles left for work before they got up in the morning and arrived home after they were in bed at night, so the children barely seemed to register that we were sleeping in different bedrooms, and on the rare occasions when they did, we put it down to Charles's need for uninterrupted sleep. There was none of the drama that one would expect in a house where a marriage was coming apart, but I worried that the meticulous politeness with which Charles and I now spoke to each other was just as damaging as raging conflict might have been. Plus Freddie's anxiety always increased if I was unhappy, which meant he couldn't sleep, which meant I couldn't sleep, which left me grouchy and irritable during the day, which then rubbed off on the other kids. Charles's suggestion that I hide my unhappiness wasn't just inhuman, it was impossible.

I managed to negotiate one night off a month, which didn't seem like a lot but was enough for Rebecca, who admitted on our third date that she found it difficult to find women who were willing to date someone in her profession. I admired her honesty—it would have been so easy to conceal the truth—but the more she told me about her life, the more I realized how vulnerable she was, and that I probably shouldn't let the affair continue if I wasn't going to get serious.

But Rebecca had woken up something inside me I needed to investigate further, and I couldn't quite bring myself to give up on the relationship. It wasn't just that she indulged my masculinity—letting me pick up the check, hold open the door, hail the taxi—it was something more, something that surfaced when we were alone in bed together. She was soft, feminine, compliant, and when she wrapped her legs around me I felt myself melt into my body, as if in sex I'd finally found the magic elixir that could soothe the anxiety that buzzed constantly through my veins. But one evening, a few months into our relationship, I accidentally strayed into new territory. I wasn't quite sure what had precipitated it—I'd let my guard down too soon, perhaps, relaxed into my body a little too much—but while I was moving on top of her, I'd been lulled into a rhythm so smooth that I slipped into an altered state, one in which I could feel physical sensations in parts of my body that didn't actually exist. It was disturbingly real: a fully embodied experience not just of making love to a woman, but of making love as a man.

I lay awake that night after Rebecca had fallen asleep, listening to the sounds of the hotel around me—the radiator clanking, someone upstairs taking a shower, a truck backing up on the street—trying to stop the aftermath of the experience from blowing up the inside of my brain. It had been the single most intense thing I'd ever experienced, and I had no idea what it meant. I wanted to be a woman with a woman—albeit a masculine-presenting one—but this was taking it all in an entirely different direction, one I had no interest in following. There might be some way for me to come out as gay in Connecticut, but there was no way I could spin a sex change.

I closed my eyes and tried to slow down my breathing. I wasn't a man—I *couldn't* be a man—there were limits to how far I'd let this go. I was five foot three. I weighed all of 110 pounds, my body was as feminine as women's bodies came. I put my hands on my breasts, between my legs: female parts, female body, female me. I needed to put this insane thought back in its box.

But Rebecca continued to tune in to my masculine energy in a way that made me increasingly uncomfortable. The way she treated me, the way she touched me, the way she exaggerated her feminine traits to highlight my masculinity. Sometimes it felt slightly performative, as if she were playing along to a gendered script she assumed I wanted to follow. Halfway through dinner at an expensive restaurant she told me she wasn't wearing any underwear and invited me to put my foot between her legs, but role-playing *Basic Instinct* in public wasn't a turn-on for me. I didn't want to be the sort of douchebag who wanted to fuck his girlfriend in the restaurant bathroom. When we were alone in private later that evening, however, her femininity enveloped me with such rich softness that I couldn't resist sinking into her, my body succumbing to its newly discovered male form.

"You want to be a man, don't you?" she whispered between kisses.

I froze. Had I misheard her? Which word had she just used, "a" or "the"?

"It's okay," she reassured me, stroking my back. "You can be the man."

My body relaxed as she started kissing me again. I could be the man. This was just a role, and we were only playing. But it didn't feel playful anymore. It was too much, too fast. I needed to slow it all down, get some control over what was happening, which I couldn't do if every time Rebecca touched me between my legs my brain kept insisting that she was touching a penis. Sooner or later, she'd figure it out, and then we'd have to have a conversation about it, and I wasn't going to have a conversation with anyone, ever, about whether I might be a man.

The only solution I could come up with was to end the relationship, so that's what I did, over the phone because I didn't have the guts to do it face-to-face. Rebecca was hurt and angry, particularly since I wouldn't give her any explanation beyond wanting to meet more queer people, which I claimed I couldn't do if I spent all my free evenings alone with her. It was a lame excuse, and I knew that by not giving her a more believable reason I risked her thinking it might have something to do with her profession—which made me look like an asshole and her look cheap—but I was too much of a coward to tell her the truth. I regretted it as soon as I hung up the phone, but when she sent me a text politely suggesting that I go fuck myself, I knew there was no way back. I felt disappointed, and deeply ashamed. If I wanted to be accepted into the queer community, I should probably start by showing its more vulnerable members a little more respect.

*   *   *

To some degree what I'd told Rebecca was the truth, though. I really did want to meet more people. I'd just effectively banned myself from the only queer bookstore in New York, and I obviously wasn't going to start hanging out in the gay bars, so it would make sense to try to find them closer to home. Connecticut was not populated only by rich, white straight people, despite what my immediate surroundings implied. There must be queer folk around here somewhere, I just had to figure out how to find them.

Once again, I went online. I ignored the dating sites and kept searching until I came to a website for a small LGBTQ center in the next town. The Lesbian Late Bloomers support group had closed due to lack of attendance, but there was an email address in case anyone was interested in reviving it. I sent a quick message and then scrolled on through the website until I came across a link to the Westport Country Playhouse. The theater was hosting an LGBTQ cocktail reception for a Stephen Sondheim musical. If I really wanted to meet local gay people then this seemed like the ideal place to do it, but could I really turn up to an event like this on my own? And if I couldn't, what was the alternative? I could bond with the women in the school playground over the subject of motherhood but not over the subject of my sexuality. I was going to have to summon the courage to go to an event like this, and then summon the even greater courage to talk to someone once I got there. I clicked on the link and bought myself a ticket before I lost my nerve.

When I arrived, the reception was humming with people, most of them over the age of forty. I could totally do this, I just had to look self-assured. Walk to the bar. Order a drink. Pick up a plate of canapés. I stood at the side of the room. Here I was, at a gay cocktail party, surrounded by gay people, with my gay canapés and my gay drink. It was excruciating. What was I supposed to do now? Just walk up to a group of people and say, "Hi! I'm Nicky and I'm gay too! Can I be your friend?"

I scanned the small groups of men and women chatting around me, simultaneously trying not to look forlorn and hoping to catch someone's eye. It would make sense to approach one of the groups of women, since I was a woman, and yet there was something about their studiously ungroomed, old-school butchness that felt excluding. They wouldn't think I was one of them because of my long hair and makeup, even though I felt just as masculine as they presumably did. And then there was the danger that they might hit on me rather than treat me as an equal, which would have been awful, not because I didn't want to be hit on by a woman but because I no longer wanted to be treated as a conquest.

I surreptitiously eyed up a nearby group of gay men. Given the choice, I'd rather look like one of them—they were so beautifully groomed and neatly tailored—and yet this appealingly dapper look seemed to require a masculine body as its starting point. If I wore a suit and tie, I wouldn't look gay, I'd look like a waitress. Someone would probably try to order a drink from me. I looked around the room hopelessly. This was absurd. What was the point in coming all this way if I couldn't bring myself to speak to anyone? I went outside to the terrace at the front of the theater, wondering if anyone might be smoking. Asking someone for a cigarette was usually a good way to break the ice.

"Nicky!"

I froze. Bearing down on me, her husband trailing at her heels, was Pandora, one of the mothers from the children's school. Another expatriated Englishwoman, Pandora had a fondness for reminiscing about the social background we both came from, which had not endeared her to me, and I couldn't think of anyone I wanted to bump into less at this precise moment.

"Pandora!" I stammered.

"What are you doing here?"

"I'm . . . I'm . . . going to the theater."

"Where's Charles?"

"Uh, he's not here."

"So, you're here with . . ."

"A friend?"

"Someone I know?"

"Uh, no . . . she's . . . he's . . . she's . . . inside." Beads of sweat were breaking out on my forehead. Pandora looked at me strangely, the smile glued to her face. "What about you, where are you off to?"

"Dinner at the Dressing Room." Pandora put a possessive hand on her husband's arm, tilting her head towards the restaurant beside the theater. "Thursday night is date night." She looked at me expectantly, as if waiting for me to continue the conversation.

"Oh, well . . . have a lovely evening . . ." I gave a stupid little wave and turned back to the theater. I could feel her eyes on my back as I walked away. Did she know it was LGBTQ night? I was shaking with panic. Why hadn't I just pretended Charles was in the bathroom? I wanted to be out, but I didn't want someone like Pandora controlling that narrative, particularly since I still had no idea who I was. I wasn't a femme lesbian, but nor was I butch, and however much I might want to be a gay man, I couldn't be one because I liked women.

And also because I wasn't a man, obviously. So, where did that leave me? Nowhere that made sense.

My next attempt at finding community took me to a small ranch house on the outskirts of a nearby town, where the Lesbian Late Bloomers group was about to hold its first revival meeting. I wasn't confident I'd find my people here either—a support group for middle-aged suburban lesbians sounded decidedly unsexy—but I promised myself I'd explore every avenue. I knocked on the door, which was opened by a small woman in her early sixties with short, salt-and-pepper hair and wire-rimmed glasses. "You must be Nicky!" She put out a hand and shook mine warmly. "I'm Eve, come in, you're the last to arrive."

I followed her down a narrow hallway into a small living room with a low ceiling. Books were stacked higgledy-piggledy on the bookshelves, the large picture window had fairy lights strung over the curtain rail, the sofas and armchairs were mismatched and informal. Beside the television a woman with a freckled face dressed in yoga clothes was talking to a dark-haired woman who'd plucked and penciled her eyebrows to look like two neat tadpoles. In an armchair a plump, motherly woman with a curly blonde perm and eighties-style blue eye shadow was nursing a glass of rosé, and on the sagging sofa by the coffee table sat a woman with purple hair and bee-stung lips, scooping artichoke dip out of a small bowl with a carrot stick. She popped the crudité into her mouth and grinned.

"Hi, I'm Lisa."

"Nicky," I replied, shaking her outstretched hand.

Eve plopped herself down in an armchair. "Help yourself, dear," she said, waving vaguely towards the bottles of wine and seltzer nestled in among the guacamole and corn chips.

I sat down next to Lisa, who kicked off her shoes and curled up her feet.

Eve broke the ice by telling us her coming-out story. I shifted uncomfortably when she said she and her wife had met through a homeschooling support group; I'd always thought people who homeschooled their children were a bit odd, but then I'd always thought lesbians were a bit odd too, so perhaps I should start being a little less judgmental. Lisa went next, relating how she'd been kissed by a drunk woman at a Bon Jovi concert, which had somehow resulted in her sleeping with her personal trainer. The woman with the shiny dark hair had just been dumped by her lawyer girlfriend, the motherly woman was having a volatile affair with her dental hygienist, and the young woman in the yoga clothes had recently started having sex with her best friend.

"I don't want my marriage to end," she said, fiddling with one of the cords from her sweatshirt, her chin dimpled with misery. "My parents went through a vicious divorce when I was young; my brother and I were completely sidelined by their hatred of each other. I've been through years of therapy trying to recover from it, and I *cannot* put my children through that." She twisted her hoodie cord tightly around her finger, tears running openly down her cheeks. "I can't do this. Any of it. I just want to give my children the best life. All the security, all the love."

"Staying married might not be the best way to do that," Eve said, gently.

"But it's what every child wants, isn't it? Parents who are happily married?"

"What if they just want parents who are happy?" I asked. I hardly knew anyone with divorced parents. Where I came from people didn't get divorced, they stayed married and fucked up their children with their misery instead.

"There's something anachronistic about traditional marriage," Lisa agreed.

"So why did we all buy into it?" I asked.

"I wanted to be a wife," the dark-haired woman said. "But a wife with a wife."

"If you say it too many times it starts to sound funny, doesn't it?" the blonde woman pointed out. "Wife! Wife! Wife! Like a little dog barking."

I remembered being invited to Royal Ascot a few months after Charles and I got married. Charles was in a top hat and tailcoat, I was wearing heels that were sinking into the grass and a large hat with bits of feather sticking out of it. Pinned to my lapel was a badge that said MRS. CHARLES STANTON, which I wore with a sense of superiority. I was married, I was a wife, I had found myself a husband. Nobody was going to bloody well tell me I couldn't do this. Nobody was going to suggest I was weird or strange or different. I was standing within spitting distance of the Queen; even she would have approved of me had she bothered to look in my direction. It was the culmination of everything I'd worked towards, and it felt entirely empty.

And now here I was, sitting on a stained sofa beneath a macramé wall hanging in a room full of bonkers women sharing ridiculous stories about their lesbian experiences to cheer up a weeping yoga instructor. When they finally managed to get her laughing, I wondered whether these were the sort of people who might start to make me feel more whole.

Chapter Seventeen

I left the Late Bloomers with five new phone numbers and promises of playdates with the kids. Finally, this felt like a start. None of the women fit neatly into either the butch or femme category, which made me feel a bit more relaxed about my own nonconforming identity. Perhaps being a masculine-leaning person with long blonde hair wasn't so weird after all. But before we could put any plans into place it was time to fly back to England with the children for the summer vacation, which presented me with a whole new set of problems. If I'd barely managed to survive a week in the closet with my parents at Christmas, how could I survive a whole summer? Tentatively, I suggested to Charles that I might come out to them, but his response was swift.

"No. Absolutely not. I won't hear of it."

"It's been almost a year, Charles, I can't go on lying to them."

"You're not lying, you're just not telling the truth."

"It's the same thing."

"England is a very small country, particularly among our people. My parents *cannot* find out about this. You understand that, don't you? My father will cut us all off completely if he finds out you're gay."

"All of us?"

"He'll do it to punish you."

"Jesus," I said, feeling slightly sick.

"My mother loathes you enough as it is," Charles muttered under his breath.

In the end I figured I didn't have to tell him—my mother and father were pretty good at keeping secrets—but I still felt queasy for the entire flight home. The children, however, were impervious to my anxiety. They bounced with excitement in the back of the car as we drove through the English countryside, past the small village church where Jane Austen's father used to preach, down the narrow country lane bordered by hedgerows of wild clematis, until we finally arrived at my childhood home, a rambling Georgian farmhouse surrounded by beech trees, oaks, and chestnuts. I turned into the drive, the crunch of gravel heralding our arrival.

"Darlings! Darlings!" my mother cried, appearing at the front door, waving her hands in the air as if we were heroes returning from war. "Goodness, gosh, it's lovely to see you!" I pulled the suitcases out of the back of the car while she shepherded the kids into the kitchen and out through the French doors into the garden at the back of the house. "Shoo! Shoo! Out you go! Run off all the jetlag!"

I followed the children into the garden, my eyes squinting against the bright sunlight. The table on the terrace was laid with bowls of salads and a jug of elderflower cordial, home-grown beans and freshly buttered new potatoes. My father had set up a carving table and was laying strips of cold lamb on a platter; my mother laid out a rug on the lawn where the children could eat their lunch. Memories surfaced of picnic teas in the garden, of daisy chains and four-leaf clovers and buttercups held under the chin, of tree houses and swings and camps made under the boxbush, of lawn mowers and tennis balls and bumblebees. I wasn't sure my father had ever read Nabokov, but in their hearts they spoke the same language: *Everything is as it should be, nothing will ever change, nobody will ever die.*

After lunch I sat in a deck chair while the children ran off to play in the tree house, trying to figure out how to tell my parents I wasn't *this* anymore, that this was no longer me. The familiarity of England in July—the smell of freshly cut grass mingling with the scent of sweet peas and roses—created a sensory overload that almost obliterated the memory of any other reality, as if my life in America had been happening to someone else, in a book I'd read or a movie I'd seen, not quite real and not quite mine. My parents' world was so permanent and reliable, and yet mine couldn't have been less so. In England I was a faithful daughter, in Connecticut an emerging lesbian, and in New York—when I lost my grip on reality entirely—a man. And yet here in my parents' garden on a sunny afternoon all these other identities seemed ridiculous, fantastical, absurd.

I decided to come out to my mother first—to get her on board before I tackled my father—so once the children settled into their summer routine, I suggested we go out for a meal by ourselves. I told her I wanted to talk to her about the reason behind my recurring depressions, the alcoholism, the mood swings. My mother chose a new pub that had opened locally. I'd hoped for a cozy and familiar environment that might offer us some comfort while we navigated this new territory, but as soon as I walked in the door my heart sank. Whoever'd been responsible for decorating the restaurant had tried to create a modern atmosphere with neither taste nor budget, and the result was a very bare, overlit room with horrible little brown tables floating around uncomfortably on a sea of pale-blond floorboards.

"Well, this is lovely, isn't it?" my mother said, sitting down at a table and smiling approvingly at the multicolored carnations that were fighting for space with the condiments. "Daddy would love it here."

I wondered if we were both sitting in the same restaurant. Daddy would not love it here; this place would make him feel seasick.

"So, Mum," I said, pushing the carnations to one side.

"Hang on a sec," she said, pulling her handbag onto her knee and scrabbling around inside it. She pulled out her hearing aid and pushed it into her ear. "Okay," she said looking up at me. "Now I can hear you properly."

I hesitated, not sure what to say next. My mother picked up the menu and started flicking through it, her spectacle cords dangling down in front of her ears. She'd put on a pair of diamond earrings for the occasion. "So." I tried to muster up some courage by moving the utensils around the table. "There's some stuff I want to talk to you about. Important stuff." My mother looked at me over the top of the menu. "Stuff I want to share with you." I glanced over at the people sitting at the table next to us. Were they close enough to hear what I was saying? Too late now if they were. I turned back to my mother. "The thing is, Mum, I understand why I've always been so confused all my life." I took a deep breath. I might as well just come out with it. "The reason I've been so unhappy . . . is because I'm gay."

Just as I said the word "gay," someone at the next table coughed. My mother's expression didn't change, as if she were still waiting for the punch line.

"You didn't hear what I just said, did you?" I asked her.

"No, I didn't," she admitted.

"Okay, then, I'll say it again." I took another deep breath. "I'm gay."

My mother looked startled, and then suddenly burst out laughing. She clapped her hand over her mouth. "Oh, my goodness, I'm so sorry, I didn't mean to laugh!" Now she looked horrified. "So, you're . . . what? I don't understand."

"I'm gay," I repeated.

"Since when?" she asked.

"Okay, maybe I should start at the beginning," I said, wondering whether perhaps that's where I should have started in the first place. "Back when I was at St. Mary's . . ."

"Were you bullied?" she interrupted suddenly. "Oh, my darling! Gosh, how awful, it must have been dreadful!"

"No, Mum, I wasn't bullied, I was still trying to figure it out back then. It wasn't as if a light just went on overnight."

"No, of course it wasn't," she said hurriedly. "It must have been a gradual realization."

"Mum, please don't, can you just let me . . ."

"Yes, yes, of course, I'm so sorry darling, go ahead."

"You don't have to leap into being immediately enthusiastic; this is hard, just let me talk it through with you. It wasn't until recently that I really understood that I was gay . . ."

"No! I mean, yes! What? Oh!" The expression on her face

started changing rapidly as if she was now trying to mask pure horror with a sort of beatific approval.

"Mum," I said, trying to talk to her calmly, like I did to Freddie when he was having one of his panic attacks. "I know it may be hard for you to process this information right now, but if you give me time to explain, I think you'll see that my being gay is not as terrible as it sounds."

"Absolutely. You're completely right. Oh, my goodness. You talk, I'll just listen." She was now wearing the expression she usually reserved for people of color, as if she were determined to overcome an innate fear by being radically tolerant. I started to tell her about everything that had happened, while she folded and unfolded her napkin across her lap, as if this would some-how help smooth out her emotional responses. Our food arrived and sat largely untouched on the table between us while my mother lost her composure again, oscillating wildly through confusion and disbelief before returning to fiercely supportive encouragement. I wished she could calm down enough for me to be able to finish a sentence without rushing in to finish it for me, but her skittishness seemed to be out of control.

"Mum," I said, reaching out a hand, "it's going to be okay."

"But Charles . . . the children!" she said suddenly, as if finding someone else who might be upset about my being gay would release her from any obligation to disclose her own feelings.

"They're going to be fine. Charles and I are going to stay together for the time being, and nothing about the children's lives is going to change just yet."

"But what about your father? We can't tell him! But how can we not tell him? How can I know this and he not know?

How can I keep a secret like this? But we mustn't tell him! No, it's okay, I can talk to him!"

"Mum, slow down, one step at a time. We don't have to tell Dad right now. Just try to get used to this yourself first."

My mother stared at the plates of food between us, and then she deflated, as if someone had blown the wind out of her. "I want you to stop talking now," she said, in a voice that sounded nothing like her own.

"Are you okay?" I asked.

She looked like she was struggling to breathe, as if she were going into shock. "I'm fine," she said. "But I want you to stop talking about it."

"Mum, we're in the middle of a conversation . . ."

"No. Please, stop."

She sat in silence, her face ashen, while I paid the bill. We drove home without speaking. That night I lay awake in bed, staring at the ceiling while I replayed our conversation in my head. I'd genuinely thought this wouldn't be a huge leap for her, because she'd admitted to me several times that she was becoming increasingly less convinced by Christian doctrine (although she tried to hide this progressiveness from my father) and seemed terribly eager to proclaim her acceptance of anyone from a marginalized community. But what if I'd misjudged the situation completely? She'd always sacrificed her own needs to the needs of my father—she believed it was the right thing to do—which meant she might support Charles's desire that I stay closeted instead of supporting me.

I turned over in bed. Maybe she just needed some time. During my childhood I hadn't understood her need to retreat while she figured out her moral position on any given subject, so it had felt like disapproval, avoidance, and abandonment. It still felt like disapproval, avoidance, and abandonment. Just this once I needed her to break through her uptight self-restraint and be a mother to me.

Two weeks passed, with lunch parties and outings with the kids and evenings sitting around the kitchen table while my mother discussed anything and everything she could think of to facilitate her complete denial that anything out of the ordinary had occurred. Events in the news, books she'd read, the various illnesses of her aging friends—all these subjects she dissected at length—but not a word about our conversation at the pub. I started to panic. What if she never reached a place where we could start talking again? What if that had been the only conversation we were ever going to have on the subject? How the hell was I going to tell my father if I couldn't even talk to my mother?

Eventually she suggested that we leave the children with a babysitter and spend the day together indulging in one of her favorite pastimes, walking around the grounds of a local stately home and looking at the plants. There was a tea shop in the orangery, and we decided to start the afternoon off with a pot of Lapsang souchong and a couple of fruit scones. I watched my mother's face as she sat across the table from me; she'd left behind the stiff mask she'd been wearing for the last couple of weeks, and in her eyes I saw sadness, defeat, and just the first trace of acceptance.

"I didn't want it to be true," she finally admitted, looking up at me.

"Oh, Mum." Relief flooded through me. "Took you a while this time, huh?"

"It's been a bit of an adjustment, darling," she replied. "I really don't have a problem with you being gay, you must believe that. I'm just upset about everything you'll have to forfeit because of it. Your husband, your family, your beautiful home—I can't bear that you'll have to give it all up."

"I don't have a choice anymore," I said, picking the currants out of my scone. "I just have to keep plowing forward and hope we'll all come out the other side in once piece."

"How will you support yourself when you come back to England? Will you go back to landscaping?"

"Mum," I said gently, "I already told you, I don't think we're coming back."

I wanted to tell her that there was no part of British society into which I could fit anymore—that the gay people wouldn't accept me because of my upper-class background, and the people from my background wouldn't accept me because I was gay—but this wasn't entirely true. Of course there were upper-class gay people in England, but following in the footsteps of the Bloomsbury Group, they were mostly found in the elite world of art and literature. Entry into these circles required either great wealth, aristocratic pedigree, or extraordinary artistic success, none of which I had. Anyway, I was tired of setting myself apart. I didn't want to belong to an exclusive club, I just wanted to be with the kinds of people I'd seen at Bluestockings, Cubbyhole, and the Late Bloomers group— normal people who happened to be queer—and that was easier to do in America. Given the choice between Virginia Woolf or Quentin Crisp, I'd rather be an Englishman in New York.

"My being a lesbian is going to offend a lot of people," I told my mother. "I can't bear to upset your friends, and I know that's what I'm going to do when I come out. I can't

toughen myself up enough for it not to hurt, my skin just isn't
that thick. Better to do it from a distance."

My mother rummaged around in her handbag for a hand-
kerchief and wiped her eyes.

"Come on, let's walk and talk," I said. I linked my arm
through hers as we walked through the gardens, listening
quietly while she told me how painful it was for her, how
she'd always clung to the hope that we might move back to
England, how desperately she missed her grandchildren. I
knew what she wanted—to grow old with all of us coming
home every weekend, to have her house and garden filled with
family, to have our lives perfectly mirror hers—but I didn't
want to point out that this vision relied heavily on both me
and my brother being exactly the sort of people she'd expected
us to be, which neither of us were. Maybe by not formatting
my life to the same template, rather than denying my children
an idyllic childhood, I might instead be releasing them from
an obligation they might not want to fulfill.

Our walk led us to a small chapel hidden on the grounds,
and we stopped to sit at the bottom of the lichen-covered
stone steps leading up to its entrance. Any residual anger
I'd been feeling at her delayed response melted away. My
coming out to my mother wasn't about me, it was about her.
I had Elisabeth and Bianca to turn to for support, whereas my
mother had no one. It had been selfish of me to think that
she should be offering me more reassurance, when in fact the
reverse was necessary. I rested my head on her shoulder. "I'm
sorry, Mum. I truly am."

A crumbling statue of Venus stood alone in the middle of
the lawn, the centerpiece in a breathtaking view across the
surrounding countryside. The statue's head was bent, and she

gazed at the ground in lonely reflection. The beauty of the countryside always filled me with an almost divine gratitude to be alive, but now I wondered whether I'd chosen a career in landscaping only because I was drawn to the solitude. Trees didn't care how I looked; plants never judged my behavior. "This is like living in an ivory tower," I said. "It's beautiful but isolating. I don't want to be protected from the world anymore, I want to be part of it."

My mother sat wordlessly looking out over the lawn. Then she sighed. "I don't know how we're going to explain any of this to your father."

I took the kids to London to see my brother, Jack, who lived in a small house in Putney with his Scottish wife, Mairi, and their five children. With all nine cousins running around the house, it was hard to find a moment of privacy, but once dinner was over and they'd all collapsed in front of a movie, we finally had the kitchen to ourselves. Jack was the most laid-back person I knew, plus he and Mairi had finished off a bottle of wine between them over dinner, so I wasn't too nervous about coming out to them. Still, I hadn't expected Jack to be quite so delighted by the news. He claimed it was possibly the most interesting thing that had ever happened to him and said that I'd just increased his cool factor by about 10 percent. His wife was even more enthusiastic. "I knew it!" she said. "I knew there was something you were hiding. I just couldn't put my finger on what it was. That whole executive-wife thing you had going was such a weird departure. I never believed it was you." I sank back into my chair, sighing with relief. I'd always known Mairi suspected I was faking it—that Celtic intuition of hers—and I'd put distance between us because of it. Now perhaps that wall could come down.

"When are you going to tell Dad?" Jack asked, opening a second bottle of wine.

"I don't know," I said. We looked at each other, not needing to voice the thought that was running through both our minds.

"It's going to be okay," he said. Then he laughed gruffly. "I think."

I returned home the next day to find my father sitting at the kitchen table with a stunned look on his face, my mother standing behind him wearing an expression of supportive concern. I hurried the children into the garden—quickly inventing a game they could play from the tree house—before heading slowly back up the lawn, pausing briefly outside the French doors while I tried to prepare myself for what was about to come. How much had my mother told him? Why hadn't she warned me? Taking a deep breath, I walked back into the kitchen.

"Okay, what's going on?" I asked, leaning my hands on the back of the chair opposite my father.

Dad looked up at me. "I've been diagnosed with prostate cancer," he replied.

My heart dropped. "Wait, *what?*"

"We got the results back this morning," my mother explained.

I sat down at the table in front of them, my brain whirring. "Dad, what's been happening? Why didn't I know about any of this?"

My father told me he'd been to a doctor after months of symptoms but hadn't wanted to worry me until the results of the biopsy came back. When my throat became too tight to get any words out, he reassured me that the tests had indicated that it was early stage and totally treatable.

"Treatable?" I repeated, unable to form a longer sentence.

"Darling, most people die *with* prostate cancer, not *of* it," he said, as if clever wordplay could somehow minimize the risk.

"Die?"

Later that evening I caught my mother alone. "We can't tell him, Mum. Not while he's going through this."

"Of course not," she agreed. "We'll put it off until he comes out the other side. Like you said, there's no hurry. It's not like anything's changing anytime soon."

Chapter Eighteen

September 2012 marked the beginning of the second year of the new sexless, loveless, shadow version of our marriage. Charles and I had become the proverbial ships that passed in the night. Alone in the house with the children, I mostly felt okay, but the minute Charles arrived home I'd tense up again. It was something in the way he looked at me—the dissonance between who I was and what he was seeing—that made me prickly and snappish, and I knew the children could feel it too. I was growing increasingly desperate to get free, tugging at my guy ropes like a hot-air balloon staked to the ground, and I couldn't understand why Charles didn't feel the same way. The amount of time he spent away from the house spoke volumes—it was clear he didn't enjoy being around me anymore than I liked being around him—so his reluctance to take the next step towards separation didn't make any sense.

Maybe he was still stuck on the problem of how to tell people. He hadn't spoken to anyone about what we were going through—not a therapist, not a single friend—which meant that however much time he spent with his work colleagues or beer buddies, he was just as isolated as I was. Was it pride? Was it fear that if he said it out loud to someone, it would all become more real? Was there still some part of him that was hoping that if he ignored it all hard enough, it would go away?

Then a woman who'd recently joined the Late Bloomers group—which was now meeting regularly—put a thought into my head. She'd been talking about how women had been so successfully brainwashed into thinking we wanted children that we all walked into the prison of motherhood willingly and without complaint and were then unable to object to the subsequent restrictions imposed upon us in case it exposed us as morally corrupt, deficient in the kind of maternal love that was meant to make us human in the first place. I couldn't quite relate to this since I genuinely liked being a parent, but I did wonder whether perhaps Charles had been using my maternal instinct to coerce me into maintaining a domestic setup that suited him from a practical perspective.

"He doesn't want to give up the privilege of being the fun dad," the woman agreed. "Why would he, when he's got you doing all the work?"

It was Elisabeth who came up with an idea for how we could break the deadlock. She'd fallen in love with an artist who lived in Mexico and was now dividing her time between San Miguel de Allende and Manhattan, which meant her East Village apartment was often empty. She suggested we split the rent and I stay in it every other weekend. It seemed like the perfect solution: if I spent two weekends a month in New York while Charles looked after the kids, then he in turn could have the other two weekends off. If we had a fixed schedule, he'd be able to start dating again, and if he started having sex he might remember what he'd been missing.

I brought up the idea one afternoon while we were walking the dog in the woods, the children scrambling ahead of us looking for rocks to jump off and trees to climb. I knew that leaping straight from one night a month to two weekends was a lot, but it had been over a year now. Any reasonable person would recognize this wasn't a big ask.

But Charles wouldn't budge. He'd allowed me to have my little affair with Rebecca—he'd even covered the cost of the restaurants and the hotel rooms—and it was presumptuous of me to ask for more. I felt slightly sick at this description of his power over me, but with no money of my own, what was I supposed to do?

"I don't think you're taking into consideration how stressful my job is," Charles was saying. "If I don't get time to unwind on the weekends, I won't be able to function, and I can't relax properly if I have to look after the children."

"I get that, but most separated parents share the childcare fifty-fifty."

"Maybe if both parents are working, but you don't actually have a job, Nicky."

"That's because I'm the only one taking care of the kids," I said, trying to swallow my frustration. "If you could look after them occasionally then maybe I'd . . ."

"You know I can't do that. I have no control over the hours I work."

"So then what do you expect me to do?"

"It's not always all about *you*," Charles said.

"What's not all about me?"

"The marriage. Our family."

"I get that, but I am in fact a part of it. Anyway, this isn't a marriage. It's a co-parenting partnership."

"Same thing, isn't it?"

I said nothing. How could I argue with a man who was unwavering in his belief that it was the structure of the marriage that mattered, not the content?

"You know if we divorce we'll both be poor, don't you?"

"We won't be poor, Charles, we just won't be quite as wealthy."

"It's the same thing."

No, it's really not, I thought, but if I didn't want to hear my husband tell me money was more important than happiness, I should probably let it go.

Rose came running back down the path. "Biscuit's in the mud! It's so much gross!"

"Don't go in after her," I said.

"You'll get stinky," Charles added.

Rose bounced in excitement. "Will I be awesomely stinky?"

He swung her up by the arms. "Terrifically stinky." She squirmed out of his grip and ran back up the path, giggling in delight. I could hear the shouts of the children as they reached a fallen tree that was straddling the shallow river ahead of us, Biscuit splashing in the water beneath them, her wet tail showering them with mud.

"They're like little sponges," I said. "They can sense something's wrong."

"And who's to blame for that?"

I didn't reply, afraid that if I tried to speak I might start to cry.

"Look at them!" he said, suddenly furious. "Look how happy they are! You want to screw this up? I will *never* forgive you!"

He strode ahead and caught up with the children, who were climbing onto the tree trunk. He waded into the water, holding a hand out towards Lily as she wobbled over the makeshift bridge. "I can do it! Go a little bit away!" she said with authority, trying to pull her pudgy arm out of Charles's grasp. Charles caught her round the bottom just as she started to slip and swung her up onto his shoulders. She kicked his chest with her heels. "Giddy-giddy, Daddy-digger!" He splashed off through the stream, hollering like a cowboy, Lily holding fast to his ears and shrieking in excitement.

When we got home I settled the children in front of a movie and turned on the gas under a saucepan to cook some eggs for their supper. I was rooting around in the cutlery drawer for a spatula when I heard Charles call from the basement. I turned off the gas and went down the back stairs, the spatula still in my hand. He was standing by the back door with an armful of coats from the car. Lily's rain boot, with its little frog eyes and green spots, lay on top.

"Where do I put all this?"

"In the mudroom," I said. "We have to talk about this, Charles. We need to find a way to move forward."

We stood facing each other across the basement. Charles's face was flushed, his whole body an accusation. I knew that stance; it was the bullish position he took when he was refusing to back down, but I wasn't going to let this drop. It was time to move forward, even if I had to use an explosive device to make it happen.

"I need us to have a fixed schedule," I said.

"And I don't want a fixed schedule. I want to be able to come home and spend time with my children whenever I choose."

"Yes, but that also means you get to leave whenever you choose. You get to have complete freedom, and I have none. How is that fair?"

"Most mothers want to stay at home with their children."

"For God's sake, Charles. They're your children too!"

"But it's not my job to parent them! That's your job, always has been, always will be!"

"Charles, *please*," I said in desperation. "This isn't working for any of us. I'm not happy, and I know you're not either."

"Well, it's not exactly a barrel of laughs living with a woman who needs constant management!"

I froze for a split second, and then I snapped. I slammed the spatula down on the top of the boot rack; the noise cracked like a gunshot and Charles leapt back in alarm. "Manage me? How dare you think you're managing me! You've been trying to control who I am and where I go and what I think and how I behave since the day we married, and I will not fucking take it anymore! You think you can just nail my feet to the kitchen floor so you swan in and out whenever it suits you? Fuck you, Charles! This is not the nineteen-fucking-fifties and I will not sacrifice my entire life to your needs!"

Charles opened his arms, dropped the pile of coats and boots onto the ground, and walked out through the basement door.

"How convenient!" I shouted after him. "You can just leave any time you like!"

I tried to get myself back under control while I gave the children their baths and got them ready for bed, shaken by the intensity of my fury. But this was what I'd been doing all my life—swallowing my needs and emotions because I didn't want to cause a scene—and where exactly had it got me? Nowhere. Nothing I could do or say would prove to Charles that I cared about my children. If he was the hero of his story then I would always be the villain, and since there was fuck-all I could do to change that, I might as well stop trying. The only people who mattered were my kids, and just because I'd failed at being a wife didn't mean I'd failed at being a mother. I was perfectly capable of taking care of them on my own, and if Charles thought I was a bad parent for breaking up the family, then so be it.

Two hours and several bedtime stories later, the children were all asleep. I closed Freddie's bedroom door, wondering whether Charles had come back home yet. I went downstairs to find him standing by the counter in the kitchen, clinging to a cup of coffee as if it were laced with valium.

I sat down at the kitchen table. "I want a divorce," I said. I focused on a piece of scrambled egg that had dried onto the table while I waited for him to respond. I could feel his presence, motionless over by the sink. I wanted to stay calm, but I wasn't going to back down.

"I don't always say things the right way," he said eventually. Something in his voice made me look over at him. He was staring down into his coffee cup, his body slumped. I'd never seen him cry before, but his face looked swollen with emotion. "I didn't mean to imply that I'm trying to manage you. I just feel like I don't know you anymore."

"That's because you don't." I wished I knew how to explain to him who I was. Telling him I was gay wasn't enough; it was more than that. It was something inside me, my soul, my identity. I shook my head. "I can't stay married to you. I'm sorry, but I can't."

The muscles in his neck tensed briefly. "I'm not ready for divorce."

Of course he wasn't. How could he be? Nothing had prepared him for this. "That's why I suggested the weekend thing, as a sort of halfway house."

There was a long silence, punctuated by the ticking of the grandfather clock in the hall. *Tomorrow, and tomorrow, and tomorrow.* Charles swirled the coffee around the bottom of his mug. Then he looked at me. "You think it would work?"

For a moment I almost thought he could see me.

"I think we'd both be better parents if we did our parenting separately."

At last we were moving forward. Charles agreed not only to let me spend two weekends a month in New York but also to get some support for himself by sharing our situation with two of his friends. William and Andy were both English—they'd expatriated to America a year or so after we did—and although I was a little worried about coming out to their wives, I knew we had to start somewhere. I wasn't close with Gabriela and Sophie, but I'd made them feel welcome when they first arrived, introducing them to all my friends and hosting them for Easters and Thanksgivings since none of us had family in the country. I assumed there would be some loyalty there. Also, Gabriela was a life coach who talked a lot about personal authenticity and mindfulness, and Sophie's brother was gay, although I had no idea how she felt about him since she never mentioned him. But that was perfectly normal—the English never talked about these things anyway—so it probably didn't mean anything.

The coming-out conversations went even more smoothly than I'd hoped—I had coffee with the wives, and then Charles went for a drink with their husbands—and a few days later I was happily heading down I-95 in a beaten-up Mustang convertible I'd bought as a getaway car for my weekends in New York. It wasn't quite a motorbike, but it was a step in the right direction, and if I was going to have a midlife crisis, the least I could do was have it in a muscle car.

Just as I passed Greenwich my cell phone rang. I clicked on the speakerphone. "Hey, Bianca."

"Where are you?"

"In the car."

"I don't know if I should talk to you about this while you're driving."

"About what?" There was a pause. "About what, Bianca?"

I heard Bianca exhale down the phone. "This is a hard phone call to make."

A truck grumbled past. I put on my blinker and moved into the slow lane. "Bianca, what's going on?"

"I just got back from lunch with Gabriela. Sophie was supposed to be there too, but she had to cancel at the last minute, so she sent Gabriela as her envoy."

"Envoy for what?"

"Well, I hoped it was going to be a 'How can we help support Nicky?' sort of lunch, but . . ." Bianca paused, as if waiting for me to say something. I could feel the questions sticking in my throat. "It seems their take on the whole thing is that you're not gay, you're having some kind of breakdown. Gabriela wanted to see if I could organize an intervention. She thinks you're bipolar."

"Bipolar?"

"She and Sophie think your behavior is symptomatic of someone having a manic episode. She says she's got the low-down on the condition because of her training."

"What training? She's a fucking life coach, not a psychiatrist!"

"I tried to tell her there's nothing remotely impulsive about what you're doing, but she wouldn't listen."

I remembered Gabriela's compassionate expression as she sat on my sofa. "You have our unconditional support," she assured me, leaning forward and touching my hand compassionately. What had she and Sophie said to each other when they'd left my house? What had they said to their husbands? What had they all been saying about me ever since? "Why didn't they just come and talk to me about it?"

"Apparently William advised them against it. Sophie told Gabriela he's worried about your ability to look after your children."

The car swerved into the hard shoulder as the muscles in my body temporarily disappeared. "He's . . . Oh my God, Bianca . . ." I gripped the wheel tightly, steering the car back into the slow lane. "Tell me everything she said." Silence. "Bianca, I need to know. I know you don't want to be the messenger, but I need to know."

Slowly Bianca repeated Gabriela's words. "She kept saying, 'After all she's put him through, and now she's doing this to him,' like she thought you were some sort of liability."

"After all I've put him through? What the hell does she know about what we've been through?"

"It's only Gabriela," Bianca tried to reassure me. "It's not like she's a close friend."

"Yes, but I've introduced her to everyone I know! Between them, she and Sophie know *everyone*! And now the first thing they'll hear when I finally come out is Gabriela's so-called professional opinion that I'm having a fucking breakdown!"

I drove the rest of the way to New York in silence, with the radio turned off, trying to piece together a picture of what had happened. It seemed unlikely that this accusation of mental illness had been conjured out of thin air by either

Sophie or Gabriela. It was more probable that it had been delivered to them by Charles. *You're not exactly a very stable person, are you?* The first time he threw this accusation at me I'd assumed it was fear, harsh words spoken in the heat of the moment, but maybe this was what he meant when he let slip that he'd been trying to manage me. If I was not gay but merely insane, then there was no reason for the marriage to end; as long as nobody knew, we could carry on as normal. And if it did leak out, he could just tell everyone I was crazy. I wondered how he'd spun it for his friends, how he'd managed to justify remaining married to me. Was he still my hero, my savior? The good guy trying to help me through a patch of mental illness? I gripped the wheel, realizing there was nothing I could do about it. If I confronted him in anger, I'd be hysterical and insane; if I asked for his compassion, I'd be pathetic and insane. This was the price of going public. There were now two narratives about my life out there, and one of them was completely beyond my control.

Chapter Nineteen

T he room we'd been allocated at the LGBTQ center was brightly lit, furnished with squishy, brown fake-leather chairs and decorated with purple posters depicting improbably beautiful people living with HIV. Eve had to retire from her role as group leader because of a sudden family illness, so Lisa and I decided to take over the Late Bloomers group and run it from the center. It wasn't as cozy as Eve's living room, but it was bigger, which turned out to be useful because we immediately started attracting more members. A shy woman who sat wrapped in a blanket talked about the conflict between wanting to be gay and wanting to support her autistic daughter; a couple of goths appeared briefly one week but hardly said a word and never returned; a woman with a strong New Jersey accent told us how her husband had found her divorce paperwork hidden on top of her wardrobe while he was hanging a picture; and a singer from upstate New York explained how she'd come out to her husband at least six times because each time he'd immediately managed to wipe all memory of it from his mind. Then the blonde from the first meeting caused a minor scandal by seducing the woman with the autistic daughter; the blonde thought the affair was just a bit of fun, but the other woman got her heart broken and subsequently left the group, which was a shame because she really needed the support. Lisa and I added a clause specifying that we were first and foremost a support group and sex between members was strongly discouraged.

One evening in October I arrived late, sneaking in with apologies to a meeting that was running itself perfectly happily in my absence. I edged around the group until I found a free chair at the far side of the room, turned off my phone, and tucked my bag under my seat. As I sat up, I found myself looking at a pair of booted feet crossed at the ankles, thrust out at the end of a pair of legs that seemed too long for the chair that was trying to support them. The stranger's fingers were resting in her jeans pockets, her dark hair tied back to reveal high cheekbones. She seemed to occupy the space around her almost aggressively, as if she didn't care that her legs were taking up half the room.

Over the next hour the conversation traveled around the circle until it finally reached the newcomer. The room turned towards her expectantly, and she shifted slightly in her seat. She told us her name was Jaime, she was married with three children, and had recently surfaced out of her first lesbian affair. She didn't believe she'd been born gay but had been gradually flowing towards women, although she was unsure how to explain this to the man she'd been sleeping with for the last fifteen years.

The floor opened up to general conversation, our two-hour timeslot never quite long enough for all the subjects we wanted to cover. Did anyone else feel isolated and terrified? Which was the best dating site for lesbians? Did anyone else feel uncomfortable around the school-mom crowd? Had anyone been rejected by a lesbian for having been married to a man? But even as we found our usual comfortable stride, I was aware something in the atmosphere had changed. The center of gravity in the room had shifted, and I was suddenly conscious of the sound of my own voice, the way I was sitting in my chair. Jaime was leaning forward, resting her elbows on her knees while she told the group how she'd studied design at college but was still waiting tables because somehow her husband's career had always taken precedence over hers. Trying to shake myself out of stupidity, I forced myself to glance in her direction, and when she looked back at me—in the split second when our eyes met—I wondered whether she'd felt the shift too.

My father underwent surgery to have his prostate removed, and by mid-December he'd received the all clear to make the journey over for Christmas. I knew it was time to tell him the truth, but I was terrified of what it would do to our relationship. If news of my sexual orientation could cause a stampede among Charles's friends, how was my father going to react? The morning of their arrival I woke with a strange feeling of apprehension, as if the date hadn't arrived yet but was still an event in the future around which I could circle from a safe distance. When the taxi pulled in through the gates, the children tumbled out of the house and into the driveway, hurling themselves at my parents like a litter of puppies, bouncing and yelping for hugs and attention. I walked carefully down the salt-strewn front steps to join my father, who was paying the taxi driver.

"Hey, Dad," I said.

"Hullo, you," he replied, putting his hands on my shoulders and giving me a perfunctory shake before putting his arms around me and hugging me hard. I swallowed my tears and offered to carry in the luggage, wondering whether this would be the last time I'd be carrying my father's suitcase into my house.

I gave my parents time to unpack and hand out treats to the kids while I bustled around the kitchen trying to pull together an early-evening meal. I was laying out an array of cold meats and salads on the counter when my mother came up to me, put her arm around my waist, and rested her head briefly against my shoulder. "I love you," she whispered. I tensed. My mother and I had had little physical contact when I was a child, so the intimacy of the gesture felt awkward. She did it again before she went to bed: a hug, a whispered "I love you." And then again when I got up the following morning. I wondered why it had always been so hard for her to say. Perhaps she'd thought our relationship had been irreparably damaged by the brutal separation that boarding school had inflicted on us. Or perhaps she'd just never learned how, since her own mother had never shown her any physical affection. Or was it me who'd put up the walls, afraid to ask for her love in case she found out who I was and couldn't give it to me? But now she seemed to want to make up for lost time. *I love you, I love you, I love you.*

I stole a moment to talk with her the next day, while we were wrapping Christmas presents. "How are you doing, Mum?" I asked, eyeing her over a sea of gold paper and red ribbon.

"I'm doing fine, darling. I'm reading a lot on the subject. And I've been trying to prepare your father as best I can."

"Prepare him how?"

"Drawing his attention to gay people he respects. Clare Balding, people like that. He doesn't seem to have a problem with Clare being gay."

Clare Balding was a BBC television presenter. Apparently she was the only lesbian anyone in England had ever heard of. "But Clare never talks about it," I said. "Everyone knows she's gay, but she never actually mentions it."

"She's very discreet," my mother said approvingly.

"She's a stealth gay. I'm not going stealth."

"I have no idea what you mean."

"Anyway, Clare's not his daughter. It's different when it's your own daughter."

"Darling, if I can learn to accept it then so can he." She fussed with a bow, trying to get the ends of the ribbon to curl. "It'll be a lot for him to absorb, but I'm sure he'll come round eventually. Even if it takes a bit of time." I wondered if she could hear the doubt in her voice as clearly as I could. She put the gift to one side and looked up at me. "You know I love you, don't you, darling?"

We decided the safest course of action would be to leave the conversation with my father until after Christmas Day, so we didn't risk the holiday being ruined for the children by the potential rapid and inexplicable departure of their grandfather. Charles wasn't happy about the situation—still frightened his parents would find out—but I told him it was happening whether he liked it or not. My friends at the Late Bloomers had given me new books to read—Monique Wittig, Simone de Beauvoir, bell hooks—and the more I read, the more I understood that if I wanted to stand on my own two feet in a queer, feminist world, first I'd have to learn how to stand up to Charles.

On Boxing Day evening Charles arranged to go out for a drink with his friends. I sat in silence watching my father eat his dinner. I felt almost empty, as if the knowledge of the impending collision between the equal forces of my father's love for me and his homophobia had created a black hole out of which I had to pull the words to tell him I was gay. I glanced at my mother; she hadn't touched her food either. Finally, my father put his fork down on his plate and wiped his mouth with his napkin. I reached over and refilled his wine glass.

"Dad, I want to talk to you about something I spoke to Mum about last summer," I said. My mother had suggested that perhaps hurling the words "I'm gay" at someone without any kind of preparation wasn't necessarily the most thoughtful way to approach the subject, so I'd decided to take it a little slower this time. "I want you to just sit and listen, because this conversation is going to go somewhere, and I want to take you there carefully."

My father pushed his chair back slightly and looked at me with interest. "Okay."

"So. When I was at St. Mary's I started having feelings that I didn't understand, that made me feel like I was different from the other girls." My father was sitting back in his chair, his legs crossed, his hands folded in his lap. I had rehearsed this so many times that I felt like I was making a speech written by somebody else. I could hear my voice as if I were listening to a presenter on the radio, feeling almost detached from the monologue. Eventually I reached the part of the story where I came out to my therapist. My father was sitting motionless, his eyes fixed on my face. "Dad, I've finally come to terms with something about myself, something that has taken me

a very long time to accept, and I need to share it with you."
My heart was pounding so hard I almost couldn't hear myself
speak. "And before I say the two words that will explain to
you who I am, I want you to remember how much I love
you, and how much you love me, and that that love is more
important than anything else in the world." I took a deep
breath and held his pale blue eyes with mine. "Dad, I'm gay."

My father didn't move. I looked to his hands, which were
clasped tightly in his lap. His fingers were slightly swollen
with age, his gold signet ring cushioned by the soft folds of his
little finger, his nails cut short and blunt. He sat motionless, as
if all his energy was being used in absorbing what I'd just said.

Then I heard him speak. "That's okay," he said.

I looked up at him. I couldn't read anything in his expression; he was sitting almost completely still, his eyes focused
on my face.

"It is?"

"Yes, it is," he said. "It's okay."

"You do understand what I'm saying, don't you?"

"Yes, I understand."

"But you . . . you don't seem . . ." I couldn't take my eyes
off my father's face. "I thought you . . . I mean, are you okay?"

"It's going to take a little time to absorb," he replied. "But
yes, I'm okay."

I tried to process his reaction. It didn't make any sense.
"I . . . you . . . Dad, you do believe me, right? You don't think
I'm having a breakdown or something?"

"No, I believe you." His face was still immobile, but his
voice was calm. "If you tell me you're gay, I believe you."

My mind whirred, running through all the possibilities that
might account for such a mild response. "Are you just waiting

until I'm out of the room before you explode? If you're upset, you can tell me. I'd rather you talked to me about it directly than hid it from me."

"I'm not upset," he said. "I just want you to be happy, and if this is what has been making you unhappy, and being gay will make you happy, then I'm happy for you."

"You're *happy* for me?" Now I was completely thrown. I'd been preparing myself to spend the evening trying to reassure him, and now here he was trying to reassure me. "I don't understand. I wasn't expecting you to be . . . at least, I thought . . . I mean, really? You're happy?"

"Darling, it's okay." He reached out and took my hand, and I saw him relax, the tension softening out of his body. "I think we have a lot of talking to do, but we have the whole week ahead of us. You can tell me everything in your own time."

I looked at his jowly face, his hands now clasped firmly around mine, and the tears came before I could stop them. "Oh Daddy, I thought you believed homosexuality was a sin."

"I did," he said.

"When did you stop?"

My father paused. "A few minutes ago," he admitted. "When I found out I had a gay daughter."

Chapter Twenty

Over the next week my parents took advantage of every opportunity to discuss what my being gay meant for both me and the family. My father admitted that most of his opinions about homosexuality were just parroted from his friends, and he'd never really stopped to consider why it should be a problem or whether he himself took exception to same-sex relationships, either in practice or in principle. When my copy of *The Gay & Lesbian Review* arrived in the mail, instead of hiding it in my bedroom, I opened it in full view at the kitchen table.

"What's that?" my father asked. I showed him the cover. "May I take a look?" He flicked through it. "Not really what I was expecting."

"What were you expecting?"

"I rather thought there might be lewd photos of men, that sort of thing."

"Dad, it's a literary review, not a porn mag."

He closed the magazine. "Do you mind if I ask you something? But it might offend you, and I don't want to offend you."

I shook my head in disbelief. *He* didn't want to offend *me*?

"Would you mind terribly not using the word 'lesbian' quite so much? I don't mind you referring to yourself as gay, but the word 'lesbian' makes me a little uncomfortable."

"Of course, Dad," I smiled. "Less 'lesbian' while you're around." I didn't tell him that using the word "lesbian" to describe myself felt uncomfortable for me too, because it was for different reasons, and that was a conversation for another time.

Now that I was out to my parents, making friends with the Late Bloomers, and spending more time in New York, the tight wires in my body started to loosen a little. Charles and I were settling into some sort of routine, and he seemed to be managing his weekends alone with the kids. According to the children Charles spent most afternoons asleep on the sofa, rousing himself only to make them meals or take the dog for a walk, but if nothing else this lack of attention was teaching them some basic survival skills. Lily learned how to make a peanut butter sandwich, Rose figured out how to use the remote, Alfie improved his breakdancing moves, and Freddie discovered video games. The only disaster that had happened so far was when Freddie and Alfie decided to perform an experiment involving a fountain pen, the carpet in my office, and a hammer, but since this had occurred on Charles's watch, I told him it was his problem to deal with.

Sometimes I shared my weekends in the East Village with Elisabeth—the two of us spending our days visiting art galleries or thrift shopping, our nights squished up together in her double bed—but when she was in Mexico, I was forced to find other ways to occupy my time. I started attending a writer's workshop run by a poet named Daisy who lived on Christopher Street, and developed a close friendship with

Maeve, the windswept journalist, who turned out to be much more approachable than anyone who'd achieved her level of success in their career had a right to be. I also joined a queer twelve-step group, where I found a new sponsor, Siobhan, an Irish lesbian who dressed like a cockney schoolboy and lived in a rent-controlled apartment with a bathtub in the kitchen. None of these women gave a damn what I wore or how I behaved or who I was attracted to, and my crush on New York and the people who lived there began to bloom into a full-scale love affair.

The twelve-step meeting where I met Siobhan was held in a large, yellow room furnished with rows of folding chairs, and I attended every weekend I was in the city, trailing around in Siobhan's shadow while I tried to muster up the confidence to make friends of my own. There was one person in particular I wanted to get to know better. Dallas was strange looking, with beatnik clothes, peroxide hair, and eyebrows tattooed with Celtic designs, but I'd never met anyone so gentle. Whenever I spoke to them they'd hunch their shoulders, look at the floor, and smile, occasionally peeking up at me but rarely making full eye contact. Siobhan told me they'd had their breasts removed, which made sense. I wasn't sure Dallas was a man, but they clearly weren't a woman either, and breasts would have looked entirely wrong on them. I was too self-conscious—and they were too shy—for us to develop a proper friendship, but whenever they talked to me I felt a flutter of excitement, some unidentifiable emotion that extended beyond merely feeling flattered that someone so wild would bother with someone so tame. I wanted to ask how they felt about their body, whether they were taking testosterone, what term they used to describe themself, but I didn't know the right language and I was afraid I might say something offensive.

In search of answers to these questions, I finally picked up *Stone Butch Blues*. It was a confusing and complicated book, and I didn't know what to make of it. Was Jess, the protagonist, male or female? Were they only taking testosterone because it was safer to pass as a cis man than as a butch lesbian, or did they want to transition? Even Jess didn't appear to know, which I found frustrating. I wanted clear-cut facts, and the book raised more questions than it answered. But one scene burned itself into my memory, the moment when Jess first straps on a dildo. "Feel how I'm touching you?" her girlfriend says as she runs her hand up and down Jess's cock. Every time I read it my eyes rolled back, as if I were feeling it in my own body.

But however masculine I wanted to be, I didn't want to cut my hair, so this whole journey Jess had taken was clearly not for me. Still, my wardrobe was slowly getting simpler as I got rid of all my more feminine clothes. I'd taken all my skirts and dresses to the consignment store, thrown out the lipsticks gathering dust in my bathroom drawer, and hadn't tried to squeeze my poor feet into a pair of heels in months. Each step felt like a small victory, and if I kept edging towards masculinity slowly enough, perhaps nobody would notice.

Lisa and I continued to run the Late Bloomers group, which was rapidly increasing in numbers. Jaime attended every meeting, sitting back in her chair with her long legs stretched out in front of her, wearing her masculine energy with confidence. She had a quick wit and a sharp mind, but although I loved the way her brain darted from one idea to the next, I was careful not to allow our verbal sparring matches to stray into flirtatious territory. Not only was she still married, but I myself had written the amendment that discouraged dating among members, and I didn't want to be the asshole who thought she could be the exception to the rule.

To distract myself, I went with a friend to see an all-female rock band called the Velvet Buzz Saws. I showed up to the gig wearing a faded green military jacket—tails, brass buttons, and gold braided epaulets—teamed with low-rise skinny jeans and an old pair of Doc Martens. By the time we arrived the band was already onstage, hurling a tornado of sound out into the auditorium. We pushed our way through the crowd until we were standing directly in front of the lead guitarist. Lean and sinewy, she hunched, snakelike, over her guitar. Through the mess of hair falling over her face I caught a glimpse of dark eyes and pale skin, a half smile of concentration on her mouth. One of the roadies handed her a violin bow and she moved to the front of the stage, where she stood with her legs apart, eyes closed as if in a trance, sawing away at the guitar strings that lay directly across her groin. As the solo reached its crescendo, she threw back her head in simulated ecstasy, and the audience erupted in frenzied applause. The woman lowered her violin bow and looked out over the audience, soaking in the crowd's reaction, before her eyes landed on me. She paused for a second, gave me a smile, and then turned back to her band.

"Jesus, you are so fucked," my friend mouthed.

After the performance the musicians came out to sign autographs by the merchandise table. I waited until the crowd of fans had thinned and then walked over to the guitarist. "That should come with a government health warning," I said, nodding at the bow, which she was holding like a whip by her side.

Her eyes traveled over my body. "I like your jacket," she said. "Very Jimi Hendrix. Can I have it?"

"No," I said.

"I'll swap it for my violin bow," she offered.

"Tempting, but still no." I felt my pulse quicken a beat.

"Have a CD," she said, handing it to me with a sly smile. "It's on me."

Back at home I checked the Velvet Buzz Saws' website. The guitarist's name was Robin Blake, and the band was based in New York, which seemed promising. I considered sending her an email. It seemed very forward. But what did I have to lose?

The next day a reply dropped into my inbox. *Nicky. So kind of you to write. Are you ready to trade your jacket for the violin bow?*

I blinked in surprise. I hadn't really expected to hear back from her. I considered my response, wondering if I should make my intentions clear. I figured I may as well be blatant.

Yes, but you'll have to take me in it, I wrote.

I think it would fit nicely, she responded right away.

I burst out laughing. What was I to do next? Casually suggest a date? This was what men did all the time; no sitting around waiting for phone calls, no having to try to make their interest apparent without seeming too forward. I could just ask her out, and she'd say either yes or no. It was that simple.

Can I buy you a drink sometime? I wrote.

She kept me hanging for more than two days before she replied, but when her email finally popped into my inbox, it was worth the wait: *There's a bar on the corner of 8th and Horatio in the West Village,* she wrote. *See you there Friday at eight.*

To say Robin was the projection of every fantasy I'd ever had was an understatement. At the end of our first date, I offered to walk her home. Out on the street the weather was bitterly cold. She tucked her hands inside her sheepskin coat, and I instinctively slipped my hand into her pocket and curled my fingers around hers, pulling her close so we were walking shoulder to shoulder. We were almost exactly the same height, her slim hips bumping mine, her long, dark hair shadowing my blonde. I could feel the eyes of the people we passed on us, our heads close together as we chatted, experiencing for the first time what it felt like to be envied. I knew we were drawing attention not just because we were both women but because we were both good-looking, and I liked the way it felt.

My affair with Robin was long and protracted. She was impossible to pin down, made herself available only at the last minute, and usually turned up late, but I didn't mind. She was one of the hottest women I'd ever met, all my former crushes rolled into one, every woman who'd ever been out of my league. I was rewriting history, and the chase only made it more fun.

Between dates I poured all my energy into the Late Bloomers group, which had now grown to sixteen women. We had members who'd been out for years and members who were just taking their first tentative steps; we had gay women, bisexual women, polyamorous women, and sexually fluid women; we had affluent women and poor women; white, Black, Jewish, and Latina women. Some women talked with confidence about previous sexual experiences before they were married, others just sat in silence and cried. There were women who attended group month after month, others who came to one meeting and never returned. It was hard not to become emotionally invested in their lives.

Witnessing them grow into themselves as the months went by was incredibly rewarding, and it felt a little heartbreaking when someone decided to return to their old life before the magic happened.

Lucy, a trans woman who briefly joined our group, was one who didn't stay. She called me before the first meeting to ask whether she'd be welcome, and I couldn't see a reason why she shouldn't come. She attended the first meeting wearing a badly fitting wig, but later admitted that she'd worn it only because she wanted us to believe she was a woman, and she didn't think it was really her look. When she turned up the next week without it, I saw what she meant; she looked cute with short hair, a little like Audrey Hepburn if Audrey Hepburn had still had a pixie haircut when she was in her sixties. She was thin, tomboyish, and I liked her style: slim-fitting pants with brightly colored silk blouses, a trace of lipstick, the occasional well-chosen piece of jewelry.

Lucy had multiple sclerosis and walked with a cane, but she was determined to make the two-hour drive down from her home in northern Connecticut to join us. She was unassuming, quietly intelligent, and didn't draw attention to herself. When she did share, she mostly talked about her gender, how she'd discovered she could relieve the pressure of being closeted within her own home by wearing pieces of silk under the men's clothes she felt obliged to wear, how a small, lacy slip hidden against her skin could release some of the tension in her body.

Lucy was committed to her marriage, but her wife—whom she loved—refused to acknowledge her identity, referred to her gender expression as "cross-dressing," and insisted on calling Lucy by her previous name. Lucy was uncertain what her future held, how to reconcile these two parts of her life. Then one day she told me that although spending time with us had given her some relief, the traveling was putting too much of a strain on her body, and she'd have to stop coming. I was surprisingly upset. There was something about the way we connected that seemed to come from a shared language, an understanding about some common experience that I didn't have with the other women. Being in her presence made me feel calmer, safer, like she was the one person in the world with whom I could relax and be myself.

We met a few times for coffee over the next few months, but between my children and her health issues our dates became increasingly hard to schedule. I couldn't explain—either to her or to myself—why I needed her in my life; many women had drifted away from the meetings before, and I'd never felt the urge to follow them. My desire for her friendship felt confusing, selfish somehow, as if she were helping me more than I was helping her, so I held back and let her go. And still, I missed her terribly.

In the meantime, Robin kept me dangling before resurfacing occasionally with an outrageously salacious text and squeezing me into her busy schedule for a quick night of sex. But the problem was less about her chronic unavailability and more about the growing disparity between what we were actually doing in bed and what I wished we were doing. Robin liked her men to be tough and her women to be feminine, which meant that when I was with her I felt compelled to be more female than I felt. And yet when I was alone and fantasizing about her, with only the fingertips of my right hand active, my brain resolutely insisted that I belonged in the body of a man.

A quick search of the internet confirmed that this wasn't unusual among lesbians—why else would strap-ons exist?—but I had no idea how to introduce the subject with Robin, since I usually saw her only at very short notice and she almost always disappeared on me immediately afterwards. I could hardly just whip out a strap-on while she was kissing me and say, "Hey, I've been fantasizing about how it would feel to fuck you like a man—want to give it a go?" What if she didn't? What if she never wanted to have sex with me again? Robin made me feel more attractive than I'd ever felt in my life, and if keeping her interest meant working my femininity, so be it.

But it still felt like my body was trying to become male against my will. An involuntary sensation of masculinity would overcome me randomly, with no warning, as if my female body was only a mirage. Sometimes it would happen in the middle of the afternoon, like the time I was curled up on the sofa watching a movie with the boys. We were watching the scene in *Spider-Man* where Andrew Garfield tries to pluck up the courage to reveal his identity to Emma Stone, and he's frightened, vulnerable, stammering. "I'm Spider-Man," he finally manages to say.

I felt it in my bones like an electric shock—the euphoria of speaking the truth—as if I were standing in front of the woman I loved, finally finding the courage to reveal my identity.

I'm a man.

I got up quickly and went to the kitchen, trying to put some space between myself and my children. I pulled the popcorn jar off the shelf and emptied it into a microwave bowl.

"Mummy?" Freddie asked, twisting round on the sofa.

"Just making some more popcorn, darling," I replied, my voice high-pitched and falsely jolly. I leaned against the kitchen counter while I waited for the corn to pop. Back on the television, the villain of the movie was turning into a lizard, a revolting process of transformation that left me feeling quite queasy. I had no idea what transition involved, but I was pretty sure it must be equally revolting, which meant it was not something I wanted to do.

But I was reaching a point of no return. I had recurring nightmares about being lost in a maze of windowless corridors with no apparent means of escape, searching for an exit while gradually becoming aware that I inhabited a male body. I tried to convince myself it didn't mean anything, that dreaming about being a man didn't mean I secretly *was* a man, any more than dreaming about stumbling down endless badly lit hallways meant I was secretly an architect or an unemployed lighting designer. I tried to persuade myself that it was metaphorical, that it was symbolic of my lack of agency in my marriage, my envy of men's power, the fact that if I hadn't been born as the oppressed sex, I might not have taken so many wrong turnings in my life. But I just didn't sound very convincing anymore.

Chapter Twenty-One

Lily and Rose started kindergarten in the fall, and I used the small gift of the few extra hours to start writing again, stealing time during the day to pen short stories and bad poetry I had no intention of showing anyone. I wanted to use the time wisely—aware that once I was divorced I'd have to get a job—and although Charles considered it an indulgence, writing was all I wanted to do. All Charles seemed to do was work, which meant he was hardly ever home. The children, remarkably, still hadn't picked up on either the change in our marital situation or the fact that I was gay, even though I'd started inviting the Late Bloomers over on the weekends when Charles was away. They didn't question why there were no fathers at the parties, perhaps because they so rarely saw theirs.

The way I parented them also began to change now that they were a little older. When they questioned authority, I let them, when they suggested things could be done differently, I heard them out. I didn't so much guide them as encourage them to guide themselves. I wanted them to trust their own instincts, develop their own moral codes, set their own boundaries, and speak their own minds. This meant there were fewer rules in my house than perhaps there might have been, but at least nobody was being shamed for having an opinion.

The winter was uneventful. My parents came and went for Christmas. It snowed, and then thawed, and as the weather grew warmer the following spring, my affair with Robin started to lose its heat. We'd been seeing each other for over a year now, and since I'd never asked for exclusivity— confident that monogamy wasn't her thing—I knew it wasn't going to turn into anything more substantial than this. It was Jaime who finally convinced me to call time on the affair. She was hovering outside the front door of the community center at the end of one of the meetings. The evenings were getting longer, dandelions sprouting up through the asphalt in front of the entrance to the Sikh temple with which we shared a parking lot. I locked the door to the community center and we fell in step with each other as we walked back to our cars.

"Jesus, you're such a goddamn giant," I said, glancing up at her. "We look like Asterix and Obelix."

"Oy, shorty, don't get frisky," Jaime replied, swatting me over the head. "You can be Han Solo and I'll be Chewy—the fur will keep me warm when it gets cold."

"You can be Gru and I'll be a Minion."

"You're not obedient enough."

My mouth twitched. "Cindy-Lou Who and the Grinch."

"You're an Aspirin and I'm a Big Headache."

"Does that mean I make you feel better?"

"Only if you do what it says on the bottle."

"Too much of me might be bad for your health," I warned her.

"That's what I'm worried about," she replied.

In a confusing turn of events, Jaime had started sleeping with her husband again. She kept returning to the question of how gay she needed to be to justify leaving her marriage. If she was completely gay then the decision would be simple, but what if she was merely sexually fluid? What if her sexuality flowed away from women and back to men again? It seemed unlikely. She seemed so resentful of the entire male species I couldn't imagine her with a man.

"Tell me more about your plan," she said as we reached my car.

"What plan?"

"The plan to prove you're as good as the boys."

"I have no idea what you're talking about."

"I'm talking about your trophy girlfriend."

"She's not a trophy."

"Sounds to me like you're into her because everyone else is into her and you just want to prove you can have her." I scowled and she laughed. "I'm right, aren't I?"

"Absolutely not."

"Do you even *want* to have a relationship with her?"

"Leave me alone."

"I'ma keep poking the bear."

"I have retractable claws. Or is that just tigers?"

"You didn't answer my question."

I sighed, leaning back against the Mustang. "I don't really know what being in a relationship means," I admitted.

"I do."

"Go on then, enlighten me."

"It's being prepared to show your soft, vulnerable underbelly to someone," Jaime said, scuffing at a weed with the toe of her boot. "The part of you that you keep hidden from everyone else. It means paying attention, noticing what gets the other person energized, learning to be interested in the stuff they care about. It means that when they're in the pit of despair you climb down in there with them. Doesn't matter how long it takes or how much it stinks, you sit in the muck with them and keep them company until they're ready to climb back out."

"Have you ever been in a relationship like that?" I asked.

"Nope."

"Me neither. I don't think Robin would want to join me in my pit of despair, and I'm certain she'd never invite me into hers."

Jaime was right, though. Robin was Georgia and Lola rolled into one, and yet I still hadn't manifested the dream I'd had in my twenties. Half of it, maybe, but what about the other half? With Robin, I'd always have to be a girl.

My affair with Robin came to a decidedly undramatic end. I explained I was looking for something more committed, she expressed mild disappointment that I didn't want to continue having vaguely noncommittal hookup sex with her and told me to get in touch if ever I changed my mind. A week later, Bianca called.

"Nicky! Pandora's telling everyone you're a lesbian!"

"Wait, she's what?" Pandora was the ghastly woman I'd bumped into at the cocktail party at the Westport Country Playhouse, but that had been two years ago, and I hadn't seen her in months.

"Apparently she spotted you at some gay event a while back. It's probably all over the school by now."

I wondered why she'd waited so long to spill the beans. Maybe she was bored. Or maybe she was one of us and wanted to join the team.

"Nicky?" Bianca sounded confused. She must have heard me laughing down the phone.

"Fuck it, Bianca. It's out of my hands. If Pandora knows, then everyone's going to know. I guess I'm coming out of the closet."

Never did I think I'd be grateful to Pandora for anything, but now I wanted to hug her. I looked at the clock. It was the middle of the night in Korea, where Charles was on a business trip with his boss, so I couldn't consult him before making my next move. Or at least, that would be my excuse when I told him what I was about to do, after I'd already done it.

A couple of evenings later Charles called from New York.

"Are you sitting down?" I asked.

"Yup," he said vaguely, although I was fairly certain from the background noise that he was walking down a busy street.

"Well, I kind of got outed by one of the school mothers, so I made an executive decision to tell all my friends before they could hear it from her. Which means I think we're officially out of the closet." I could hear horns blaring in the background, something that sounded like an ambulance.

"Okay, that's fine," he said. "I already told my boss anyway."

"Told him what?"

"About us."

"What, that we're . . ."

"I told him our marriage was over. I called it an in-house separation."

"Did you tell him why?"

"Sure."

I blinked in surprise. "What did he say?"

"He didn't seem that bothered."

Was this the same man who had raged at me that his career would be finished if anyone found out he was married to a lesbian? "Well, that's great then," I said somewhat limply, unable to muster a better response. Perhaps he'd been making more progress in accepting the end of our marriage than I'd given him credit for. Or maybe he was getting laid. Just because he hadn't told me about it didn't mean it wasn't happening, and if he was finally having sex it might account for his generous mood.

When he got back from work that evening, Charles said nothing about our phone conversation, which only proved how far apart we'd grown. The next morning, he surprised me again. "I think we should get divorced," he said as he picked up his keys and wallet to leave for work. "I've put some thought into it. Staying married just doesn't make any sense." He looked at me, frowning when he saw my expression. "If you're okay with that,"

Was this how it was going to end after all this time, not with a bang but with a whimper? I wondered what he'd told his boss about me. If the truth about our marriage was finally out, now was the time he'd probably start discrediting me in public. Maybe that's why he suddenly wanted a divorce; it made no sense to stay married to a woman who was mentally unstable.

"And I think we should keep sharing the house for now. Give the kids time to adjust."

I hesitated. I'd have preferred a clean break, but angering Charles might not be a good idea right now. Despite his calm countenance, I was afraid of him. He was so good at coming across as the mild-mannered English gentleman that his accusations against me would hold water—I knew this from my experience with Sophie and Gabriela—and I didn't want to make things any worse. Sooner or later Charles would meet a woman who wouldn't be okay with our arrangement, which would give him the incentive to end it himself.

"Okay," I said. "For now."

Only Alfie cried. Big, fat tears, rolling silently down his face. We told the boys on their own while Bianca took the girls to the playground, because they were too young to understand. Freddie and Alfie sat side by side, wide-eyed on the sofa, while we explained that Mummy and Daddy didn't have romantic love anymore so we couldn't stay married.

"Honey, I'm sorry," I said gently. "It's okay to be sad, we're all sad, this *is* sad."

"Is Daddy going to leave?" Alfie sobbed.

"No, nobody's leaving you. We're all going to carry on living here, just like we are now. Very little is going to change."

"Does this mean Grandma isn't my grandma anymore?" Freddie asked.

"No, everyone in the family still belongs to you."

"But not to you?"

"Well, not really. Grandma belongs to you and Daddy now."

"Daddy can't have Granny?"

"No, but Granny will always love Daddy."

"But Grandma doesn't love you?"

"Uh, that's a little complicated," I said. "But she still loves you."

There was a pause while Freddie considered all this. Then he reached for Alfie's hand. "Come outside, I want to talk to you." He pulled his little brother up off the sofa and over towards the kitchen door. Opening it, he turned back. "Just us, not you."

Charles and I stood by the window, watching them climb up onto the large rock down by the lake, deep in conversation. Whatever Freddie was saying, it seemed to be calming Alfie down. I'd predicted and prepared myself for Alfie's quiet tears, but I'd been bracing myself for yelling and hysterics from the more combustible Freddie, expecting to be told—with all the force that an anxious nine-year-old could muster—that I'd ruined his life. I hadn't expected a conversation about the family tree, nor had I expected him to be the one comforting his younger brother. Eventually they climbed off the rock and came back towards the house.

"Can we have a snack?" Freddie asked as he walked in the door. I opened the cupboard and gave both boys a bag of Goldfish. "When you were looking all serious, I thought you were going to tell us we were eating too much junk food," he said.

"Would that have been worse?" I asked.

"Yes," he said, popping a handful into his mouth. "Much."

Word about my sexual orientation spread quickly across the Atlantic. I mapped its geographical progress across England that summer as old friends I hadn't seen in years started reaching out to me on social media, casually asking me what was new in my life or commenting on how great I looked. I knew I was just the latest bit of gossip, but it was so far removed from my fear of permanent social ostracism I hardly cared what they might be saying to each other behind closed doors.

My mother called to update me on how it was going with her friends. "The Beaufort-Smiths came for lunch, they've just left," she told me. She was wearing a silk scarf secured around her neck with a large brooch, and appeared to be sitting at the kitchen table, although it was difficult to tell because her iPad camera was angled at the ceiling.

My father's face appeared over her left shoulder. "Hullo, darling!"

"Hey, Dad," I said.

"We told them all about you," my mother continued. "All about the . . . *you know*."

"You did?"

"Yes, it was rather fun, actually. The Beaufort-Smiths have always seemed so sophisticated, but they can't beat a gay daughter, can they?"

"Oh my God, Mum. Are you telling everyone now? How are they all taking it?"

"Well, we've had a fair amount of 'Oh, poor you' and 'Aren't you being frightfully brave,' but most people have pretty much taken it on the chin."

"I'm sorry I'm not there to help," I said.

"Don't be," my mother replied. "To be honest, we're quite enjoying being renegades."

"It's certainly perked up a few dinner parties," my father agreed. "Everybody else's lives seem thoroughly boring in comparison."

"Has anyone . . . not been okay with it?"

"One or two people," my mother admitted. "Anthony wasn't fully on board."

"What did he say?" I asked, bracing myself. Anthony had been like a second father to me, and his disapproval was going to hurt.

"He quoted that actress from the twenties who said, 'I don't care what they do, so long as they don't do it in the street and frighten the horses.'"

I winced. I'd heard the quote before. It epitomized the British way. Keep it behind closed doors, be discreet, have some common decency. In short, stay invisible. I tried to swallow the bitter taste in my mouth. "Shame me into hiding?" I asked.

"Nobody's hiding anything anymore," my father said stoutly. "And we don't give a fig what our friends think."

Freddie and I were driving back from the skate park. His skateboard was lying across his lap, and he was spinning the wheels absentmindedly. "Mom, is Dad going to get married again?" he asked.

I snorted, then tried to turn it into a sneeze. Charles was having way too much fun with the apparently inexhaustible supply of single women in Connecticut to be thinking about settling down.

"I don't think Dad's planning on getting married any time soon, honey," I reassured him.

Freddie swiped the flat of his palm along the top of the wheels again, making the ball bearings buzz with a satisfying hum. "What about you? What if you get a boyfriend and have more children?"

"I'm much too old to have any more children."

"But what if you got a boyfriend and *he* has children? Would we go and live with him, or would his children come and live with us?"

My hands tightened on the steering wheel. Freddie's growing interest in adult conversations meant that I was increasingly having to monitor what I said around the house, and I battled daily with my conscience over whether to tell the kids the truth. Was my desire to come out to them entirely selfish, or was my obsession with transparency justified?

"Mom? What if you got a boyfriend?" Freddie pushed.

I turned off the radio and adjusted the rearview mirror so I could see his face. "I'm not going to get a boyfriend, honey," I said. "When I have another romantic relationship, it won't be with a man, it'll be with a woman."

Freddie stopped spinning his skateboard wheels. "Does that mean you're gay?"

I held his eyes in the rearview mirror for a second. "Yes, sweetheart, it does."

He turned and looked out of the car window. The road was covered with leaves scattered from the maple trees, the sidewalks bordered by low stone walls behind which lush green lawns sloped up to handsome colonial houses. The scene couldn't have been more richly suburban, and I wondered what was going through his mind. Was he trying and failing to fit a gay parent into this picture? Was he wondering whether he even belonged here himself anymore?

Freddie looked back at me and shrugged. "Nothing wrong with being gay, Mom."

"Nope," I said, smiling with relief. "Nothing wrong with being gay."

Back at home, Freddie ran up the back stairs to find the three younger children eating dinner at the kitchen table. Freddie hopped from one foot to the other in excitement, waiting for the babysitter to leave, and as soon she closed the door he stood up on his chair. "Mom's got something she wants to tell you!" he yelled.

"Sit down, Freddie." Freddie climbed reluctantly down from his seat. I pulled up a chair at the head of the table. "Freddie and I were having a conversation in the car that we'd like to share with you."

"Mom's gay!" Freddie shouted.

All the kids stopped eating and stared at me. Alfie's face was a cartoon expression of astonishment. "Cool!" he breathed.

Lily and Rose looked at each other in confusion. "What's 'gay'?" Rose asked.

"Well, if a man and a woman love each other, that's called being straight," I explained. "But if a man loves a man, or a woman loves a woman, that's called being gay."

"Are you being gay with Bianca?" Lily asked.

"No, honey, Bianca's got a boyfriend."

"What about Elisabeth?"

"No, Elisabeth's straight too."

"If you're being gay with someone, do you have to tell them first?" Rose asked.

"Generally, that's a good idea," I said.

Lily suddenly perked up. "If you married Bianca, Willow would be my sister?"

"Yes, but I'm not going to marry Bianca. I'm not planning on marrying anyone right now. This is all very hypothetical."

"What's 'hypothetical' mean?"

"Wishful thinking." I turned to my younger son. "Alfie?"

Alfie's brow was furrowed in concentration, as if he were trying to formulate a question he didn't know how to ask. "Okay, Mom," he said tentatively. "Just think about this before you give me an answer, okay?"

"Okay," I promised.

"I know I'm not allowed Pokémon cards at school, but I really want to show everyone my new Charizard. So can I take it in if I promise only to bring it out at recess?"

"No questions about me being gay, then?"

Alfie shook his head, smiling shyly.

"Cookies!" Freddie yelled, jumping down from his seat. "Mom's gay and everyone gets cookies!"

By the time I finished handing round the cookie tin, the conversation had moved on to whether astronaut or knight was a better career choice, and if neither profession paid well, whether a side hustle as a builder would come in handy. I put the cookie tin back in the cupboard. It had all seemed too easy—suspiciously so. I wasn't sure they really understood what it all meant. Perhaps it didn't feel like a very big step to them right now, but what if I changed the way I looked? What if I cut my hair? What if . . . I stopped myself. One step at a time. The next step would be to introduce them to a girlfriend. Anything beyond that would have to wait.

Alfie was sitting on my bed, solemnly watching as I packed my suitcase. Jeans, T-shirts, Chucks. Women's Week in Provincetown didn't require much in the way of wardrobe.

"How long will you be gone?" he asked, putting one of my baseball caps backwards onto his head and pulling his hair out of the hole at the front.

"Only four days," I told him.

"Can I come too?"

"It's only for gay women, I'm afraid."

"Will it be fun?"

I stopped folding my sweatshirt, remembering how Bianca had explained it to her son. "Imagine you'd lived your whole life in a town where nobody played soccer, or watched soccer, or talked about soccer, and some people even thought that soccer was bad and dangerous and that children shouldn't know about it in case they wanted to become soccer players too. And then one day you found a town where everyone loved soccer, and played soccer all the time, and walked around all day wearing their team jerseys. Wouldn't you love that town?"

"Yes, I would," Alfie agreed.

"That's what Provincetown will be like for me."

I drove the Mustang through sheets of rain up to Cape Cod and arrived in Provincetown just as the sun broke through the clouds. I checked in at the hotel and set out to explore the town. I ambled past stores selling buckets and spades, lobster rolls and ice cream, knickknacks and T-shirts. Women were wandering hand in hand down the middle of the street, sitting in groups outside the coffee shops, relaxing on the benches in front of the town hall. Reaching the far end of town, I cut across a small alley onto the beach, took off my shoes, and started walking back on the sand. The beach was mostly deserted, but ahead of me two women were standing on the pebbles at the shoreline, the sea licking their toes, their chinos rolled above their ankles. They were silhouetted by the sun, so I couldn't see their faces, but I could read their body language, heads close, hands touching, deep in a conversation I couldn't quite hear. I felt a pang of envy. The closer I got, the more out of reach it seemed. There was nothing stopping me now—I was out of the closet and within a few months I'd be divorced—and yet for some reason a relationship like this still felt unattainable.

Back at the hotel, I stood in front of the bathroom mirror. I had my father's features, which was presumably why I always looked so masculine when I wasn't wearing makeup. I pulled my hair back so I could see myself better. This was the problem: my hair. I tried to imagine myself with short hair— God, the relief!—but short hair would make me look more masculine, which would make me less attractive. Instinctively I thought of Jaime, who was away in Maine with her husband this weekend. I remembered something she'd said recently at one of the Late Bloomers meetings: *I can't imagine a future where I don't crave someone's breasts against mine, someone's hair trailing across my stomach.* This was something I had that her husband didn't. I let my hair go, allowing it to fall back over my shoulders. My hair had always been my best feature; maybe I shouldn't cut it just yet. There was no need to do anything drastic.

I met up with the Late Bloomers at the wet T-shirt competition at the Crown & Anchor later that evening. The mood was aggressive, the music deafening, the women drunk. I scanned the room, looking for a distraction from my thoughts of Jaime. My eyes landed on a girl who was standing on a chair, hollering with excitement at the women onstage. She was in her midtwenties, with long platinum-blonde hair, a tiny angora sweater above a bare midriff, slim legs in tight white leggings. She looked like a cross between Anna from *Frozen* and a *Playboy* centerfold, her boyfriend standing self-consciously by her side, trying to look game.

I tapped one of my friends on the shoulder. "I'm bored of this. Let's go somewhere else." She followed me outside into the cool, dark quiet of the street, but before we had a chance to decide where to go next, the door to the bar opened and the *Frozen* girl and her boyfriend walked out. The girl was giggling, looking straight at my friend and me, who were blocking her path. The opportunity was irresistible, and I stepped forward.

"You can't walk into a bar like this with a woman who looks like that and then expect to leave with her," I said, ostensibly speaking to the man but looking directly at the girl. She blushed and dipped her head. "Seriously, you're not going home with *him*, are you?" She stepped away from her boyfriend and I put my arm around her waist and scooped her towards me. "Oh my God, you're delicious. You're like a cream bun, I just want to bite you," I said, running my hand over her naked waist. Over her shoulder I could see my friend blocking the boyfriend, giving me the chance to make my move. I pushed her hair away from her neck and kissed her cheek. "Come back to my hotel with me," I murmured into her ear. She turned her face towards me—smiling, playing the game—and I kissed her on the mouth.

The minute she started kissing me back, I realized I'd made a mistake. I'd become an ape-man, beating my chest at the successful snatching of another man's woman; she, in turn, was probably only kissing me to titillate him, while he, by the look on his face, wasn't sure what part he was meant to be playing—voyeur, participant, cuckold? The pendulum of my masculine performance had swung to its furthest extreme, and the whole charade had become demeaning. I dropped my arm from around the girl's waist, and she teetered slightly, unsure what to do, before turning back to her boyfriend. He put his arm quickly around her shoulder, turning to glance back at me as he led her away.

"Why did you let her go?" my friend asked.

I shrugged. "I wasn't feeling it." This parody of masculinity felt empty and insubstantial—dehumanizing—and I didn't

want to do it anymore. I didn't want to be the sort of person
who turned women into objects, and I didn't want to be with
the sort of woman who'd allow herself to be turned into one.

"I'm tired," I said, faking a stretch. "I think I'll go back
to the hotel."

I walked back down through the town on my own, leaving
the girl and her boyfriend and the frenzy of the party behind
me. I wanted to be more like a man, but I wasn't going to tread
on the backs of women to get there. I just wanted to be able
hold my own views, speak my own mind, and live life on my
own terms. In short, I wanted to be who I'd been when I'd
been hanging with the bikers, only this time sober and with
the benefit of maturity. It would be so much easier if I was
with someone who felt the same way, someone who'd been
navigating this space for a while and seemed to be getting it
right. Someone who balanced their masculinity with radical
feminism, who was meticulous about putting women first.
Someone like Jaime.

Impulsively I pulled out my phone and typed her a text.
*Thinking of planning a night out in New York when I get back.
You in?*

I pressed Send before I could change my mind and then
stood under a streetlamp, holding my breath, until her response
pinged through.

Hell yeah, I'm in.

Chapter Twenty-Two

It was Women's Week in Provincetown three years later, and Jaime and I were walking back to our hotel after seeing Kate Clinton eviscerate the forty-fifth president at the Crown & Anchor. We were walking slowly because there was no reason to hurry. The street was as dark and empty as it had been during that solitary night all those years earlier, and yet everything seemed a different color, the front gardens of the houses bathed in a rosy-pink glow that didn't come from the streetlamps. At the beginning of our relationship, I understood that this golden glow that haloed us was part of a temporary love bubble, one that would eventually burst, but somehow the pop never came. Or perhaps the pop had come, and we simply hadn't noticed.

Our first kiss had been outside a gay bar in the East Village. I told her I'd wanted to kiss her for ages; she said she'd had no idea. I told her she was a fool and kissed her again. From that moment, we seemed to have only one speed, and we blew through everything standing in our way, including her marriage.

"We may be going too fast," I warned.

"You steer, I'll check the road," she said.

"Which of us has their hand on the hand brake?"

"Not me," she replied. "I've got my head out the window like a puppy."

I had some minor concerns about our dynamic at the beginning—her height made me feel slightly emasculated, my long hair perhaps gave her the impression I was more femme than I was—but these fears had quickly fallen away. Masculinity was a matter of confidence, not stature, and I solved the problem of my hair by finally cutting it all off. Jaime swore she'd find me attractive however I looked, and it didn't matter if short hair devalued me in the eyes of my heterosexual friends, because now that I was with Jaime I didn't need their approval anymore. I didn't need anyone's approval, except hers.

And Jaime felt the same way. "I don't think it can get any bigger than this," she said the first time she told me she loved me. "It's a pervasive fluency, maybe it's in the shape of our souls. When I'm with you I feel all the hard places inside me start to breathe and untwist. It feels like an unfurling."

I stored up the things she said to me like pebbles, fingering them incessantly when we were apart, carrying the smooth coolness of her words with me wherever I went. The words she spoke to me and the ones she wrote to me, the ones she whispered in my ear, the ones I'd always be able to summon from memory, and the ones she didn't say, the ones I heard in the silence when I lay with my head on her chest, feeling her language through her skin. Trust became a pocket full of words into which I could dip my hand whenever I liked. And even when we didn't have the words, I could feel it every time she kissed me, as if every cell in our bodies demanded the connection, as if kissing were the only thing to be done, which it was, so we did, whenever we could, for hours and hours.

Unfortunately, "whenever we could" wasn't quite as often as I might have liked. Charles's plan to keep sharing the house had stretched on for three years beyond our divorce, which I'd allowed to happen only because Jaime was in a similar situation. Jaime and I did our best to integrate our families by vacationing with the children in England, Cape Cod, and Spain, and when the lease on the New York apartment ran out I took over a small cottage by the coast, near where Jaime lived, so we could be closer to each other on the weekends. But now, finally, Charles had fallen in love and wanted to get married, so we were putting the house up for sale. The terms of the divorce meant I had to stay local, but at least the town where Charles's girlfriend lived was bigger and more diverse. It was beginning to look like my patience was finally paying off. The kids were happy and stable, Charles and I were on relatively good terms, and the future Jaime and I had dreamed of was now so close I could almost smell it.

Jaime stroked the short hair on the back of my neck, and I rubbed my head against her palm like a cat. She always did this if our conversation got too heated; just a touch, some small gesture to reassure me that we still belonged together, even if we didn't always agree. This time we were discussing a recent news story—Rose McGowan blowing the whistle on Harvey Weinstein. I'd been praising her for her public bravery; Jaime wasn't so impressed.

"She should have come forward when it happened," Jaime said. "She might have prevented other women from being raped."

"That's a bit harsh, isn't it? Criticizing the survivor doesn't sound like female solidarity."

"Women need to be tougher than that."

I raised an eyebrow. "Not everyone can be as tough as you."

"I know, but they should be. When you start a conversation about something as crucial as this, you have to start from an extremist position. If you start from a place of compromise, that's where you'll stay—in the middle."

"So you're saying fuck the middle ground," I clarified.

"Yes, I am."

Jaime slipped her fingers through mine, and I held on to her hand even as I held my tongue, glad to be on the right side of this warrior. Jaime's shift away from men started slowly, but her move towards lesbian separatism seemed to be intensifying with each year. I had slightly ambivalent feelings about this, although I had to concede that her antipathy towards men was unsurprising, given what was coming to light around us. Elisabeth admitted she'd been sexually assaulted by a famous actor when she was in her teens, Maeve was researching a story about sexual abuse in the workplace that would go on to win her team a Pulitzer Prize, and I'd confessed to Jaime that I'd once (or possibly more than once) had nonconsensual sex during an alcoholic blackout.

"Couldn't you feel it, back at the Kate Clinton show? The relief of being in a room filled only with women?" Jaime asked as we passed Captain Jack's Wharf.

Yes, I could feel it, being with women was comforting to me too, but this touched on a difference of opinion that I kept secret from Jaime: I quite liked the company of men. Particularly the gay ones. I'd grown so close to the men at my Connecticut queer twelve-step group that they now felt as much like family as the Late Bloomers did. While I understood this was slightly out of step with Jaime's fearless, women-only mindset, I didn't worry that it would come between us. None of our differences mattered, because what we had together transcended opinion.

Anyway, second-wave feminism was over. Everyone nowadays was talking about intersectional feminism. While Jaime and I had been waiting to blend our lives together, the world had been changing. Edie Windsor triumphed over the Defense of Marriage Act, which led to the Supreme Court legalizing gay marriage across the country, and everyone's Instagram feeds being showered with a profusion of rainbow confetti. What once seemed radical was now mainstream, a bumper sticker declaring LOVE IS LOVE IS LOVE on the back of an SUV. So the media had started to focus on the trans community, a percentage of the population so small it found itself on the wrong side of the decimal point. The word "queer" now referred to gender identity as much as it did to sexual orientation, Laverne Cox graced the cover of *Time* magazine, the Pentagon announced it was lifting the ban on transgender people serving in the military, and more books written by trans writers started appearing in the bookstores. I even had a few on my nightstand, although I hadn't read them yet. I still had too many thoughts about my own identity swirling around in my head, and I wanted to go at my own pace, ask questions only when I was sure I was ready to hear the answers. But thanks to Jaime it was nearly time. I loved her, I trusted her, and I wanted to be able to talk to her about what I was going through. It was simply a question of when, and how.

We arrived back at the hotel to find an envelope taped to the outside of our door. I opened it while Jaime groped around in her pockets for the key. *Thank you for the bottle of champagne! So happy to share our good news with you!* It was from the women in the room next to ours. The walls were thin, and it had been impossible not to overhear them getting engaged earlier that afternoon—the emotional tears, the shrieks of excitement as they telephoned their families. Jaime and I left a bottle of bubbly outside their door as a gift, a cute idea even though I had ambivalent feelings about marriage.

The first time Jaime brought it up was near the beginning of our relationship, while we were lying on a picnic blanket in the park, watching our seven children climbing in the trees around us. I tried to explain that my reservation wasn't a fear of commitment; I just didn't like the idea that someone might feel obligated to stay with me because they'd signed a contract. What I wanted was to wake up every morning and actively choose to be with Jaime, and to know that for as long as we were together, she was actively choosing to be with me. Also, I didn't like how binary weddings were, with all the men in suits and women in dresses. It gave me the creeps.

Then Rose got stuck in a tree and needed to be lifted out. As I climbed to my feet to go and rescue her, Jaime rolled onto her stomach and called out, "You'd better get over your hang-up about weddings, because one day I'm going to ask you to marry me." I felt it in my toes as I walked away from her, the warmth traveling up my body like a vine and blossoming in my cheeks until I couldn't stop smiling. I was going to spend the rest of my life with Jaime, and if she wanted proof of commitment, that was okay with me.

Jaime unlocked the door to the hotel room, sat down on the bed, and started unlacing her boots. The bedsprings squeaked as she lay back on the quilt, her chin arching in the air as she stretched her neck back into the pillows, her long legs sticking off the bottom of the bed. She patted the comforter beside her, and I lay down, slipped my hand under her T-shirt, and started stroking the soft skin of her stomach. Jaime murmured sleepily, her eyes closed. Her forehead was freckled with sun-spots, her lips twitching in that way she had when she was thinking of something funny. I leaned over and kissed her.

"Hmmm," she said suspiciously.

"Hmm what?"

"You're thinking. I can feel it."

I picked a piece of seaweed off her T-shirt and flicked it across the bed onto the floor. "Are you climbing in here with me?" I asked.

"Wandering sleepily around the interstices of your mind. Lost in the labyrinth of your brain."

"Let me know if you find anything interesting."

Jaime smiled, her eyes still closed.

"I'm going to brush my teeth," I said, pushing myself up off the bed. A few minutes later Jaime appeared by the bathroom door. She stood, leaning on the doorjamb, watching me lazily with that steady beam she had.

I spat the toothpaste into the sink and looked up at her in the mirror. "Uh-oh," I said.

She shook her head slightly. "You're going to have to tell me eventually."

"Tell you what?"

"The thing you still haven't told me."

"I've told you everything."

"No, you haven't."

I want to see it all, she'd said at the beginning of our rela-tionship. *Show me your tender underbelly, the parts that scare you, all the things you've been too afraid to show anyone else. I want to see it all so I can love you better.*

We held each other's eyes in the mirror. Her expression wasn't challenging, it was solid, reassuring. *I love you*, it said. *You're safe.* For three years she'd been patient, like someone waiting for an oyster to open rather than trying to crack it with a knife. I knew she'd go on waiting for as long as it took. I also knew I was almost ready.

"You're not going to ask me to marry you until I do, are you?" I asked.

She smiled and shook her head. "Nope."

Chapter Twenty-Three

S tanding in the bathroom of the cottage a couple of weeks later, drying myself off with a towel, I tried to figure out how to tell Jaime the thing she'd been waiting to hear. At least when I'd come out as gay, I'd been able to say, "I'm gay," and everyone had understood what I was talking about, whereas I genuinely had no idea where to start when it came to talking about my gender. But the longer I put it off, the more anxious I would become, so tonight was the night, regardless of whether I was ready.

I supposed I could describe what had been happening inside my head while we were having sex, but I didn't want Jaime to think her game was off. The feel of her hands on my body wasn't the problem; it was more that I couldn't get my body to align properly with her hands anymore. The minute I started to relax under her touch, my body would morph into its male form, which meant she'd be touching my body as if it were female when my body wanted to be touched as if it were male, and the confusion this caused in my head prevented me from being able to climax unless I left my body entirely and escaped into a fantasy completely removed from anything we were actually doing. And Jaime had started to notice. "You disappeared on me again," she'd say, or, "I lost you for a bit there." I was breaking the connection, and she could feel it.

I sat down on the edge of the bath as I dried my feet. I didn't like having to separate from my body during sex. I wanted to be fully present, I wanted to give my body permission to feel everything, even in parts of it that didn't technically exist. Because it had got to the point where I could no longer deny that I had a penis—not that I wanted a penis, or wanted to fuck her with a strap-on, or wanted to role-play being a man, but that I *actually had* a penis, one I could physically feel every time I got aroused.

I had ambivalent feelings about this. On the one hand it seemed to answer a question that had been stuck in my head since my early twenties: Why had I always felt so much like a boy? On the other hand, the answer to that question led to another question which was a little scarier: What did "feeling like a boy" actually mean? I wanted to ask Jaime, but I was too afraid of what she might say, and my silence had started to create a gulf between us.

One evening a few months earlier, we were having dinner at a table outside a small Italian restaurant in the East Village. I was facing the interior of the restaurant, and I had a clear view of the iconic cabaret artist Justin Vivian Bond, who was enjoying a meal with a group of friends. I'd seen them onstage a few months previously, displaying more charm, wit, and charisma than anyone I'd come across in recent history, and had since become mildly obsessed with them, searching for clips on YouTube and returning to their Instagram page more often than was necessarily healthy. I tried to keep my eyes from straying in their direction—conscious that they were just trying to have a quiet dinner with friends—but at the end of the meal, instead of exiting through the main door of the restaurant, the party of friends decided to take a shortcut between the tables on the sidewalk. As Vivian squeezed past my table, they looked down at me and beamed me a smile so dazzling, so generous, so *lavish* it caught me completely off guard. Suddenly I felt brimful with emotion: not only *I love you*, but also *You're my people*, and finally *If you can do it, I can do it too.*

The thought was so shocking I almost choked on my seltzer. I spent the rest of the evening in mute silence, unable to hold a proper conversation with Jaime because this thought was so huge it drowned everything else out. What was I trying to say? Did I want to transition? Did that mean I was a trans man? I didn't know any trans men, I knew nothing about trans men, the only prominent trans people in the media were all femme, like Justin Vivian Bond. Trans men were so invisible it was sometimes hard to believe they even existed.

Except, of course, for Joe, but Joe was only a kid. I'd known Joe since he and Alfie started kindergarten together, but it wasn't until a year or so previously that I got an email from his mother asking if we could meet for coffee. I assumed she wanted to talk about my sexual orientation—because Joe looked like someone who might grow up to be interested in girls—but over coffee and bagels Tina revealed that since he was old enough to speak, Joe had insisted he was a boy. She'd allowed him to dress in boys' clothes and play with boys' toys, but now he wanted to drop the name Joanne entirely and start using the boys' restrooms, try out for the boys' sports teams.

I couldn't do much during that first coffee beyond lending a sympathetic ear because I knew nothing about trans identities, but as our friendship developed Tina started to open up more.

Listening to her talk about how she and her husband had been
trying to navigate this impossible territory with little to no
help from anyone in their community, my respect for her
rocketed. Determined that she shouldn't go through it alone,
I started looking for organizations and support groups that
might be able to help her. But if anything, Joe's experience
only reinforced my belief that I wasn't trans, because I'd never
had the conviction he had. I knew I'd wanted to be a boy
when I was a kid, I knew I felt like a boy, I knew I felt more
comfortable presenting as a boy, but there was no way in
hell I was ever going to make this add up to the fact that I
actually *was* a boy.

And now here I was, standing naked in the bathroom of
a cottage in Connecticut, wondering whether that was pre-
cisely what I was. I went through to the bedroom and pulled
on some jeans. There were almost no mirrors in the cottage.
I was sick of mirrors. I didn't need to see my reflection to
know what I looked like. Skinny shoulders, small breasts,
slim waist, round buttocks, a neat pubic triangle. I'd covered
my forearms in tattoos over the last couple of years, so the
view of my arms when I was typing at my desk looked sat-
isfyingly male, but it wasn't enough. I wished I could scrape
the curves off my body like wet clay, leave myself hard and
straight. It was *me* that was wrong. It was this invisible penis
that wouldn't go away.

I picked up one of the memoirs sitting on my nightstand.
It was written by Thomas Page McBee, a trans man who'd
come to terms with his masculinity by learning how to box.
The photo on the dust jacket showed an attractive dark-haired
man with kind eyes and a beard. Did Thomas have an invisible
penis? I wished I could call him up and ask. *Hey, you don't*

know me, but do you have a dick you can feel during sex? Like, not just imagine you can feel, but actually feel?

I needed to talk to Jaime about it. The body issues were only really a problem in the bedroom anyway, so maybe it was a kink thing. And anyway, Jaime was right, we couldn't possibly commit to spending the rest of our lives together if I was withholding something like this. I'd figure out a way to explain it to her, we'd find a way to work around it, and finally there would be no more secrets between us.

I couldn't find an immediate inroad into the conversation when Jaime arrived at the cottage; she was too busy telling me a story about a guy she'd sat next to at the diner the night before who'd tried to compliment her on her culinary sophistication—she'd asked for jalapeños with her omelet—and almost ended up with hot sauce in his eye. We had dinner, and my body issues didn't seem like a suitable subject to bring up while we were eating, and then Jaime had to deal with some minor work crisis, and I suddenly felt the overwhelming urge to take a long bath, and then we were in bed and still I hadn't said anything. Perhaps it would be easier to discuss after we'd made love rather than before, because I was on top of her now and she was kissing me and I didn't want her to stop. I closed my eyes and allowed my body to morph into its male form: muscled arms, pecs, a hard stomach, tight buttocks, a penis. I kept my eyes closed as I moved above her, feeling myself growing, feeling myself harden, feeling myself inside her, I was inside her, I could feel it, I was inside her . . . oh God . . .

When I opened my eyes Jaime was staring up at me in astonishment. "Did you just *come*?"

"Yes," I admitted, looking down at her.

"But we're barely touching!"

"I know."

"What the hell just happened?"

I rolled off her and lay on my side, propping my head up on one hand. "Okay." I took a deep breath. "You know how you always thought there was something I wasn't telling you?" Jaime lay there, waiting. I was going to have to tell her now, there was no going back. "Well, you were a little bit right. There's been this one thing . . . It's a bit difficult to explain. You know how when some people have their arm amputated they can still feel it, like their central nervous system sends messages from the brain to the arm as if the arm actually exists? The phantom limb thing? Well . . ." I looked down at my pubic triangle, putting my hand around the space where my penis should be. "I kind of have a phantom penis. I can see it's not there with my eyes, but my brain believes it's real, and I can feel it. I can actually feel it. I felt myself inside you."

Jaime lay still, looking at me. She seemed tense. "You have a phantom penis?"

"Yes, and actually I have phantom pecs too, only I don't have so much sensation in them. It's just, my brain seems to think I have pecs and is constantly irritated by my breasts, like they're not really meant to be there."

There was a long pause during which I waited for Jaime to tell me that this was completely normal and she'd heard of lots of lesbians who had phantom pecs and penises.

"Nicky, this would make you transgender."

"No, no, it wouldn't," I said, sitting up and pulling the bedclothes around my waist. "I'm not transgender, I just seem to have a brain that believes my body is male."

"That's the definition of transgender."

"No, no, it's not." Now that I was having this conversation out loud it suddenly seemed much more real than it had in my head, and Jaime's expression was beginning to scare me. "I don't have all that backstory about growing up knowing I was a boy, so I can't be transgender."

"But you have a phantom penis."

"Yes."

"That you can feel."

"Yes."

"And that doesn't make you transgender?"

"No. Absolutely not."

The lead-up to Christmas was so busy with kids and families and friends that Jaime and I didn't have the chance to talk much about what happened. All seven of our children were in my kitchen decorating our annual Christmas train cake when Jaime mentioned in passing that perhaps I should start reading up on trans identities—that maybe the phantom penis wasn't the end of it—but I ignored her. Alfie was sticking red-and-green candy up his nose so he could "sneeze out Christmas," and Lily was getting competitive with Jaime's eldest daughter, which wasn't wise since she was five years younger, and I didn't have time to think about phantom penises when I had to deal with mountains of icing and the dog eating M&M's off the floor and fights breaking out over who got to decorate the caboose.

Anyway, I didn't *want* to read about trans identities; that's why all the memoirs on my nightstand were still untouched. This had to be something else, something that didn't involve me being trans, because I couldn't imagine that trans was something Jaime would want me to be. Also, the proof that I wasn't trans lay in the fact that I didn't know I was trans, because if I were trans, surely I would know? So best to avoid the books for now. I didn't want to be confused by other people's rhetoric, or risk being led into believing I might be something I was not.

On New Year's Eve we met up with the Late Bloomers at the local gay bar. The place was already heaving by the time we arrived; half-naked barmen were chucking around bottles of spirits and spraying people with soda, the dance floor pulsed with bodies. I danced with a beautiful gay man who was wearing a blue velvet smoking jacket with a white silk scarf. "I want your wardrobe!" I yelled at him over the deafening music.

"You want my what?" he yelled back.

"Your wardrobe!"

"My what?"

I pulled the silk scarf from around his neck and wound it around my own, ducking away from him as he tried to snatch it back, laughing. I didn't just want his wardrobe; I wanted his everything. His beautiful jawline, his small, tight torso, his slim buttocks, his manicured presentation. So chic, so dapper, so cute. Why couldn't I look like him?

Just before midnight the dance floor became a stage for the drag show, the revelers clearing a space for the queens to strut and shimmy their way across the floor. The final act was an artist with an incredibly beautiful body; she had pink flowers in her hair and was wrapped in a blue silk bikini made from what looked like an Hermès scarf. She was exquisite, like a bird of paradise. I looked at Jaime to see if I could gauge her reaction. I knew she had a problem with what she considered to be the misogyny of drag, but surely no one could think this woman was anything other than heavenly. "She's so beautiful!" I mouthed. Jaime just smiled and shrugged.

In bed later that night I curled around Jaime's back. She was falling asleep, but I couldn't stop talking about the drag artist, trying to work out whether she was in drag or identified as female. Since she was wearing so little, I figured she must be trans. "How much work must it take to get a body like that?" I wondered aloud. "She was incredible. But she must have been through so much to get there. You really have to admire it, don't you?"

"A lot of surgery," Jaime said sleepily.

"Yes, but worth it if you end up looking like that," I said.

Jaime didn't reply, possibly not wanting to get sucked back into an argument we'd had recently about whether trans women benefitted from male privilege. Jaime's position was that trans women could never claim equal status with cis women since they'd spent a portion of their lives as men, and therefore had managed to avoid the formative misogyny that had shaped the rest of us. My position was that trans women had never been men, they'd simply been *viewed* as men—which was a different thing entirely—and of course they'd experienced misogyny prior to transition. Hadn't she seen how effeminate gay men were treated by the cis-het population? But I figured it might be wise to stay away from the subject, because if I continued to press my point Jaime might accuse me of sounding like I cared too much. Or maybe I was overthinking it and she'd just fallen asleep.

"Are you asleep?" I whispered.

"No," Jaime murmured. "I was just thinking it must suck to be trans."

"I'm not trans," I said.

"That's lucky," she replied, "because I'm a lesbian."

Jaime left early the next morning, leaving me alone in the anxious sweat that had kept me up all night, her words swimming round and round my head. But recognizing some kind of gender-nonconformity about myself wasn't like saying I was a man, was it? I didn't have to be trans just because I had a phantom penis; there must be some other term I could use. I needed to do some research, figure out exactly what I was so I could explain it to Jaime in a way that didn't sound so scary. I got up, made myself some coffee, sat down at the kitchen table, opened my laptop, took a deep breath, and started trawling the internet for information.

As I searched, I began to realize how little I knew. Why hadn't I read more on this subject? Because I didn't think it applied to me? But it was the same fear that had kept me from talking to the lesbians at art school. I hadn't wanted to hang out with the lesbians because I didn't want to be a lesbian, and now I was avoiding reading about trans people because I didn't want to be trans. But the whole thing seemed to be absurdly complex, which just made it all the more frightening. Like when I first picked up *Stone Butch Blues*. I thought I was reading a book about lesbians, because it had "Butch" in the title, and then Feinberg had blurred the line between butch lesbians and trans men—or failed to draw a line where I thought a line should be—which left me obsessing over where I could stand that was still safe. Without that line firmly in place, what was to stop me from accidentally becoming trans?

The best argument for me not being trans was that I hadn't known I was trans when I was a kid. Except there was one moment from my childhood that in retrospect might have been a red flag. I was six years old, standing naked in the bathroom of my family home while Jack—who'd just come back from his first term at boarding school and was now the authority on everything—splashed in the tub. "D'you know there's a thing called a sex change?" he said. "There are girls out there who think they're boys and one morning they wake up and they're actually a boy. Like, *bam*, sex change. It's true. One of my friends told me."

My mother burst out laughing, seeing the alarm on my face. "Your brother's talking nonsense," she said, rubbing me briskly with a towel. "Sex changes don't just happen in your sleep." But for a split second I'd been certain this was going to happen to me, because I was that girl my brother had described. But I wanted to be a boy like my brother was a boy; I wanted to have been *born* a boy, I didn't want to turn into a boy having been born a girl first. That was the grossest thing my six-year-old self had ever heard.

As I did my research, and plumbed my memory for more red-flag moments, I began composing an essay to organize my thoughts and feelings. It seemed increasingly likely that the chronic anxiety I'd always suffered from was gender dysphoria; this persistent itching and crawling in my skin, the torturous desire to peel my flesh off my body. According to the internet, the solution was to align my body more closely with my internal gender, but I still wasn't entirely sure what my internal gender was. If gender roles were culturally assigned, and someone believed they'd been assigned the wrong one, surely the answer was just to switch roles, and bingo, problem solved. But however masculine I became, the dysphoria was still present. I felt it whenever I took my clothes off, or when I caught sight of myself in a mirror, or when Jaime touched me in bed. But that was a problem with my body, not my gender, wasn't it?

So, maybe it wasn't about masculinity or femininity, it was about whether I was male or female. My brain said quite clearly that my body was male, but every time I looked in the mirror my eyes said otherwise. I wondered whether there was a possibility I'd been born with a male brain in a female body. Not a male brain that thought stereotypically male thoughts as if it had been socialized as a man, but a male brain that believed that the anatomy of the body to which it belonged should also be male. Perhaps this might explain why I'd never liked penetrative sex: if someone was trying to put their dick into my vagina, and yet my brain insisted I didn't *have* a vagina, how could that feel good?

And yet my childhood still didn't make sense. I couldn't see an obvious bias towards either gender when I was a kid, but maybe that was because most of my everyday clothes were my brother's castoffs, whereas the clothes I played dress-up in didn't represent my gender, they represented my imagination. I didn't care whether I was a fairy or a cowboy or a pirate or a princess; I just liked pretending to be someone I wasn't.

I sighed and closed my laptop. Look where that had got me.

I'd been pretending to be someone else for so long, I had no idea who I was.

Late the following Friday Jaime and I met back at the cottage. I lit a fire in the hearth and put on some music. Jaime stretched out on the sofa in the living room and told me about her

week while I made us a pot of tea in the kitchen, the essay I'd
written during my research hidden in my bag on the kitchen
counter. I came back through to the living room with the
mugs of tea, passed one to Jaime, and sat on the arm of the
sofa. "So," I said.

Jaime looked up at me, warming her hands around her mug.

"I wrote a thing about gender. I want you to read it and
tell me what you think."

Jaime put her mug down on the coffee table. "Okay."

I hesitated, and then went back into the kitchen and pulled
the essay out of my bag. I came back through and handed it
to her. "I'm going to take a walk down to the coffee shop to
pick up some pastries while you read it," I said.

"Okay," Jaime repeated, sitting up on the sofa.

I pulled on my coat and boots and opened the front door.
"I won't be long," I said, looking back at her. She was still
sitting on the sofa, holding my essay in one hand, looking
slightly surprised.

Walking through the snow to the coffee shop, I reassured
myself that given the conversations we'd had about gender
over the years, Jaime would probably find the essay quite
interesting. I maintained that I definitely wasn't a trans man,
but I might perhaps have a male body primarily activated by
sex. My identity seemed to be dictated by my environment,
which meant that when it was necessary for me to be a girl, I
could be a girl, but if I were allowed to be a boy, that's what
I'd gravitate towards, and when I relaxed so much that I
lost my grip on myself entirely—like in the moments before
orgasm—the sensation of being male would swallow me up
completely. But I could totally come back into my female
body when I resurfaced, even if it felt a little uncomfortable

for a while. It was important, I felt, that she understand this, because she clearly wanted to be in a relationship with a woman, and I didn't want her to think I was saying I wanted to be a boy *all the time*, only that I wanted permission to be a boy *occasionally*, if I needed to be, which I sometimes did, mostly when we were in bed. That was a very long way from being trans. Reassuringly far away. As far as essays on gender went, I was quite proud of it.

When I got to the coffee shop the queue was longer than I'd anticipated. I bought some pastries and started to walk home, realizing I'd been away from the house for longer than I originally planned. I sped up slightly, hurrying as fast as the snow would allow, until I was almost running as I neared the house. I took the porch steps two at a time, stomped my feet quickly on the doormat to get rid of the snow, and opened the front door.

Jaime was sitting on the sofa, completely still. I stood in the doorway. She looked up at me. "Why did you leave me to read this on my own?" she asked.

"I wasn't . . . I thought . . . I didn't want to . . ." I pulled off my coat and boots and sat down on the sofa with her, leaving the pastries on the coffee table. "It's not that scary, Jaime."

"It *is* that scary. You're talking about being trans."

"Not *transgender* trans, though," I said. "It's not like I think I'm actually a boy, it's just there are some elements I want to . . ."

Jaime put up her hand to stop me. I sat, waiting, but she appeared to be struggling to speak. "This is only the beginning," she said eventually.

"What d'you mean?"

Jaime shook the pages at me. "You don't just write some-thing like this and then say, 'That's it,' do you? You're not going to just *stop* here, are you? This is only the tail of the tiger!"

I frowned. "I don't understand. What's the tiger?"

"You being trans! I don't believe for a minute this is 'pri-marily activated by sex'—it's more likely that it's just got to the stage where you can't shut it down anymore. This is who you are all the time. I can see it in you already, I've been watching it happen. The minute I read this I could see it: I could see the boy."

"Wait, what?"

She threw the essay onto the coffee table. "Do you have any idea how different you look now from when we first started dating? If I showed someone a photo of you from three years ago, they probably wouldn't even think you were the same person! Your whole body has changed!"

"That's because I've been working out . . ."

"You even smell different!"

"Wait, *what*?" I stared at her. Where was all this coming from? Jaime had never commented on my gradual shift in style before, and I'd assumed it was because she didn't care. How many other changes had been secretly bothering her? How many other changes had there actually been? "I don't think this is as big as you're making it out to be," I said. "I mean, I don't think where I'm going to end up is very far from where I am now. This isn't the beginning of some huge transition—really, it's not—I'm just trying to find the right language for it all. Like maybe 'nonbinary' . . ."

"A phantom penis is pretty fucking binary." Jaime looked angry, but there were tears in her eyes. Jaime never cried.

Jaime *never* cried. "You're completely dismissing the magnitude of what's happening here. I feel like I've fallen for a bait and switch."

"Jaime!"

She shook her head, cutting me off. "You're going to have to leave this with me for a while." She turned and picked up the essay that was lying on the coffee table, holding it in her hands as if it were the test results for an incurable disease. "You shouldn't have left me alone while I read this," she said under her breath. "You should have been here with me."

Chapter Twenty-Four

Over the next few days Jaime withdrew into an uncharacteristic silence. I waited, not knowing what the silence meant, afraid of making the wrong move. I couldn't get the words "bait and switch" out of my head. What did she think I'd been faking? This was my body, and however much my brain might think I had a penis and pecs, I still had breasts and a vagina. These were unchangeable biological facts.

I went to the bookshelf and pulled down my copy of *Stone Butch Blues*. I turned to the page where Jess, the protagonist, describes her girlfriend touching her cock, and immediately felt the heat rise between my legs, as I did every time I read this passage, which I'd obviously done quite a lot given that this was the place where the spine was broken. I squeezed my eyes shut, wondering how many layers of denial it was possible for one person to bury themselves under. I wondered whether I'd been resisting my own transness because I thought that, with the exception of a handful of rarities like Justin Vivian Bond, trans people were lesser. I believed there was a sliding scale down which a woman slipped as she got progressively more masculine, and if I felt that way, then other people must too. I didn't want to lose my status, become something worthless, a person on the lowest rung of the ladder.

I put the book back on the bookshelf, feeling something in my chest tighten. I wasn't just a homophobe; I was a transphobe too. And yet reading about Jess being expelled from the warmth of the lesbian community into miserable isolation after taking testosterone had been genuinely distressing. I had surrounded myself with lesbians; I understood lesbians; popular and success-ful and glamorous lesbians were all over the media. But where were the trans men? Beyond Thomas Page McBee I couldn't think of a single one, except Brandon Teena, and he'd ended up dead. I sat back down at my computer, staring at it in panic. I didn't want to be trans. I wasn't a revolutionary communist like Feinberg, I hadn't developed the tough skin of a hard-line extremist, I wasn't ready for any of this.

I took a deep breath, trying to calm myself down. Nobody said taking testosterone was a requirement. And even if I could no longer be a lesbian, who said I had to be a trans man? Why couldn't I just be vaguely boyish? I started dig-ging through social media for visuals, but none of the trans men on Instagram—all beards and muscles and buffed-up torsos—fit the image I had in my head. Then I found a link to the page of an artist called Chella Man, who had started transitioning a year earlier, and I stopped. He reminded me of Daniel, the boy I'd dated in high school: the same smooth skin, the same dark hair, the same angular jaw and full lips. He was the most beautiful person I'd ever seen. He was clearly taking testosterone, because he tracked his own changes on his Instagram account, but there was no trace of stubble on his skin or hair on his chest, which was marked with two perfect scars beneath the shadow of his pecs. I sat, scrolling through his photos, imagining what it would feel like to have a chest like his. This was possible. This boy had done it.

I went back through to my bedroom and stripped off my clothes, forcing myself to look at my naked body in the mirror. As I started to push through the discomfort, I realized it wasn't so much that I disliked the image I saw; it was more like being a small child who didn't realize that the person in the mirror was actually him. As long as that body belonged to another person, it looked perfectly fine; it was only when I tried to make it belong to me that it became problematic. Because that wasn't my body. I closed my eyes and allowed myself to see my body in my mind: flat chest, smooth pecs, wide abs, slim buttocks, the penis dangling between my legs. I opened my eyes and looked in the mirror. Staring back at me was the body of a woman. It was too weird. I pulled my breasts into my armpits and stood sideways, looking at myself with a flat chest, my hips jutting forward, my groin in shadow. It wouldn't take much; if I got rid of my breasts and grew my leg and armpit hair, I'd look like a teenage boy.

I let my breasts go and turned to face myself, my spirit deflating. Would my baseline mood rise permanently if I had slim hips and a flat chest like a man? But even if I did get rid of my breasts, nobody could create a dick where there wasn't one, or at least not one that worked the way I wanted it to work. I pulled my clothes back on, my skin prickling with apprehension. If this had been the root cause of all my unhappiness, then I would never be truly happy until I found some way to resolve it. But how? This wasn't something I could fix by changing my partner, like I'd done when I came out as gay. I'd have to change myself.

*   *   *

Early the following week, Jaime called to ask whether I had time to drop by for a coffee; her eldest daughter was home sick from school, so she was stuck at home folding laundry. I perched on a stool by her kitchen counter while she sorted her children's clothes into piles. I didn't want to talk to her about my thoughts on top surgery yet, so instead I told her about some of the other articles I'd been reading. Jaime listened as I spoke, contributing little.

"Tell me how you're feeling about all this," I said eventually. "And tell me the truth. I need you to be honest with me."

Jaime folded a pair of sweatpants and put them on the pile at the side of the counter. "My main concern is that this'll take up all of our attention," she said. "I thought I was finally going to get to focus on my work, but if all our energy is getting sucked up by this, my career's going to get sidelined."

"Then we won't let it. I'll make sure it doesn't take over." Jaime's face was a closed book. "Jaime," I pressed. "What is it?"

Jaime picked up a pair of jeans, shook them out, and folded them into a square. "I'm worried I'm going to prevent you from doing the work you need to be doing," she said carefully.

"My writing?" I asked.

Jaime shook her head. "No . . . the work on yourself. I'm worried you're going to form your new identity around me rather than around who you actually are."

Ah, so that was it: Jaime's obsession with autonomy, her fear that our individual personalities might somehow get sucked into a black hole created by the relationship.

"I don't think that's going to be a problem, Jaime," I reassured her. "I think I'm already pretty close to who I'm going to be."

"Okay, but I really just want you to feel whole," she continued. "And in order to see that happen, I'm willing to risk a net loss to myself."

"What d'you mean, 'net loss'?"

Jaime stopped folding and leaned with her hands on the counter. "If you'd already made the decision to transition, I'd be calling it now. I'd pull the rip cord."

I lurched backwards on the stool as if I'd been shot. "Jaime, don't! Please, don't!"

"Christ," Jaime sighed. "Come here." She came round the counter and wrapped her arms around me. I leaned into her, burying my face in her sweater.

"Mom? Nicky?" Jaime's daughter appeared in the doorway. I pulled myself out of Jaime's arms.

Jaime turned and shook her head. *Not now*, she mouthed. Her daughter just nodded, wide-eyed, and disappeared back through the door. Jaime turned back to the laundry, wiping her forehead briefly with the back of her hand. "I shouldn't have said that," she said. "I know this is scary for you and I don't want to make it worse."

I was still trying to digest what she'd said. Surely there was nothing I could do that would result in Jaime actually *leaving* me. Jaime's greatest fear was having her feelings invalidated, being told that what she thought or felt wasn't real, and I was acutely aware that if I tried to contradict anything she said, I'd be on dangerous ground. But I needed to try to correct her understanding of what was happening here. "I'm not turning into a man," I managed eventually. "A boy, maybe, but that's not such a stretch from where we are already."

Jaime put down the shirt she was folding, looking exasperated. "If you begin to prioritize the things about you that are male and let the female parts atrophy, I'll be left loving someone who no longer exists."

"But I'm not changing on the inside," I said, my voice tightening against the impulse to fight with her. "I'm the same person you've always loved. I'm just being clearer about who I am."

Jaime's face hardened. "You *are* changing. I can see it happening. I've been watching it happen. So far, I've been okay with it—I don't give a damn how short your hair is or what clothes you wear—but masculine energy is a different beast. That's not a superficial change." She shook out a shirt and laid it flat on the counter, then started doing up the buttons almost aggressively, her fingers fumbling. "I'm sick of men. Sick of them. If I wanted to be with a man, I'd have stayed in my marriage. I left because I wanted to be with a woman. And so far, we haven't had a problem, but there is a tipping point where masculine energy aggregates into an identity, and I may not be able to love you beyond that point."

"What d'you mean, masculine energy?"

"I mean, you can't hold me accountable if you turn into something I can't love."

I stared at her, appalled. I should have never told her about the phantom penis. If I'd never mentioned it, none of this would have happened. I could have made our relationship work without telling her, I *could* have. This was horrendous. I leaned across the laundry, trying to get her to look at me.

"Jaime, three years ago you specifically told me that you wanted to see all of me. All the bad parts, my dark underbelly, all of it. You said you wanted to see it all so you could love me better."

Jaime met my eyes. "Neither of us could have predicted that your dark underbelly would turn out to be this."

For the next few days, I tried to distract myself by climbing into the backs of all the cupboards and closets in the house I shared with Charles and clearing out all the shit that had accumulated over the last ten years. Old car seats covered in dust, boxes of cables that belonged to nothing, broken toys, empty spray bottles, ripped bath towels that might have been useful for something once. All of it hauled out and sorted into piles—toss, save, donate—until my home looked like it belonged to the demented hoarders in E. L. Doctorow's *Homer & Langley*. My tea breaks were spent reading Jaime's emails and texts, which came in randomly, confused and contradictory: anger in one message, fear in the next, words of encouragement, predictions of a catastrophic end, promises of enduring love, accusations of betrayal. Finally, she sent me an email asking me not to contact her for a couple of weeks. She needed some time away from me to deal with her feelings on her own.

I felt like someone had drawn a blade up from my stomach to my throat. Was this her first step towards ending the relationship? How could it have happened so fast? I remembered something written by the Buddhist monk Thich Nhat Hanh: *Finding truth is not the same as finding happiness. You aspire to see the truth, but once you have seen it, you cannot avoid suffering.* Was this my path now? Did I not get to be happy anymore?

Early the following week I found myself back at the LGBTQ center. The room that usually hosted my twelve-step meeting now had a sign saying TRANSGENDER SUPPORT GROUP taped to the door. I pushed it open to find three people sitting in a small circle of fake-leather armchairs.

"Is this the transgender support group?" I asked, somewhat pointlessly.

The woman in the facilitator's chair looked up at me and smiled. "It is, please take a seat. My name's Theresa." She was older, dressed modestly in a long skirt and a blouse, teamed with no-nonsense spectacles, a spinster-aunt look. I'd seen her around the center before; she exuded a quiet intelligence, as if she were the sort of person who'd offer measured, practical advice, and I was relieved she was running the meeting.

I sat down and the woman sitting opposite me leaned forward, her hand outstretched. "I'm Marilyn!" she said. "Great to have you on board!" She wore heavy makeup and colorful clothes stretched over a curvaceous body, spaghetti straps falling off rounded shoulders, a vast bosom heaving out of her tight pink top. Next to her sat a third person, of indeterminate gender; they sat bunched up in their chair like a frightened hamster, chewing the inside of their cheek nervously, a fuzz of dark hair evident on their upper lip. I smiled and they gave me a half smile in return.

Theresa opened the meeting by asking me what pronouns I used. I said I hadn't got that far yet, but if there was a bridge between woman and man, I was probably more than halfway across. Marilyn lit up, as if delighted by the prospect of having a newbie to educate, and she launched into a medley of questions and suggestions and answers, apparently accustomed to holding both sides of a conversation. Theresa briefly tried to interrupt by bringing the hamster into the conversation, but Marilyn was commandeering the stage with the confidence of a born diva, covering subjects as disparate as her marine boyfriend, the effects of estrogen, the music of Bauhaus, and the merits of polyamory, until suddenly she asked me whether I planned to have top surgery.

It was such an abrupt question that I blurted out "Yes" before I had time to think.

Everyone sat looking at me while I tried to come to terms with my answer. Eventually Marilyn broke the silence by asking how I thought my girlfriend would feel.

"I don't think it'll end our relationship," I replied. "Although perhaps she might need some time to adjust."

"But she's a lesbian, right?" Marilyn said.

"Yes."

"And you yourself are only attracted to women?" she clarified.

"Yes," I admitted.

Marilyn sat back and crossed her arms in front of her bountiful chest. "So how would you feel if you woke up one morning to find yourself lying next to Tom Hanks?"

"Well, I wouldn't, I . . . Wait, am I Tom Hanks in this scenario? Why do I have to be Tom Hanks?"

Marilyn shrugged her ample shoulders. "Who d'you want to be?"

"David Bowie, of course."

"So how do you think your girlfriend would feel if she woke up next to David Bowie?"

"There's not a human alive who'd have a problem waking up next to David Bowie!"

"You're missing my point."

"No, I get your point," I said. "But maybe it's not even a physical thing. Maybe she's just worried I'll usurp her role. She's meant to be the more masculine of the two of us, and my becoming more boyish is probably upending her idea of who she's supposed to be."

"Or her idea of who *you're* supposed to be." Marilyn said, refusing to be mollified. "She may genuinely stop being attracted to you. Haven't you seen *The Danish Girl*? Do you want to end up in a relationship with someone who can't love you sexually?"

"Oh my God, Lili Elbe transitioned nearly a hundred years ago! There weren't any choices back then—two genders, two options, that was all they had! It's not like that now, is it? I don't have to go all the way; I can find somewhere in the middle where I'm comfortable."

"But wouldn't that feel like a compromise?"

That's what I'm trying to find out! I wanted to yell, but I didn't because I knew she was just trying to be helpful. "All I know is I can't go on indefinitely waking up in this body every morning just because it's what someone else wants." I said instead. "I mean, who does my body belong to? Who is my body *for*? It's like my femininity's a gift I've been giving to other people for so long that they've just come to expect it, and if I take it back now, everyone's going to accuse me of being selfish."

This was true. My father wanted a pretty daughter, my ex-husband wanted an attractive wife, and Jaime wanted a feminine girlfriend. What *I* wanted was apparently irrelevant because everyone else's claim on my body exceeded my own.

"*It's my goddamn body!*" I exclaimed. "Isn't it my right to do with it as I please?"

"Yes," Marilyn said, cupping her hands protectively over her breasts. "Yes, it is."

*   *   *

I was leaning with my forehead pressed against the bark of a tree, staring at a leaf stuck to the end of my sneaker, trying to breathe through the pain. Whatever happened, I couldn't let the girls see how upset I was. We were out in the woodland beside the house, gathering sticks to use as kindling. Freddie and Alfie had declined to join us. Alfie was sulking in his bedroom because he didn't want us to sell the house—he had a tight-knit group of friends at his school and was furious at me for breaking them up—and Freddie, now thirteen, wasn't interested in anything that didn't involve comics or video games.

"Is this one too big?" Lily called out, dragging a branch behind her.

It was early March and the house had just gone on the market. So far Lily and Rose hadn't seemed bothered by the prospect of moving; they were more concerned about where Jaime was, and why her daughters hadn't come round for so long, and I was beginning to run out of excuses. What if Jaime left now, in the middle of all this disruption? The queer-friendly world of the Late Bloomers was all the girls could remember, so while they might be prepared for conversations about gender, they were not remotely prepared for the possible loss of Jaime and her daughters.

I tried to reassure myself that the more space I gave Jaime, the sooner she'd come back, but it had been weeks since we'd seen each other. I punctured the silence occasionally with a text telling her I loved and missed her, but her responses were evasive. *I feel like a bomb's gone off and I don't know what's going to be left when the dust clears. We need more time to let this settle.* I asked her how much time, but she couldn't—or wouldn't—tell me. *I want to be able to ask for space when I need it. It doesn't mean*

I'm leaving you forever. When I said I was concerned that the cracks appearing in our relationship would never get repaired if we continued to avoid each other indefinitely, the message became firmer. *What you're going through is overwhelming, but it's not about me, it's about you. And it's too much for me right now.*

I went over to where Rose was piling twigs into the wheelbarrow, forcing a smile onto my face. "This one's too long, honey. You can break it over your knee like this." I showed her how to snap the branch in half and then started moving the twigs from the wheelbarrow into the kindling basket. The question of what, exactly, Jaime was running from seemed crucial. If I could figure out which part of this had pushed her over the edge, I could fix it. *You can't hold me accountable if you turn into someone I can't love.* Was it just that she wouldn't be physically attracted to me anymore, or was it more than that? What if she thought I would try to undermine her female power? What if she saw me as a legitimate threat?

We carried the kindling basket back into the house and laid the fire, and once the girls were settled in front of a movie I went through to my office and turned on my computer. The only solution was to keep moving forward, figure out who I was, and see if Jaime could still love me. I went online and found a therapist in Brooklyn who specialized in gender affirmation, a company selling binders for people who wanted to strap down their breasts, and a monthly meeting for trans men at the LGBT Center in New York. I wasn't messing around this time; I was going to get shit done.

My next mission was to resolve the issue of my invisible penis. Trying to align my physical body with what my brain believed it should look like wasn't going to be easy, but it would make sense to get comfortable with it while Jaime and I were on this extended break. If people who'd had limbs amputated could learn to live with prosthetics, I could do the same. There was a sex store near Bluestockings—I'd walked past it several times—so I earmarked a day in my calendar to head down to the Lower East Side to find my dick.

Pushing through the front door of Babeland a week later, I was confronted by shelves of red and pink silicone, pots of creams, and tubes of gel that made the place look more like it was selling expensive cosmetics than sex toys. I made my way past objects that looked like microphones—or eggs, or hair straighteners, God only knew what they actually were—to the prosthetic penises lined up on a shelf against the back wall. For a moment I was overwhelmed by the sheer quantity of dicks on display. Large, small, multicolored, rainbow-striped, realistic, synthetic, long, stubby, smooth, veined—every type of penis I could have possibly imagined and quite a few I couldn't have. It didn't take long to find mine. The right size, the right shape, the right color—I recognized it as soon as I saw it. I opened the box and pulled it out; it was heavy, not exactly hard but not quite floppy, like something that would bounce if I dropped it. It was like finding something I'd lost, something familiar for which I'd once felt great affection. It was so absolutely my penis it seemed strange it wasn't already attached to me.

I glanced around, suddenly realizing I was holding my dick in my hand in the middle of a store in broad daylight, but the trans woman behind the counter was busy on her cell phone and the rest of the store was empty. I put it back in its box, chose a pair of ring briefs and a harness, and carried them over to the checkout, trying not to feel self-conscious. "Found what you were looking for, honey?" the store clerk asked, and I nodded, suddenly awash with love for this woman who treated prosthetic penises like they were everyday items. As she started chatting to me about the new shipment they had coming in—whether I'd be interested in a trans-masc suction pump or a mini stroker—I wondered why I'd been afraid of this for so long. I could see a pattern emerging: the things I most feared often turned out to be the things I most wanted. Perhaps I should start paying slightly closer attention to my fears in the future.

Later that night, after the children were asleep, I shut myself in my bedroom with my new dick. The binder had arrived in the mail a couple of days earlier, so I pulled it out of its packaging and unrolled it. A flesh-colored garment made from heavy-duty elastic, it bore a close resemblance to an armored vest. I maneuvered it on and looked at myself in the mirror: it squashed my breasts into two flat mounds that resembled a pair of well-formed pecs. It wasn't comfortable—to be honest, it was a little hard to breathe—but it made my chest look amazing. I pulled off my jeans and positioned the rubber penis against my pelvic bone. The effect was instantaneous, as if someone had hit a switch in my brain, the nerve endings in my groin reaching out like tentacles to claim it. It perfectly filled the space where my eyes insisted something was missing; it belonged to me, it belonged to my body. I was a man.

I sat down on the bed and leaned forward, my hands on my knees. No wonder I'd always shied away from using a harness. I must have known that strapping one of these onto my body would have made it impossible for me to deny what I was. I felt a sudden burst of euphoria—*this was real*—followed by a wave of nausea as I realized what that meant. The panic I'd felt in the bathroom when I was six wasn't some unfounded childish fear. This sex change was going to happen whether I liked it or not.

Chapter Twenty-Five

I was sitting at my desk paying bills when I heard the school bus pull up at the end of the drive. Feet thundered up the back stairs into the kitchen, cupboard doors banged open as the kids helped themselves to snacks. A few minutes later Rose appeared in my office. She threw her book bag into the corner and slumped down on the swivel seat that faced my desk, put her feet up on the desk, and started swinging her hips back and forth in the chair, popping potato chips into her mouth as she swung. Long hair tucked under a baseball cap, red Levi's T-shirt, twiggy legs in cut-off jean shorts: now in third grade, she was so young-American-hipster it made my heart ache. They were all growing up way too fast.

"How was your day, sweets?" I asked as I filled out a check.

"Liam's such a loser," she said. "He spent the whole bus ride trying to convince me that Vans are cooler than Converse. I said you shouldn't wear Vans unless you were an actual skater or you'd look like a hypebeast, but he said nobody skateboards now anyway so if that was the case Vans would go out of business. I said you haven't met my older brother, and that shut him up."

"I prefer Converse," I said, as if my opinion mattered.

"Me too, and anyway I'm getting all of yours when my feet are big enough."

"You'll have to fight me for them." Rose watched as I tore the bottom of the electricity bill along the perforated line. I slipped the stub and check into an envelope and sealed it.

"So, Mom," she said.

"Yes, honey?" I asked, peeling a stamp off the roll.

"D'you think you're basically a man now?"

I stopped, the stamp suspended in midair. Rose was still swinging the seat of the chair in a small arc, pressing a finger into the bottom of the chips bag to find the crumbs.

"Well, maybe, sort of, a little bit," I said, carefully sticking the stamp onto the corner of the envelope.

"Does that mean you're trans?" she asked, sucking the crumbs off her finger.

I put the envelope down and looked at her. "Maybe."

"Because you really only do man stuff now. You act like a man, and you look like a man, so that basically makes you a man, doesn't it?"

"D'you think so?"

"Yeah, although actually you mostly look like a gay man. Are you a gay man?"

I sat back in my chair. "No, because I only like women."

"So you're a gay man who likes dating lesbians."

Lily came wandering in. "What are you two talking about?"

"Mom's transgender," Rose said.

"Wait, are you?" Lily asked, looking at me.

"I'm not sure that we need to—"

"Because you're basically a man now?" Lily said.

I narrowed my eyes. "Have you two been discussing this without me?"

"Come on, Mom, it's pretty obvious. I mean, look at you," Rose said.

"Jesus, you're *nine*, how are we even having this conversation?"

"We're too cool for school, Mom," Rose said, spinning the chair around in a circle. "It's your fault; you raised us."

"So, you used to be a girl who dates boys, and then you were a girl who dates girls, and now you're a boy who dates girls?" Lily clarified.

"Well, I'm just me and I'm dating Jaime, but yes, I guess so."

"Jaime's almost a man too, so perhaps you *are* a gay man," Rose said.

"Does Freddie know?" Lily asked.

"No, I haven't . . . this is the first time . . ."

"He's going to freak out," Rose said, looking delighted at the prospect.

"You think?"

Lily rolled her eyes. "It's Freddie, Mom."

But Freddie wasn't interested in the conversation when I broached it during dinner that evening. "Whatever, Mom, we don't need to talk about it," he said, avoiding my eyes. I knew my son; if he wasn't ready, he wasn't ready, and I wasn't going to push it. Anyway, I still didn't have all the information I needed for the sort of conversation Freddie would want to have. I had research to do, books to read, people I needed to meet.

When the day of the trans-masculine support group in New York arrived, I took the train down early so I could spend the afternoon with Daisy, the poet who ran writers' workshops from her apartment overlooking the Stonewall

Inn. The suburban landscape rolled past the window like a series of snapshots in a family album—backyards and swing sets and patios and grills—while I replayed everything the girls had said in my head. They seemed to have accepted my potential transition as if it were a natural part of an organic process, like what they themselves were going through as they approached puberty. But children were supposed to change. Part of the deal was that the mother would remain the same. I was meant to be the one constant in their unstable lives, and yet even if on some level they understood my transition as a betrayal of the mother-child contract, how could they voice this to me? I wasn't just an authority figure; I was their primary parent, and their dependence on me might stop them from being honest about what they really felt. I'd seen them being careful about what they said around Charles—toning down their left-wing views so they wouldn't offend him—which meant they'd already learned the value of censoring themselves to earn favor from a parent. I might never know the full truth about the impact my transition would have on them.

I leaned my head against the train window. The girls were growing up so quickly, not only emotionally but physically too, their bodies already starting to mature. How could I teach them to love their bodies when I was considering surgery to alter mine? And how could I talk to them about any of this without putting fears they might not have into their heads? The rapidly approaching teenage years were going to be fraught enough already, with four kids going through adolescence at the same time, and now here I was, planting more mines in the field.

I arrived at the stoop of Daisy's apartment, but before I had the chance to ring the doorbell my phone pinged. I pulled it out of my pocket.

I can't find my shin guards, Alfie texted.

They're probably with your cleats, I texted back.

Where are my cleats?

A shadow fell across my phone. "Excuse me, do you think you could buy me something to eat?"

I glanced briefly at the person standing in front of me and then looked around to see if there was a deli or grocery store nearby while trying to text Alfie back. "I don't know . . . I can't see . . . maybe I could just give you some cash . . . ?" I reached into my back pocket and pulled out my wallet.

"No, no, I don't want your money." Her voice cracked. I looked up into her face and quickly put away my wallet, feeling like an asshole. She was very thin, with long silver hair, a short, neatly clipped beard, and fuchsia lipstick. A three-quarter-length purple velvet coat hung from her shoulders, a pleated skirt fell to her calves, and on her feet she wore a pair of men's brogues with no socks. "Hey, are you okay?" I put my hand on her arm as she dissolved into tears. "Hey, hey, it's okay, what do you need? Do you need help?"

She wiped her eyes with the back of her hand. "I don't have anywhere to stay. I only arrived in New York a few days ago and I've been sleeping on the F train and I heard that Christopher Street was where people like me came, but now that I'm here I don't know where to go. And I'm so hungry, I just need something to eat."

"Okay," I said, getting practical. "For a start, you shouldn't be sleeping on the F train. Have you tried to find a shelter?"

"I can't go to a shelter, it's not safe for someone like me."

"Neither is sleeping on the F train. What about the Center on Thirteenth Street? They might be able to help find you somewhere to stay." I pulled up a map on my phone. "It's only about a ten-minute walk from here." She stared at the phone blankly. It was clear she'd never make it there on her own. "Okay, come on, I'll take you. We'll go together."

She looked down at her feet. "I can't walk very fast. Someone gave me these shoes, but they're too small and they're rubbing my toes and I've got blisters."

"Then we'll walk slowly." I took her elbow and she half leaned on me while we shuffled down the street. She told me her name was Michael and that she'd moved here from France after her mother passed away, today was her birthday, and she'd managed to put herself together on the train from Brooklyn before coming to Christopher Street. She was carrying an I-heart-New-York shopping bag, which she held open to reveal a tube of lipstick, a bottle of nail polish, and a book. "I always put on my lipstick in the morning," she told me. "I don't want to look like I'm down and out. You don't have to let yourself go, do you?"

"You certainly don't," I agreed. We hobbled on down the road together until we came to a deli, where we stopped to buy something to eat. While the deli clerk made her a sandwich, Michael pulled out the book—a queer punk reimagining of the Peter Pan story—flicking through the pages while she explained how she identified with the characters. She put the book back in her bag, paused for a moment, and then said, "I've got a secret I want to tell you." She leaned down and whispered in my ear, "I'm not really a man."

"I have a secret to tell you too," I said in an equally confidential tone. "I'm not really a woman."

Michael pulled back and stared at me in amazement. "You're transgender?"

"I am." I smiled, amazed to find myself saying it out loud to this magical person.

"But you're so beautiful!"

"And so are you, Michael."

Her face lit up. "We are all beautiful!"

"Yes! We are!" I said, laughing.

When we arrived at the Center, Michael started crying again. While the receptionist was contacting the crisis counselor, I scribbled my phone number down on a piece of paper. "Call me if you need me," I said, giving her a hug and feeling surprisingly reluctant to leave.

I headed back to Daisy's apartment, texting an apology for being late. I'd grown close to Daisy over the last few years, so it was easy to open up about my encounter over a pot of tea and chocolate cake, but when I got to the part where Michael told me her secret in the deli, Daisy stopped me. "I know what you're going to tell me," she said. "I'm sorry, I can't stop smiling because I know what you're about to say."

"You do?"

"It's in your writing. It's all there if you know what you're looking for." Daisy paused, as if waiting for my permission.

"Go on," I encouraged.

"You're transitioning, right?" she asked. I started to laugh. "Of course you are. Look at you. It's so obvious." She leaned back in her chair, looking me up and down. "You've grown into yourself. You look exactly like you should." We spent the next hour reading through my latest writing assignment, but I couldn't stop smiling, elated by Daisy's easy acceptance. Sounds from the street outside filtered in through the open sash window: a chirping bird, a muffled shout, the compressed air released from a braking truck. Daily life on Christopher Street, where people like me were a dime a dozen.

Eventually it was time to head back to the Center for the meeting. "Look out for a friend of mine who works there," Daisy said as she kissed me goodbye at the apartment door. "His name's Oliver. If you see him, tell him hello from me."

I paused after Daisy closed the door, taken by surprise. As I walked back down the narrow stairs of the apartment building, the name bounced off the plaster walls like someone had just released a giant soap bubble that was shimmering rainbows around the hallway. It felt as if I'd just been reminded of something I'd forgotten I already knew. Oliver. That was my name. I opened the front door and stepped out into the street. Oliver. I'm Oliver. I'm a boy and my name is Oliver. I walked past the red-brick facade of the Stonewall Inn, seeing the person reflected in the dark window. This was the boy who'd gone on that first date here six years ago, only now I had a name: I was Oliver. I felt like skipping. I hadn't even known I'd wanted a new name, but now here it was, and it was perfect, and it was mine. I was Oliver. I was Oliver! It felt ridiculous and brilliant and exciting and new and entirely familiar, as if I'd always been Oliver but somehow someone had got my name wrong at birth and I'd spent my life being called something else. And now I had the right name, my own name, my real name, the one that belonged to me.

The meeting at the Center was held in a large, high-ceilinged room with enormous windows, in which thirty or so men in various stages of transition sat in a circle on folding chairs. We went round the room introducing ourselves by first name and pronouns. When it was my turn, I said my name was Oliver and I still didn't know what my pronouns were. I spent the rest of the meeting sitting in self-conscious silence. The other men were sharing about finding the courage to become their most authentic selves, to live their truth and reclaim their power, but I felt like I'd already covered this ground with the Late Bloomers. The stuff I was interested in now was more abstract, such as whether we were on thin ice when we talked about reclaiming our power if the tool we were using was a syringe full of testosterone. If, as Jaime claimed, testosterone was the drug of the patriarchy, how could we reconcile ourselves with taking it? But most of these men were clearly already on testosterone, and I was fairly certain none of them would react well to having their right to power challenged by a newcomer. A couple of the men stopped to talk to me after the meeting, but I made my excuses, citing a train to catch, a long journey home. They were all so much younger than I was, and the problems they were facing—how to come out at work, how to find space in the lesbian bars—were different from mine.

As I walked back to the subway, I wondered how much of my experience I'd share with Jaime. I'd felt almost weightless all day—as if the disguise I'd been wearing all my life hadn't been mere lipstick and clothes but heavy steel armor that had been lifted off my shoulders—but I couldn't tell her how happy I felt without upsetting her, and the fact that she'd be upset by my happiness would immediately puncture it, leaving me unhappy again. If Jaime couldn't accept my masculinity, sooner or later I'd be forced to choose between the two, and I wasn't sure that was a choice I could make.

A couple of weeks later Jaime broke her silence, texting to suggest we meet at the cottage the following Friday. I wasn't sure what this new move might mean. When she arrived, she knocked instead of letting herself in with her key, an unusual and slightly foreboding formality. I opened the door, and she stepped inside.

"So," she said as I closed the door behind her. "Are you ready? Can we do this now?" I hesitated, uncertain what she was asking. She stepped forward, cupped my face between her hands and kissed me. She must have felt my legs go weak, because she stopped and looked at me.

"Are you scared?" she asked.

"I didn't think you wanted this," I admitted, trying to remember how to stand upright.

"Do you think I'm not attracted to you anymore?" she asked, taking off her coat.

"It's a legitimate fear."

"How about my fear that you might not be attracted to me?" She sat down on the sofa and started pulling off her boots. "If you're male, you might want to be the desirer, not the desired. You might find yourself desiring someone else more than me."

"Do you think it's innate? That the desirer is masculine and the person being desired is feminine? Or is that part of the social construct? I still want to be desired by you."

"Maybe your problem with being a man is tied to a fear that masculinity isn't desirable."

"Or maybe my problem with being a man is that I'm not a man."

Jaime sat back and looked at me. "Then what are you?"

"Can I be David Bowie?"

"If we could choose who we wanted to be, I'd have chosen to be a supermodel."

"I very much doubt that."

Jaime smiled. "How do you want me to see you?" she asked.

"More like a boy, maybe?" The only thing I was sure about was that I was meant to have pecs rather than breasts, a penis rather than a vagina. The basic definitions of "man" and "woman" seemed to be disappearing, like familiar words that start to mean nothing if you stare at them for too long. Jaime listened in silence while I tried to explain this, but when I told her I felt like I was trying on different parts of gender for size, she stopped me.

"I don't think you can select your gender like you're choosing clothes off a rack in a clothing store," she said.

"Why not?" I asked.

"Because you can't choose your identity. It's innate."

"I'm not saying it's a choice, I'm just trying to find out what belongs to me and what doesn't."

"And you feel like you know this now?"

"I'm getting closer."

I told her about my trip to the sex store and the package I'd come home with. Jaime stood up and held out her hand. "Come on," she said. "Show me."

Upstairs in the bedroom I removed my clothes shyly, as if I were taking them off in front of her for the first time. I sat on the bed, the box containing my dick on the bedspread in front of me. I'd been getting to know my new appendage in the privacy of my own bathroom, but bringing it out in front of Jaime felt terrifying. What if she didn't like it? What if she didn't want to spend the rest of her life with someone who had a prosthetic limb?

Jaime sat down on the edge of the bed. "Put it on," she said. I knelt up on the bed and strapped it around my pelvis, and then quickly sat back down, hugging my knees. "Show me." When I didn't move, she said it a little more firmly. "Come on, show me." I uncurled myself and lay back on the bed, covering my face with my arm, allowing her to see me for the first time. I felt stupidly virginal—exposed, vulnerable, and completely defenseless. I heard Jaime move over the bed towards me.

"Open your eyes," she said. She was lying beside me, propped up on one elbow. I looked down to see her stroking my cock with her hand. I watched her fingers travel slowly up the shaft, move gently over the head and back down again, her touch as light as a feather. I held my breath as my nerve endings sparked to life, the heat inside my body blossoming out into her hand as she cupped her fingers around me. I wasn't just seeing it; I could feel it. She was holding me, and I could *feel* it.

Freddie and I were in the car driving to the local comic store a few days later, listening to Panic! at the Disco. Freddie was an inquisitive and curious thirteen-year-old—he wanted to know everything about everything—but change made him jittery as hell, so he had to pace himself when it came to new information. I hadn't forced a conversation about my transition because I knew he'd be more comfortable figuring it out in his own time. He'd be ready to talk when he was ready to talk.

"Mom, I think I have a straight-boy crush on Brendon Urie," Freddie said, gazing out of the car window.

"That seems unsurprising," I said.

"Do you ever get straight-boy crushes on people? Like crushes that aren't sexual?"

"Sure, at the moment I've got one on the actor Andrew Scott."

"Do you want to date him?"

"I don't think so. I'm attracted by something he has. I can't quite pinpoint it; it's a sort of femininity, an ambiguity in his gender."

"Brendon Urie has that."

"Yes, he does." I hesitated, wondering where this conversation was leading. "I used to find it hard when I was a teenager. All the signals got mixed up. I never knew whether I was attracted to someone or whether I wanted to be them."

Freddie was silent as I pulled the car up outside the comic store. He opened the car door, but instead of getting out he sat for a moment, his body turned away from me. I unbuckled my seat belt, waiting. "Mom, do you have mental health issues?" he asked.

"No, I don't," I said cautiously. "Why?"

"I was watching this thing on YouTube about transgender stuff, and someone posted in the comments that all transgender people have mental health problems."

I swallowed hard. "We should talk about this."

"I don't want to talk about it," he said, his voice rising. "It's just stupid. You're my mom. You're a woman. You can't be a man."

"But if you're struggling with it . . ."

"Of course I'm fucking struggling with it!" He got out of the car and slammed the door. I watched him through the car window as he walked into the comic shop. Unlike the girls, Freddie was old enough to have found his voice. He was beginning to understand that I wasn't an omnipotent being, I was human and flawed, and this discovery was going to be complicated by my transition. Through the window of the comic shop, I could see Freddie's shadow moving around the store. He had every right to be angry; I was prioritizing my own needs over his. I couldn't have chosen a worse time to do this.

And yet I couldn't not do it. The thought of trying to put myself into reverse was untenable, as if any move back towards femininity might kill me. Henry once told me I shouldn't try to protect my children from pain; instead, I should support them through it, help them adjust. But what did it say about me as a mother that I could convince myself this wasn't going to damage them? Could I convince myself of anything if I wanted it to be true badly enough? What if this was, in fact, a zero-sum game, in which all my wins were my children's losses?

I got out of the car and went into the store. Freddie glanced at me as I came in, a frown flitting across his face. I paid for his comics, and he followed me back out to the car. We drove in silence until he was ready to speak again.

"I don't care about you being trans," he said eventually. "It's everyone else. Everyone online thinks you're a freak. I wrote something on Reddit about my parent being transgender and this guy wrote back telling me how sorry he was. He said I should tell the authorities. He said I shouldn't be looked after by someone who was mentally ill."

"Jesus."

"I don't care if people are assholes, but I can't stand them feeling sorry for me." I heard his voice break. "I don't want any of this, I don't. I just want you to be my mom."

I pulled the car over to the side of the road and turned to face him. "Freddie, I am always going to be your mom. Freddie, look at me. I'm always going to be here for you. Nothing about what you and I have is going to change. I will always be your mother."

He slumped forward and I hugged him as he buried his head in my shoulder. "I love you, honey. I'll always be here."

I kept repeating the words until he started to calm down, but I felt myself shiver, as if someone had walked over my grave. Who knew what the future held for us? I couldn't fathom the effect my transition would have on my kids, but I'd been a parent for long enough to know that every action has an unintended consequence, and however hard I might try to persuade myself that their lives would be enriched if we allowed ourselves to break free from gender norms, I couldn't guarantee it. My transition wasn't just going to affect my children; it was going to affect other people's opinions of us, which meant that from now on the slightest sign of dysfunction would automatically be blamed on me. If their grades slipped or they fell out with their friends, if they suffered from depression or eating disorders or—God forbid—addiction, it would all be because I was trans. And I'd never know for sure whether I was the scapegoat or the cause.

Eventually Freddie pushed himself upright and wiped his eyes on his sleeve. I put my hand on his arm as he sat back in his seat. "You okay?"

He shrugged a yes. I started the car, looking over at him once more to check that he was ready before I pulled out into the road. "We need to keep talking about this," I said. "It's a lot to absorb, and I don't want to leave you to do all the research online. There's a lot of stuff out there you shouldn't be reading."

"You're not gonna ban me from Reddit, are you?"

"Not if you promise to talk to me about what you read."

He looked out of the window. "Would it be okay if I tell my friends you're nonbinary?"

"Tell them whatever you like," I replied. "I don't care about the labels."

"Or the pronouns?"

"I really don't care about any of it; I just want you to be comfortable with who I am."

"Okay," he said. "I get it. I do want you to be happy, I just also want you to be my mom."

Chapter Twenty-Six

J aime and I decided we needed a break from Connecticut, so we headed to Brooklyn in the Mustang. It was early May, the weather was starting to get warmer, and I was beginning to realize that at some point I'd have to make a choice between psychological and physical discomfort if I wanted to carry on wearing a binder during the summer. Despite being told by the doctor that I should keep it on for only a few hours at a time, I was now wearing it all day every day, because it was worth any amount of discomfort to have a body that looked the way it was supposed to. But once heat and humidity were added to the equation, the discomfort was going to increase exponentially, and I wasn't looking forward to a summer of crushed ribs, bruised skin, and rivulets of sweat dripping down my back.

Jaime didn't comment on my newly flattened torso, deftly managing to avoid the subject of gender for the whole morning even though we spent it at the David Bowie exhibition at the Brooklyn Museum. Bowie's entire career seemed to have been one long experiment with identity. I paused in front of a music video in which a Berlin-era Bowie, dressed in sequined drag, ripped the wig from his head and smeared the makeup off his face: *Boys keep swinging*, he sang, *Boys always work it out*. It was hard not to believe I was being sent a direct message from the sky.

Leaving the museum, we headed round the corner to the Botanic Garden. The lawn was covered with couples on blankets and families having picnics, the cherry trees so heavy with blossom it looked like someone was getting married, their boughs weighed down under globules of rich pink icing. Jaime stretched out on a spot under a tree, leaning back on her elbows, her long legs in front of her. I sat down opposite her, cross-legged.

"So, talk to me," she said. "Tell me what you've learned since we last saw each other."

"That we're not sexually incompatible?" I suggested, trying to keep the tone light.

Jaime shook her head. "The fact that it worked like that once doesn't mean it's going to work like that every time."

"It doesn't need to work like that every time, we can switch it up."

"You say that now, but one day you might not want to."

"We don't know what I'm going to want, Jaime."

Jaime gave me a look and I bit my tongue. Instead, I changed the subject, and told her the story of how I found my name.

"What does it feel like?" she asked.

"Like I've spent my life groping around in the dark not knowing what I was looking for, and now that I know it's 'Oliver,' everything is falling into place so quickly I don't know how to slow it down anymore."

Jaime's expression was unreadable, but I knew something must be going on inside that head. "Does losing Nicky make you sad?" she asked.

"No. Your sadness makes me sad." I wasn't going to tell her that finding Oliver made me euphoric. I didn't want to rub it in.

"I feel sad all the time," Jaime said.

"Perhaps it's grief," I said. "Like mourning a death. A lot of parents feel it when their children transition."

"I'm not your parent."

"I know."

Jaime rolled onto her side and looked at me. "The sadness is always with me. I can't compartmentalize it like you can, I can't separate myself from it. It's like living with a constant feeling of loss. I almost wish we could speed the process up and get through to the other side, so we know what we're dealing with. And then I worry that there'll never be an end, that you'll never stop changing. Or worse, that you'll say you're done but you won't be there yet, and eventually you'll end up somewhere else. Sometimes I feel like it's never going to go away."

I said nothing. There was nothing I could say.

"Are you scared?" she asked.

Only about losing you, I thought. "I'm scared of how other people are going to see me. My image is going to become more important than I want it to be, because everything about the way I present myself to the world is now going to be a statement about who I am. That feels like a lot of pressure. Plus, I'm worried I'm going to be forced to become something I'm not because the rest of the world doesn't have the capacity to see me as I am—like, I won't get to choose which clothes I wear anymore, because if I wear anything too feminine, it'll reinforce people's belief that I'm a woman. And I hate the whole pronoun thing. If we didn't have gendered pronouns, it would be so much easier. I could just be Oliver and that would be that."

"We should have as many names for gender as the Eskimos have for ice."

"I know. And unless I take hormones, everyone will always see me as a masculine woman, which I'm not. I'm a feminine man. That's the missing piece, the bit I've been getting backwards. But try explaining that to people. It's going to be impossible."

Jaime was lying on her side, her head propped on her hand, making a pile of cherry blossom petals on the grass. I rested my elbows on my knees, picking the moon-shaped petals off a piece of clover while I told her about Chella, the trans man I'd been following on Instagram. Trying to keep it as simple as possible—to counteract the feeling that I was confessing to a crime—I admitted how much I envied his chest, how often I kept returning to his feed, how sooner or later I'd probably make the decision to have my breasts removed.

"And testosterone?" Jaime asked, her face impassive.

"I don't know," I replied.

Jaime wasn't looking at me; no part of her body was touching mine. I could have reached out and stroked her leg, flicked a bit of grass at her head, rolled down beside her for a kiss, but I didn't. I was afraid that any gesture would be seen as a trick, that deep down inside Jaime didn't trust me anymore.

"I'm afraid of losing my femininity," I said. "I've worn it my whole life, it's part of me, I don't want to give it up. I identify with women. My allegiance is to women."

"Yes, but you're *not* a woman."

I winced. Even though she was right, I understood the point she was trying to make. She'd built a fence around herself to keep out all the men—even the good ones—and now she was trying to push me out through the gate. It suddenly felt like such an arbitrary way to categorize people, such a nonsensical method of discrimination.

"Imagine if you'd figured all this out back in your twenties when you were still hanging out with the bikers," Jaime said. "If you'd been socialized as a man, it would've shaped you into a completely different person."

"Meaning?"

"Meaning, I think you're going to find your allegiance changes."

And there it was. It wouldn't matter what I did or said, because from now on Jaime would always believe that instead of fighting for the rights of women, I was fighting for my own right to be a man. Finding the lesbian feminists—the writers, the musicians, the artists—had felt like finding my people, but Jaime was now claiming these people for herself. And if what was hers could no longer be mine, then where did that leave me? I should have known this would happen. Leslie Feinberg had warned me. I should have fucking known.

We left the park as it closed and headed back to the car, walking side by side but slightly out of step, neither of us reaching out to take the other's hand. Dusk was falling. By the time we got home it would be dark.

"I'll drive," Jaime said as we reached the Mustang.

I threw her the keys and climbed in the passenger side. While she was adjusting the seat to accommodate her long legs, I reached across to turn on the headlights.

"Whoa," Jaime exclaimed, leaning back as if I were invading her space. "I think I can find the lights without your help!" I froze, startled by the harshness in her voice. She jammed the key into the ignition and revved the engine. "Things that were cute in you as a girl aren't going to be so cute if you're a boy," she said, half under her breath.

Rain was falling by the time we reached Connecticut. The streaks of water on the windshield lit up rhythmically with the orange reflections from the streetlights; puddles on the road, splashes from the tires, water streaming down the side windows. Jaime turned off the interstate at her exit and pulled up outside her house. I sat still, facing forward as she unbuckled her seat belt. "You're not coming back with me?" I asked.

"No," she replied. "It's too much."

I swallowed, willing myself not to cry.

Jaime turned and looked at me. There was accusation in her eyes. She paused, and then she said, "Have you ever considered that what you're doing to me is violently cruel?"

My muscles spasmed in shock. She reached towards me, but I flinched away. She hesitated for a moment, and then opened the car door and got out. I sat in the passenger seat, staring out through the rain, unable to move.

The following weekend was Mother's Day, and Abby, one of the Late Bloomers, was throwing a lunch party. She'd invited most of the women from the group, and her house was bursting at the rafters with children racing up and down the stairs from the attic to the basement while their mothers prepared the food in the kitchen. Lily and Rose asked where Jaime's daughters were, but I explained that Jaime had to work, and they accepted it with the confidence of children who hadn't yet learned that people could disappear and not come back. I watched my friends stirring pots and chopping vegetables and decanting sauces, wondering how I would have made it through the last seven years without them.

"Hey," Abby said, pushing a large vase of flowers across the kitchen island towards me. "I forgot to give you these. Jaime left them for you yesterday."

"For me? Oh my God, they're beautiful!" I buried my nose in the petals and breathed in the scent. "She's never given me flowers before."

"We figured you might find Mother's Day hard."

"You did? Why?"

"Because in the future you might not be a mother."

I pulled my face out of the flowers, blinking in surprise. Just because I was trans didn't mean I was any less of a mother, did it? I'd survived three pregnancies, nearly fifty hours of labor, a torn vagina and a near-fatal hemorrhage. I'd pushed four children out of my birth canal—two of them within three minutes of each other—and then spent the next thirteen years single-handedly tending to their physical, spiritual, educational, and emotional needs. Nobody was going to tell me I wasn't a mother.

Abby bent down to slip a tray of vegetables into the oven.

"How was she? Jaime, I mean," I asked, picking up one of the cloves of garlic I was meant to be peeling.

Abby straightened up and wiped her hands on her apron. "All right, I guess," she replied, not quite looking me in the eye.

"Only all right?"

"Well, what you're going through is hard, isn't it?"

Sure, it was hard, but Jaime had sent me a message with these flowers. I knew her well enough to look for small signs, not grand gestures, and this one was clearly meant as an olive branch.

"When are you going to start taking testosterone?" Abby asked. She picked up an avocado and started slicing it in half.

"I don't think I am," I said, picking the skin off the clove with my fingernail. "I'm pretty sure I can become who I want to be without it."

Abby looked doubtful. "Look, I know you must be afraid of the side effects—the aggression and everything—but you won't know how bad it is until you start taking it, will you?"

I put the garlic down. "What d'you mean, aggression?"

"You've seen that episode of *The L Word*, right?" Abby said, trying to wrestle the pit out of the avocado. "When the trans guy gets all violent and starts breaking things?"

I stared at her, momentarily lost for words. "Have you ever actually *met* a trans man?" I asked.

"No, but everyone knows that testosterone increases aggression," she said, scooping the avocado into a bowl.

"Oh my God. Okay, firstly, it doesn't; that's steroids, not testosterone. And secondly, whether I take hormones—or have surgery—is an entirely personal choice, and only I get to make it."

Abby looked up. "Are you going to have surgery?"

"Yes," I said. "I probably am."

"But isn't surgery usually the second stage? After hormones?"

"Yes, it is, but I'm doing it first, because *that's what I want to do*."

The next day Jaime sent me a text suggesting we meet at the park that evening. I booked a babysitter and arrived early, laid out a picnic blanket and opened a basket, which I'd packed with cans of seltzer, a bunch of grapes, and a box of chocolate Florentines. This was the park where she'd first told me she wanted to marry me, so it seemed apt to meet here now that we'd hit rock bottom; it would remind us what we were trying to get back to. I lay on my back eating one of the Florentines while I waited for Jaime to arrive. I understood that our relationship was undergoing a process of change, and I also understood that this particular change was more dramatic than most; I wasn't a fool. But I also knew we'd find a way through it. This was what you did when the person you loved was in the pit of despair. You sat with them in the shit, keeping them company, until the two of you could figure a way to climb up out of it together.

My skin prickled with a sixth sense, and I sat up to see Jaime walking across the park towards me. "Hey," I said, reaching into the picnic basket for a can of seltzer. Jaime sat down on the other side of the blanket. When she didn't reply I looked up. "What is it?" I asked, seeing the expression on her face. "What's happened?"

Her long legs were stretched out in front of her, and she was leaning back on her elbows, staring out into the middle distance. She looked burned out, dog tired.

"I'm done," she said, her voice flat.

"You're done what?" I asked.

She looked at me. "I can't do this anymore."

"This what?"

"This relationship."

I blinked at her. What was she talking about?

"I feel like I've already lost you," she said. "I can't just sit by and watch you disappear."

My mouth opened and closed as I realized what she was saying. "But I'm not *going* anywhere, Jaime! I'm here! I'm right *here*!"

"Yes, but you're not *here* anymore," she said, putting her hand on her chest. The gesture was almost beseeching. "The place where you lived inside me—where I could always find you—it's gone."

I stared at her, speechless. This wasn't happening. It couldn't be happening yet. It wasn't time.

"I don't think you understand what I mean when I tell you I wake up crying every morning," she said. "I can't do it anymore."

"You're pulling the plug?"

"Yes."

There were no words. Perhaps this was what people meant when they talked about being stunned into silence. Jaime's gaze returned to that spot in the middle distance, as if she were trying to dissociate from what was happening. I tried to find the words to reason with her, to convince her not to give up on us yet, but I found nothing. If Jaime said she was done, she was done.

I stood up, emptied my can of seltzer onto the grass and put it back into the picnic basket. Following my lead, Jaime stood up so I could gather up the blanket. I folded it tightly and put it in the basket with the food. Then I picked up the basket and started walking towards the parking lot. Jaime followed, a short distance behind me. I threw the picnic basket into the back of the Mustang, turned and leaned against the car door. Jaime stood a few feet away from me, as if waiting for permission to leave.

"I don't understand," I said.

"Neither do I," she replied.

Our eyes fixed on each other across the empty space between us.

"That doesn't help me," I said.

She held my eyes. "It doesn't help me either."

Stone coldness bloomed inside me like ink spreading through water.

"So this is it?"

Jaime said nothing.

I got into the Mustang, slammed the door, and drove away.

Chapter Twenty-Seven

One Saturday when I was in my early twenties I'd been standing on the perimeter of a muddy field at an air show with my six-foot-four biker buddy, watching a Harrier jump jet preparing to take off. The pitch of the engines climbed to a high whine until with a shudder the beast started to rise vertically from the ground, hovering above us for a moment before roaring off into the distance. We watched it circle round and head back towards the crowd, moving in low to the ground until it silently screamed past us at a distance that felt like mere feet. There was a brief, noiseless pause before the sound hit us with such force that it knocked our bodies backwards, propelling the air out of our chests as if we'd been punched by an invisible fist. Regaining his balance, my biker friend put his hands on his knees and leaned forward, laughing so hard I thought he was crying.

That's how breaking up with Jaime felt. For two days I soared above the earth, giddy with relief that I'd finally been released from the effort of trying to be something I wasn't. It was only on the third day, when I was sitting at my desk scrolling through my morning emails, that it occurred to me—almost in passing—that I wouldn't see Jaime's name in my inbox anymore.

I folded over as if I'd been slugged in the stomach. I started to cry, and once I started, I couldn't stop. I cried all the tears I'd been bottling up inside for the last few months, cried until my body was shuddering, cried until my face was swollen and bloated, my nose so clogged with mucus and my throat so ragged and raw I could hardly breathe. Jaime was gone.

Having never been in love like this before, I'd had no idea that loss wasn't just a missing thing, it was a physical assault that could shatter your body from the inside. Nobody had told me that grief would feel like being trampled by a horse daily, or that for months—years—afterwards a random kick would suddenly appear out of the blue, an unexpected hoof to the chest knocking the wind out of my lungs. I sleepwalked my way through the few weeks after Jaime left, trying to help my children through their own grief at her sudden and unexpected departure, but I was starting to break under the pressure of trying to hold it together on my own. If I didn't get help soon, I'd be risking my sobriety. My twelve-step group was the only thing standing between me and a drink, but my silence about my transition was standing between me and my queer Connecticut twelve-step group.

I lingered in the doorway at the beginning of the next meeting. Walking into this room each week felt like walking into a room full of puppies who bounced with joy every time I arrived, as if I weren't full of despicable character defects to which I confessed every time I saw them, as if I were truly lovable, through and through. I'd never worried before that

I could do anything to interrupt this all-forgiving flow of love—after all, the litany of crimes committed by my fellow members far exceeded anything I could realistically match—but what if my being trans was just too much? I knew I'd been able to get away with certain things as a woman by being charming; what I didn't know was how much of that charm depended on my being female. Jaime had said I couldn't hold her accountable if I turned into something she couldn't love; would this be true of everyone now? Would I have to forgive everyone their rejection, even the people I needed the most? I knew my identity was confusing, and confusion could turn into avoidance, and if my gay friends started avoiding me, I had no idea how I'd survive.

Lori, the tough old butch with the dry sense of humor, was hobbling across the room on her cane, trying to make it to her chair before her hip gave out. Andrew and Ryan, the beautiful twinks with the perfectly sculpted muscles, were looking at pictures of something on Andrew's phone. Dave the old-timer was sitting quietly in the corner as always, while Jessie and Krysten, who'd met in rehab, were squished up next to each other holding hands. Mark, the diabetic nurse with the chronic gout, was sitting with his leg stretched out, his foot encased in an orthopedic shoe, next to Chris, the hairdresser with the bright blue eyes and cute lips. Chad, the laborer with the enormous red beard who looked like he could break a tree in half with his bare hands, was talking to Jim, the introspective intellectual who sold carpets, while Jim's husband, Will, the cabaret singer, made the coffee. Anthony, the French interior designer, was motioning something across the room to Tom, the extrovert marketing executive.

The only trans person currently attending the meeting was Julie, an old hippie who lived with her aging mother and who turned up each week in a different outfit from Goodwill as if she were channeling Stevie Nicks. I was drawn to Julie's gentleness, but if someone referred to the group as a gay meeting, she'd get spiky. "Please don't exclude the *T* from the rainbow," she'd say, and I'd often wondered how excluded she must have felt for this to be such a prickly issue.

I walked into the room, stopping to plant a kiss on top of Tom's bald head as I passed. "Nicky, my darling. Come sit with me. Tell me what's been going on." Each person in the room broke conversation to say hello or wave or blow me a kiss as I took my seat, but the relief I usually felt when sinking into my chair was tainted with anxiety. Christian, young and thin with the upright posture of a dancer, opened the meeting and after a short qualification introduced the discussion topic. "It's easy to forget the importance of truthfulness in sobriety," he reminded us, "so honesty is our theme for this evening."

My heart started racing. This must surely be a sign, and yet as Tom raised his hand, I had no idea how I'd find the courage to speak. The clock started ticking away as the other members of the group shared their thoughts, and yet I still couldn't bring myself to say anything. I was beginning to sweat. The hour was almost up. My heart was beating so hard I could hardly hear the speakers anymore. There were only five minutes left before the end of the meeting. I felt like my chest was going to rise up into my head and explode out through my ears.

"Nicky?" Christian was looking at me expectantly.

"Hi, I'm Nicky and I'm an alcoholic," I managed to say. The room swam in front of my eyes, my friends blurring together into one big circle of faces. "I have a secret I've been keeping, and I need to share it with you because if I can't tell you this I can't be honest about what's going on in my life and if I'm not being honest I'm going to relapse." The words came out in a rush, as if the faster I could say them, the sooner I could be done. "You know Jaime and I have been having some problems and I haven't been able to tell you why and each week I've been promising myself I'll tell you and each week I chicken out and now I just have to do it. Jaime left me. She left me because I started transitioning. I'm transgender. My name isn't Nicky anymore, it's Oliver. I'd like to be able to introduce myself as Oliver going forward. That's it. That's all I've got."

There was a brief silence and then everyone mumbled, "Thanks, Oliver." Krysten put up her hand. "Hi, I'm Krysten and I'm an alcoholic," she said, giving me a look as if to say, *It's okay, I'll take it from here.* Out of the corner of my eye I saw Tom mouth to Anthony, *Did you know?* and Anthony shrug back, *I had no idea.* I wanted to bolt from my seat. It was too much. I'd shared too much. This whole thing was excruciating. I'd blown it. Nothing would ever be the same again. Krysten finished her share and Christian called the end of the meeting and I stood sandwiched between Tom and Dave as we said the serenity prayer. When the circle broke up, I turned for the door, but Tom wouldn't let go of my hand. He pulled me round and enveloped me in a giant hug. I could hear the laughter emanating from his chest, and as I surfaced out of his arms, I found myself surrounded, the group closing in around me like a giant basket full of puppies wagging their tails, everyone talking at once. *Oliver! Oliver! Oliver!*

Half an hour later I picked up my bag to leave while Tom turned out the lights.

"You can stop shaking now," Dave said, walking beside me down the hall.

"I was so frightened," I admitted.

Dave smiled. "Hadn't it occurred to you that we might enjoy being part of your journey?"

Outside in the parking lot, I was about to get into my car when Jim, the intellectual carpet salesman, appeared by my side. "Sometimes God will pluck out of your path someone who's standing in your way," he said, giving me a shy smile. I looked at him curiously. "You get to have a different life now. You're just too close-up at the moment to see it." He paused for a moment, then he kissed me on the forehead and turned away.

I stood for a few minutes watching the cars pull out. I'd heard people talk about being grateful alcoholics, but this was the first time I fully understood what they meant. This is what it felt like to be loved by a family that never said no. That never said, *You're too much.* That never said, *Go away and deal with this on your own.* A family whose support was unconditional, whose reassurance was constant. *We love you, we've got you, keep coming back.*

It was early summer, we'd found a buyer for the house, and I had to find somewhere new for us to live before school started in September. The housing crash of 2008 had left us with little equity in the property, and a series of bad investments made by Charles left us with little savings, so once the proceeds of the sale had been divided between us, I'd be left with a small amount in a share account, a few years of alimony, and enough capital to buy a home for myself and the kids. I knew this meant I'd have to start counting pennies again, but I didn't mind. I left the marriage with roughly the same amount of money as I'd come in with, which almost came as a relief; I didn't belong with people who prioritized wealth, and I didn't want to have profited financially from the marriage. Charles would continue to support the children financially while I figured out how to make some money, for which I was grateful, and if anything was going to force me to start submitting some of those stories I'd been writing, the need to earn a living would.

I started to try out my new identity in public, although it was proving a little harder than expected. At the local coffee shop the barista called out "Oliver?" and then said, "Here you go, ma'am," as he passed me my coffee. I tried to use the men's bathroom, but waiting for a stall took longer than waiting for a urinal, so I had to stand in mortified shame as every man who entered the bathroom did a double take on seeing me, checked the door to make sure he was in the right place, and then looked uncomfortable peeing in my presence. I was beginning to understand that the bathroom issue wasn't just about safety; it was about trying to maintain some basic level of dignity and self-respect.

The isolation was the hardest, though. I knew of other people from my childhood who'd gone through life-changing events as adults—who'd got divorced or lost jobs or moved countries or suffered bereavements—and even a handful who'd come out as gay. But when I looked back at all the thousands of people I'd met during the first half of my life, before I moved to America and found my queer community, not one of them had transitioned. Not a single one. It was a shockingly lonely thought, and it made me feel even more disconnected from the world than I already was.

But I could either sit around feeling sorry for myself or I could get up and get on with it. Reach out to the handful of trans people I'd met through my recovery programs, find more gender-nonconforming friends, read more books, join more support groups, follow more organizations. And thanks to the savings I'd managed to set aside after my divorce, I could afford to start the process of medical transition. I opened up Chella's Instagram page and looked for the name of the surgeon who'd given him his new chest.

Later that month Elisabeth flew back to New York for a short trip, so we arranged to meet for dinner with Maeve at a macrobiotic restaurant in the West Village. Walking down Prince Street, I allowed myself to believe that the people around me could see I was a boy, my jeans loose around my groin to accommodate my new cock, my breasts flattened into provisional pecs by my binder, my hair short and spiked on top. Hands in pockets, I sauntered through the Village, experiencing the same sense of exhilaration I used to get while racing my motorbike. Maybe this was why I'd felt so alive on my bike; it was the only time my body worked with me rather than against me, the only time I got joy out of having a body at all. Now I could achieve the same feeling just walking down the street.

I walked into the restaurant, grinning at Elisabeth and Maeve, who were already sitting at the table. They got up when they saw me. "Oh my God, Oliver! Look at you!" Elisabeth cried, holding out her hands. "You look completely different!"

"Have you been working out?" Maeve asked. "What is it? What's changed?"

"I don't know." I shrugged. "Maybe my body just got the memo."

"You look incredible," Elisabeth said.

"I look like a gay man," I replied.

"Jesus, they're going to eat you up with a spoon. You've got the body of a seventeen-year-old boy with the maturity of an adult woman."

Elisabeth sighed. "All the men our age are balding and paunchy."

"And hairy," Maeve added.

"You'll be the only man left without a beard."

"Every straight woman on earth wants to have the kind of sex lesbians have, and now they can. All of them. With you."

"They're going to devour you."

"Because it won't be all about the dick."

"You'll *have* a dick, but it won't be all *about* the dick."

"If they don't feel like dick that night, you can just leave it in the box."

"And they won't even have to give you a blow job!" Elisabeth concluded.

I waited for Maeve and Elisabeth to stop laughing. "Seriously, though, can you see it?" I asked, tipping my pelvis forward and peering down at my groin.

"See what?"

I straightened up. "Well, that was a waste of money. I'm packing. I think I got a size too small." I put my hand down my pants and shuffled it around to see if I could position it better. "It's a starter penis."

"There's a starter penis?" Elisabeth asked in amazement.

"Yeah, it's the one for teenagers, and I figured . . . since I'm a boy . . . But there's no point if you can't see it. I mean, it's not for me—I know I have a penis. I want it to be visible to everyone else."

"You need to get the next size up," Maeve said.

"I might be better off with a pair of socks. Silicone gets kinda sweaty down there."

The waitress arrived and I sat down. Maeve ordered our food for us—being the only one who understood the menu—while I tried to explain how euphoric I felt about finally being free to wear my identity in public. "Remember all that makeup I used to slather on my face? I think I spent my whole life worried that someone would notice I was a man if I didn't cover it up well enough. Isn't that weird?"

"It's weird that it's weird, but yes, it's weird," Elisabeth agreed. "It's so obvious now that you're male, and yet I totally believed you were female before."

"I know, right? How could I have fooled everyone for so long?"

"I have no idea," Maeve said. "But it would explain why you never looked right in lipstick."

"How are the kids?" Elisabeth asked.

"They're doing fine, taking it all in stride," I said, although I wasn't sure how true this was. I told the kids that no question was off-limits, no subject out of bounds, but I suspected there might be a blind spot we were all quietly stepping around, something so sensitive nobody dared say it out loud. However much I reassured my children that my relationship with them wouldn't change, none of us knew whether this was true. The elephant in the room was that they weren't going to have a female parent anymore. How could they tell me to my face that they didn't want to lose their mother, when they'd already seen how much Jaime's rejection had hurt me? I didn't want to stop being their mother either, I just wanted to be a mother who was a man, but I knew from my experience with Jaime that I'd underestimated the extent to which my outside affected how other people treated me. And not only that, but how they would allow me to treat them. Would my daughters let me brush their hair and paint their nails now that I was a man? Would it change the way we hugged each other, or how often they'd come to me for cuddles, or the way we curled up on the sofa together while watching TV? The thought of losing that kind of physical intimacy with my kids was almost more than I could bear.

The waitress arrived with our food, and we stopped to rearrange the table to make room for everything. "Another drink, ma'am?" she asked me before she left.

I shook my head, feeling something in my throat knot up. Maeve noticed. "Does it bother you?"

"Yes, it does," I said, relieved to have somewhere to deflect the pain. "But I do get it. She can't ask every person what their gender is. Seriously, look at all the people in here. Who knows how they all identify? And my body's still female, so of course she's going to assume I'm a woman." I looked around at the other people in the restaurant, wondering if it mattered to them whether other people identified their gender correctly. I wished it didn't matter so much to me, but after a lifetime of feeling invisible, I was desperate to be seen.

Chapter Twenty-Eight

As July edged closer to August, the need to find somewhere for us to live became more pressing. Charles and his fiancée lived in the wealthy part of town, near the beach, but I was looking for something more affordable, in the area where the houses were a little closer together and the population a little more diverse. Eventually I came across a fixer-upper with a small backyard that looked promising. It was unprepossessing from the outside—dirty shingles stained with lichen, a roof covered in moss, a front drive of broken asphalt barely big enough for one car, an overgrown backyard surrounded by a rusty chain-link fence, and a garage with doors that didn't open—but although it hadn't been updated in over fifty years and the heating system was rattling its death sigh, I loved it the minute I walked through the front door. If we did up the attic for Freddie, the kids would each have their own room, and although the kitchen and bathrooms would need replacing, I could just about make it work with my budget. Turning circles in the empty hallway, I could already picture the finished interior in my head. I'd paint it in rich, dark colors and fill it with all my books and my pictures and the ratty old antiques I'd inherited from my grandmother.

If I was going to defy convention with my body, I might as well do the same with my house. It would be a slice of New York in the suburbs, a sanctuary with no gender-policing, no limits on the imagination, and absolutely no discrimination.

My parents were arriving in mid-August to help us move, which gave me the next deadline I needed. If I really wanted to move forward with my life, then it was time to cut ties with the old one completely—not with the people themselves, but with the ties that bound me to their conventions—and that meant explaining to both Charles and my parents that I was no longer prepared to go on masquerading as the woman they believed me to be.

I decided it might be sensible to start with Charles, use him as a jumping-off point, so to speak. Also, I wondered whether it might help us with a bit of a roadblock we'd run into. We'd been having some problems coming to an agreement over the parenting schedule now that we were going to be living in two separate houses. Charles insisted that the children should live full-time with me, and he'd drop in to see them as his schedule allowed. I'd been hoping he might step up a bit more on the parenting side, particularly now that I needed to start earning some money, but Charles refused to budge from his position that parenting was a woman's job. The current system worked for him, and he was determined to keep it in place. But if Charles and I were both men, how could he refuse an equal division of labor?

The next time he dropped by to check on the progress of the house, I made him a cup of tea, sat him down at the kitchen table, and told him I was about to start transitioning.

"Why d'you have to be Oliver?" was his first question. "Why couldn't you just shorten your existing name to Nick?"

"Because that's not my name," I said. I didn't bother to explain that "Nick" was too close to "Nicky," that I needed to create as much distance between myself and my old name as I could so people would understand I wasn't that person anymore. I had a pretty close read on my audience.

"But this means I'll have to tell Sandra," Charles complained.

"Given that she's going to be the kids' stepmother, I think that might be a good idea."

"But it's embarrassing, Nicky."

I didn't want to point out that saving my ex-husband from embarrassment hadn't exactly been at the forefront of my mind when I'd decided to transition, because I could understand why he might not want the news widely broadcast. After all, this meant he hadn't just married a lesbian; he'd married a man. But I was fairly certain his reluctance to acknowledge my identity came from something deeper than mere insecurity over his sexual orientation.

"Well, if it's really what you need to do, then fine," he said with a shrug. He stood up, shooting me a look of magnanimous sympathy. I knew that expression, I'd seen it a few months previously when I asked him if he minded me writing about our family or, more specifically, about him in my writing class. He said he didn't mind in the slightest, since he was confident I'd never get published. I could playact at being a writer—or a man—if I wanted to, but it was all just make-believe. It wouldn't change the reality of my unpublished status or my female body.

Charles reaffirmed this position at every opportunity, reacting to the threat of my proposed change in gender by acting as if it weren't happening. Slow victory by erasure, with the deliberate misuse of pronouns and repetition of my deadname as his weapons of choice. The whole thing fit so neatly into his narrative of the crazy ex-wife, the woman so deranged she now thought she was a man. At first I corrected him whenever he misgendered me, but when I realized it was intentional, not accidental, I gave up trying. He could never allow himself to believe I was a man, because that would mean having to accept that I was not only sane, but also someone he would have to recognize as his equal, which was untenable. He needed me to counterbalance his identity: for him to feel masculine I needed to be feminine, for him to feel successful I needed to be ineffectual, for him to feel powerful I needed to be dependent. And if I were to become the children's father as well as their mother, what did that make him? The bank account? The question of whether he'd been pushed out of the family or whether he'd removed himself from it was a deeply subjective one, but whichever way you looked at it, he was never going to call me by my name.

I also knew that this was only the beginning, that by transitioning I'd be exposing myself to a lifetime of erasure, and not only from Charles. And yet, I was still certain the gains would outweigh the losses. Now that Charles had safely retreated to his position as purveyor of pizzas and pocket money, I reminded myself that long before I married him I'd known I was better suited to being a solo parent than a married one. He had given me my children, and then given me the means to support them. I had no reason to bear any resentment against him.

Next, I needed to figure out how to explain it to my parents in a way that wouldn't damage the new relationship that had been strengthening between us over the last few years. By some miracle, my parents had managed to successfully straddle two worlds without losing their footing in either: one in England, where they still held tight to their old customs and values, and one in America, where they bore unflinching witness to their daughter creating an entirely new life for herself. I had no idea how I was going explain to them that this *her* was now a *him*—a son, not a daughter.

My parents arrived to find our old house in chaos, half-packed cardboard boxes everywhere, furniture in disarray, an overflowing dumpster in the front drive. By late afternoon they were exhausted and decided they'd earned themselves a glass of wine, so they sat down at the kitchen table and asked when they were going to see Jaime.

My heart sank. I pulled up a chair at the table, resigning myself to the fact that everything about this conversation was going to be difficult. My father, in a short-sleeved button-down shirt, looked as fit as he had a decade earlier, no trace of the cancer that briefly destabilized him; my mother's hair was a little more silver at the temples, her eyes a trifle more creased, but otherwise she looked pretty much the same at seventy as she had at sixty. How had I changed so much over the last ten years, while they had changed so little?

"So," I said. "Jaime left me."

I tried to explain everything using language they'd understand, talking in binary terms and trying to keep it as simple as possible, aware that any inner confusion would sound dangerously like doubt to anyone who believed in absolutes. This wasn't the time to try to explain that my gender was constantly evolving, that the type of trans I'd been as a kid wasn't the same type of trans I was today, and the type of trans I was today probably wouldn't be the same type of trans I'd be tomorrow. I stuck to the basics, watching my parents' faces closely as I talked, wondering if they understood what I was saying and praying they'd find it in their hearts to believe me.

My mother spoke first. "I think I get what you're trying to tell us. I'm just not sure how we're going to explain it to our friends." I was wise enough by now to know that when my mother spoke of "her friends," she meant herself but was too embarrassed to say so. "I'm worried they'll think it's just another phase," she continued. "One minute you're riding motorbikes and the next you're a housewife and then you're a lesbian and now this. 'Where does it all end?' they might ask."

This seemed like the hardest question to answer, partly because I wasn't sure it was going to end anywhere. I was tired of the constant expectation that I stop changing. What if I didn't want to?

"I know it looks like I never settle," I said, "but you're just going to have to trust me when I say this is something I need to do. I need you to support me, even if you don't understand."

"Does this mean you're going to have a sex change?" she asked.

"The term 'sex change' isn't really used anymore."

"That's what they call it in the *Telegraph*."

"The *Telegraph* is a deeply transphobic newspaper," I replied, bristling. "Please don't believe everything you read in it."

"Darling, I'm sorry, I didn't mean to offend you . . ."

"No, no, it's okay." I didn't want to start by getting defensive. I began to explain the various processes of transition—legal, emotional, surgical, and hormonal—while my parents listened quietly. Far from recoiling in horror, they appeared to be rising to the occasion. My father looked a little bemused but perfectly relaxed, and instead of shutting down, my mother was interjecting with practical questions that betrayed none of the fearful reservation I'd expected.

"What happens if you get arrested?" she asked. "Will you have to go to a men's jail?"

"I have no idea. I hadn't even thought about it."

"Don't worry, I'm very good at prison visiting."

"I'm not planning on getting arrested, Mum."

"And what about women-only spa days?"

"Wait, one day I'm in jail and the next I'm at a spa?"

"I'm just trying to work out how this is going to affect your life."

"I'm raising four kids by myself. When on earth would I have time to go to a spa?"

We talked our way around the subject for a while longer before my mother could bring herself to return to her original question, the one I still hadn't directly answered. "So will you have a . . . What's it called?" she asked again. When I told her that I'd sent in my application for top surgery, she sucked in her breath sharply. "Already?"

"Technically speaking I've been waiting all my life, so why wait any longer?"

"I just don't want you to . . . I'm just worried that once you start, you may not be able to stop," she replied carefully. "Isn't it a little like the women who get Botox? First, they're only worried about a few wrinkles, but next it's fillers and then it's a face lift and then suddenly they're the Bride of Wildenstein."

"Someone who gets a face lift because they want to look young is trying to turn themselves into something they're not," I explained, trying to stay calm. "I'm trying to turn myself into something I am. It isn't vanity, it's necessity. I may never find total harmony between my body and my brain, but at least I can try."

"I just want you to be happy," my mother sighed.

"I know you do, Mum," I said, although I struggled not to read her words as an accusation: that it was my job to be happy, that by not being happy I'd failed her. I wanted to be able to tell my parents I had no idea what my future now held, to ask for their support even if I couldn't guarantee happiness, to ask them to love me regardless. But I didn't know how.

The following week we finally took possession of our new home. The move felt symbolic, as if I were leaving my identity as a heterosexual woman buried in the dumpster in the driveway of our old house, along with all the unwanted garbage from my previous life. Walking through my new front door, I felt giddy with freedom; this would be the house in which I could allow my queerness to overflow. I would line the bookshelves with my queer books, cover the walls with my queer art, fill the kitchen with my queer friends. I'd write more queer stories sitting at the queer desk in my queer office, and once my name-change application had been approved, I'd see my own queer name on the bills in my queer mailbox.

The movers hauled in the furniture while the kids ran in and out of the house in the sweltering late-summer heat, taking breaks from unpacking their treasured possessions to scour the neighborhood for other kids their age. My father busied himself filling the kitchen cupboards while my mother started unpacking my books so I could stack them onto the bookshelves, a job that took twice as long as it should have because I kept stopping to read bits while I was unpacking. I picked up *Gender Outlaw* by Kate Bornstein, which fell open at a paragraph I'd circled in red ink: *The choice between two of* anything *is not a choice at all but rather the opportunity to subscribe to the value system that holds the two presented choices as mutually exclusive alternatives. Once we choose one or the other, we've given up our imagination in favor of buying into the system that perpetuates that binary.*

"Look at this," I exclaimed, showing it to my mother. "And look, here . . ." I flicked through the pages. "*If I attempt to decide my own gender, I am apparently transgressing.*"

My mother was holding a copy of Judith Butler's *Gender Trouble*, looking mildly terrified. "I don't know how I'm going to explain any of this to my friends," she said again. "Everyone's going to ask me questions I won't know how to answer."

"Okay, well, perhaps let's not start with Judith Butler," I said, taking the book out of her hands. "Would it help if I wrote down a list of frequently asked questions for you?"

My mother looked at me helplessly.

"Okay, let's do this." I opened my laptop. "I'll write something you can send out in an email. Hit them all in one go, get it over and done with. How's that sound?"

We came up with a brief paragraph explaining my transition, along with a list of answers to any questions they might have, which my mother duly sent to all her friends. The responses trickled in one by one over the next few days while we finished the unpacking. I could tell when my mother had received another email, because I'd come across her sitting on a box, reading something on her phone, sometimes frowning, sometimes sighing.

On the final night of their stay, my parents and I sat down for a late supper in the now unpacked kitchen. The children were asleep in their new bedrooms, so while my father nursed a glass of after-dinner port, my mother showed me the replies she'd received from their friends. I skimmed through the emails, most of which were from people I hardly knew. The messages largely centered on my parents' bravery, peppered with sentences that betrayed the senders' real feelings through the polite veneer: *I can't possibly comment . . . The email you sent came as quite a shock . . . I don't suppose any of it is easy for anyone . . . I do find the current gender issues very disturbing . . . It must be terribly hard for the children . . . Frankly I'm mystified by it all . . .* I searched for responses from my parents' closest friends—the tight-knit group who'd been my extended family when I was growing up—but there was nothing.

"I guess transitioning was just a step too far," I said, trying not to let my parents see how much the rejection stung.

"Some people are going to find this difficult," my father said gently. "Particularly the ones who know you best."

"*They're* going to find it difficult?" I said, trying to keep the resentment out of my voice. "They should try going through it!"

"But look at this one here," my mother said, scrolling through the emails. "This one's quite positive, isn't it?"

It was the only one written by a close friend. She congratulated my parents on their bravery, continued by asking whether my children were in therapy and getting adequate care, and ended with her concerns for Charles.

"Seriously?" I said, looking up at my parents. "Your friends are worried about Charles?"

"Well, no, I think they're mostly worried about us," my father pointed out.

"Why is the mark of everything I do still measured against how hard it is for Charles?" I asked, suddenly enraged. "Charles is fine, he's moved on to a whole new life, he *can* move on! Don't you think your friends might stop to consider where this leaves *me*? Being a divorced father is a piece of cake compared to this! Being *gay* is a piece of cake compared to this! There's a solution to being gay: you find yourself a partner and bingo, you've got gay marriage, rainbow confetti, women with beautiful hair kissing on Instagram! But what's the solution to being trans? There isn't one! What are trans people? Nobody really knows! Who are they supposed to date? Nobody knows that either! We just get shut out of everything—oh, I can't date you because you're not a girl, and I can't date you because you're not a boy, and you can't come in here because you're the wrong gender, you're not welcome anymore, you're not in our gang, go away, find somewhere else, you don't belong, don't use the bathroom, keep away from the children, you're not even real, you motherfucking *freak*! And I have to spend the rest of my life being half of nothing because there's no perfect medical solution and do you want to know why I'm not taking testosterone? D'you want to know *why*? Because testosterone can't give me the one thing I want, which is a *working fucking penis!*"

I stopped abruptly. My parents sat frozen in their chairs as the word "penis" echoed around the room. I turned to my father in horror. He looked at me calmly over the top of his half-moon glasses. "If it's any consolation," he said, "my penis doesn't work anymore either."

Chapter Twenty-Nine

My parents returned to England with the severed ties that bound me to my old life packed away in their luggage, but their love for me still, thankfully, intact. "Oliver," my mother kept saying as we drove to the airport. "Son," my father repeated, as if they were determined to prove that they could see me, even if their friends refused to. I found it harder than usual to say goodbye to them, and wished they'd been able to stay longer. For the next month I barely spoke to another adult, my energy focused on getting the house into a workable condition and the children settled into their new schools. I wanted them to concentrate on the sorts of things kids should be concentrating on—making new friends, choosing new activities, finding new sports teams, decorating new bedrooms—so I tried to sideline my transition as much as possible. We agreed that I'd introduce myself to the neighbors as Oliver, but beyond that I let each child make their own decision about how to approach the subject with their new friends. I didn't want them to feel any pressure, or to have to worry about my needs during this critical moment of change in their lives.

I started to get to know the other families in the neighborhood. My immediate neighbor, Sydney, was going to be a friend; we hit it off the moment we met. Sydney was light-skinned and straightened her hair, so people often assumed she was white, despite her Black husband and two Black daughters. As she described her experiences living as a biracial woman in a Black-and-white world, I realized that being read incorrectly was something some people had been dealing with for their entire lives. Sydney and her husband's easy acceptance of my gender felt like a breath of fresh air; a few weeks after we moved in, her five-year-old daughter, Jojo, squeezed through the gap in the fence and ran across our backyard to the trampoline. "My mom says your mom's a man," Jojo said, reaching out her hands for Rose to pull her up. "Yes, he is," Lily replied as they hauled her on board. "Oh, okay," Jojo said as she started to bounce, and from then on, to Jojo I was simply Oliver.

But Sydney understood that however much we tried to normalize our families, our children still had to navigate spaces that other kids didn't. Jojo had grown up watching her parents code-switch between their Black and white friends, and now my children had to learn this skill too, code-switching between the queer and straight adults in their lives. I noticed them looking for the signs and signals of whom they could trust, who would get it and who wouldn't, how much information to provide, and when to avoid explanation altogether.

Each child chose a different approach. Freddie's strength lay in his verbal skills, his ability to collate vast amounts of information and weave it into an argument so complex that anyone trying to counter his position would be left tongue-tied. He didn't lead with the fact that he had a trans parent, but I knew it reassured him to have these verbal weapons in his arsenal. Alfie seemed to be taking it all in stride, which epitomized his pragmatic nature. Rose was less interested in my being trans and more interested in persuading me to come to the school with my sleeves rolled up so her friends could see my tattoos, a small act of rebellion-by-proxy against the bland conformity of suburban style. Lily was still holding back, waiting to see the outcome of everyone else's approaches before she committed to her own.

I knew Lily was afraid of being singled out as the kid with the weird family, and I minded that this was a problem they all now had to contend with. I was supposed to disappear into the background, to be the invisible support system, and I couldn't do that if every time I left the house my children had to explain who and what I was. One evening I came into her bedroom to find her curled up in bed, weeping quietly. "Hey," I said, sitting down on the bed. "What's up, sweetie? What is it?"

Lily scooched up until she was sitting with her back against the headboard. She rubbed her eyes with the heels of her hands. "I don't want to tell you. You'll be upset."

"No, honey, I won't. You can tell me anything."

"But you'll try to fix it, and you can't."

"How about I promise I won't do anything you don't want me to?"

Lily's face creased up. "I don't want you to be transgender," she said, burying her face in her hands as if ashamed she'd even said it. "Nobody understands what transgender is and I don't know how to explain it. And I thought Sloane was going to be my new friend, but ever since I told her you were trans, she acts different. Like every time I say the word 'Mom,' she puts her hand over her mouth and starts giggling."

"Honey, I'm so sorry."

"She was doing it at lunch today, giggling and whispering with the other girls as soon as I started talking about you. And I wasn't even talking about you being trans, I was just saying that you make the best chocolate chip banana bread."

"It's true, I do make the best chocolate chip banana bread."

Lily started crying again. "Nobody is going to be my friend. Everyone is whispering about me. And you can't fix it. Don't say you can, because you can't."

I stopped myself from leaping in with reassurances. The children had found it relatively easy to explain having a gay parent, but a trans parent was different. The whispering would end only when people like me were normalized, but the only way to normalize my identity was through exposure, which would have unavoidable repercussions for my family.

"D'you want an armchair hug?" I asked. She nodded and I pulled her onto my lap and wrapped my arms around her, resting my chin on her shoulder while I hugged her. "It's okay, honey. I love you, I've got you," I said, rocking her while she wept.

"You won't tell the teacher, will you?" she asked when she finally stopped crying.

"Not unless you want me to. My guess is that Sloane's going to get bored of this pretty quick and then everyone will move on. Today's news is tomorrow's fish 'n' chips paper."

"Are you upset that I told you?"

"No, of course not," I said as I tucked her back into bed. "There's nothing you can't tell me. That's what a mom's for."

I couldn't sleep that night, anxiety running through my veins like an electric current. I'd dog-eared a line in a book by bell hooks—*It is impossible to nurture one's own or another's spiritual growth when the core of one's being and identity is shrouded in secrecy and lies*—but was I just using this as an excuse to prioritize myself? If we'd lived in New York, the kids would have been exposed to all different types of families. But we didn't live in New York; we lived in Connecticut. I didn't have a partner, most of my queer friends were childless, my family lived three thousand miles away, and I was getting more serious about my writing now that I had to earn a living. Which meant that most of the time my kids weren't being raised by a village of adults, they were being raised by one adult alone. What if I couldn't give my kids everything they needed? What if I lost my children, not because someone took them away but because they turned on me for not being the right kind of parent?

I turned my pillow over, trying to find the cool spot, wishing I had a sleeping body next to me who I could shake awake and ask for reassurance, another adult human being who could tell me that I was doing okay, that I was a good parent, that the kids were going to be fine. I worried that I couldn't trust my own judgment. History was littered with people who had managed to justify doing terrible things, and if I ended up damaging my children, I'd never forgive myself.

It was early November, the weather outside my bedroom window was cold and blustery, and I was lying on my bed with my hands behind my head watching Elisabeth try on all my old underwear. She was pulling on various flimsy bits of lace—lingerie that looked ridiculous on me but gorgeous on her—while the warm light from the table lamps bathed her in a smoky glow as if she were in an old movie. It was good to have her back again, even for a short visit. I needed to spend some time with someone who knew me as intimately as she did.

When we finished sifting through my old clothes, we took the dog for a walk. Wet leaves covered the sidewalks, Halloween decorations hung from the porches, the sky was porcelain blue. As we passed each house, I described my neighbors to her: gay, straight, married, widowed, Black, white, Jewish, Asian, young children, grown children, adopted children, no children, and an awful lot of dogs.

"Are you making friends with the women or the men?" Elisabeth asked.

"Both," I said. "The guy across the road invited me to join his men-only backyard fit club, so now I'm over there every Thursday doing push-ups on his lawn with the other men. I love the fact that they're so inclusive, but I know they don't really see me as one of them. It's almost like I can be myself only when nobody's looking, and as soon as someone looks at me, I'm reminded that what they're seeing is not who I am. It's really jarring. And it's hard not to feel inferior when they've all got such gorgeous bodies."

"Why not start testosterone? Build some muscle?"

I shook my head. "I don't know, I just . . ." I paused, still struggling to voice my reservations. "I was at a literary event a few weeks ago and this woman asked me whether I was taking testosterone, and when I said I wasn't, she said I'd made the right choice because a friend of hers had started transitioning and had gone from being 'a really attractive woman to an ugly-as-shit man.' And that's a direct quote."

"Jesus Christ, who says that to someone who's trans?"

"I know, but what if she's right?"

I pulled Biscuit away from a tree, wishing I could unhear what the woman had said. "I'd be perfectly happy to identify as nonbinary, but it doesn't solve the problem of my dysphoria. And I think it might be the cause of all the physical symptoms, which means they're not going to disappear completely until I fully transition." Elisabeth looked at me, frowning. "You remember all that pain in my limbs? When my hair started falling out?"

"That was because you're trans?"

"I think so. It makes sense, doesn't it? That my gender might start physically attacking my body for being the wrong sex? It's just a theory, but it might explain why the more closely I align my body with my gender, the less pain I feel. I just have to hope that surgery will be enough to get rid of the symptoms completely."

"Wait, the surgery's scheduled?" I told her that NYU had called with a date for early January, and she sucked in her breath. "That soon?"

"I know, that's what Mum said. But now that I know I *can* do it, I can't wait." Elisabeth didn't respond. I didn't blame her. Everyone seemed to think the surgery was the biggest step—that it should be the scariest part of my transition—so it was hard to explain how simple the decision had been.

"But you don't feel that way about testosterone?"

I shook my head. "I like being boyish, and testosterone would turn me into a man."

"Are you sure?"

"About what?"

"That you want to be boyish? Or is it just that 'boy' feels safe?" Elisabeth paused, as if wondering how far she could push this. "I mean, when you were in a girl's body you did your best to be a girl, and now that you're in this boyish body you're doing your best to be a boy. But what if you could be whatever you wanted to be? What if you could have the muscles and the mass to be a man?"

I remembered a paparazzi shot I'd once seen of David Bowie walking down the street outside his apartment in Soho. He was wearing a T-shirt and a pair of khaki shorts, and he looked just like a regular bloke. I don't know why I was so surprised by this, because of course he was. Beneath all the performance he was an ordinary man, like all the other ordinary men.

But instead of answering her, I changed the subject to my concerns about how I was going to get through the recovery period. For two weeks I wouldn't be able to lift anything heavier than a teacup, and I didn't have anyone lined up to help me yet. My parents were back in England, all my friends either had kids or had full-time jobs, and there was this lovely guy in AA who'd offered to take care of me, but he'd also recently shared that he tended to answer every question with the word "yes" and often regretted it, and I didn't want to take advantage of him. Elisabeth started laughing. "Oh my God, Oliver, you're not going through this on your own. I'm booking my ticket now. How long do you need me for? Two weeks? Three?"

A month later I was perched on an exam table at the gender clinic at NYU, dressed only in a pair of boxers and a paper gown, waiting for the surgeon to tell me what she'd be doing to my body in a few weeks' time. Maeve sat in a chair in the corner, her laptop balanced on her knees, earbuds in her ears, interviewing someone for an article she was writing. She was twisting her hair into a thick rope over one shoulder as she talked, occasionally pausing to let it unravel as she typed something into her computer.

I repositioned my paper gown, which was falling open at the front.

Maeve looked up at me. "Nervous?" she mouthed.

I shook my head. I was just grateful I didn't have to wait months for insurance approval. I knew paying out of pocket was an absurd luxury, but it didn't seem frivolous.

There was a knock at the door and the surgeon came in, a petite woman with blonde hair who looked more like a preschool teacher than someone who spent her days helping people surgically transition. We smiled and shook hands and introduced ourselves, and then I slipped off the table and removed my gown so she could have a proper look at the material she had to work with. My breasts hung limply, as if already resigned to their fate—two pounds of superfluous flesh I no longer needed and hadn't wanted in the first place. Removing them would be making an irreversible statement that I wasn't retaining anything for anyone else's pleasure, that my body belonged solely to me. The surgeon started to trace imaginary lines across my chest, explaining how she'd cut away the flesh and stitch up the skin, removing my nipples and grafting them back on over the muscles that would then become my pecs. I liked how she discussed my breasts with such clinical precision. It made me feel seen.

"Do you have any questions?" she asked. I shook my head. Maeve and the surgeon started talking about post-op medication—discussing how to limit my access to opioids given my history of addiction—while I stood, inspecting my half-naked body in the mirror, trying to imagine the shape the doctor would create with her knife. I could almost see the boy gazing back at me from the other side of the looking glass, holding his breath, waiting for the signal that it was time to step through.

Elisabeth flew to New York the day before the operation. Charles had agreed to take the kids for a week, so we checked into a hotel near the hospital, where we'd stay until I'd been cleared by the doctor to return home. It was early January and icy cold. We had dinner at a local restaurant, where we talked about everything except the surgery. I'd spent the last few months focusing so hard on the outcome that I'd managed to prevent myself from thinking about what it was going to take to get there; now that it was actually happening, I didn't want to think about it at all.

We walked to the hospital the following morning. I was bundled up in clothes that I could put back on without having to raise my arms. In the hospital I lay on a gurney in a small room near the operating theater, clutching Elisabeth's hand. We'd been waiting like this for about an hour, speaking in whispers. I was glad Elisabeth was here. This step was symbolic, and I needed her to witness it.

Suddenly the room was full of people—nurses, anesthetists, interns, and finally the surgeon, her eyes smiling above her mask. I looked up at Elisabeth, who was half laughing, half crying. "I love you, Oliver," she said, letting go of my hand so the nurse could wheel me away.

Surfacing from the anesthetic, the first thing I felt was a tight constriction in my chest, as if a pair of giant hands were crushing my ribcage. Then I realized my chest was flat, my breasts gone. A nurse appeared at my side. "Are you in pain?" she asked. I shook my head. "So, the tears are emotional?" I nodded dumbly. She smiled as if she were used to this answer. "Okay, I'll give you some space."

I woke in the hotel room the next morning, dimly aware of Maeve and Elisabeth lying on the bed beside me as I drifted in and out of consciousness. It hurt to breathe, it hurt to move, so I lay still, listening to them chatter, comforted by the sound of their voices. Over the next couple of days a steady stream of friends dropped by while I lay propped on the pillows, high on pain medication. One friend brought cake; another brought a book of poetry. On the third day I returned home wrapped in thick layers of clothing, protection from the pressure of the car seat belt and the cold. Elisabeth unlocked the front door and kicked it open, already accustomed to its habit of sticking at the bottom. The house was dark and silent, the children away with Charles. Elisabeth turned to help me over the threshold, holding me by the elbow as I made small steps down the hall.

"Where d'you want to go?" she asked.

"The bathroom," I said. "I want to take it all off, just for a few minutes, so I can breathe."

Elisabeth stood behind me and lifted my coat off my shoulders, then turned me around to untie the belt on my cardigan. I sat down on the side of the bath while she unbuttoned my shirt and helped to ease my arms out of the sleeves. I lifted my elbows a couple of inches so she could get to the Velcro that was holding the medical binder around my rib cage, trying not to wince while she pulled it apart. Then she unwound the bandages from around my chest.

I stood in front of the mirror. Two gashes ran across my chest, as if someone had ripped into me with a large knife, cleaving me in two. Thick black stitches held the folds of my skin together, dark clots of dried blood lined the wounds. Below them snaked two drainage tubes, siphoning fluid into bags under my armpits, the stents stained orange with iodine. Squares of surgical tape held my nipples in place, the areolas black with blood, the flesh around them mottled with yellow-and-purple bruises.

Elisabeth gathered up my discarded clothes from the floor and then sat on the edge of the bath, holding them in a bundle in her arms. "What do you think?" she asked.

We were looking at the same thing—the wreckage of my chest—but what I was seeing wasn't surface, it was form. I tried to find the words but there weren't any. What I was experiencing existed beyond language. My eyes were finally seeing what my brain had known all along, my femininity peeled away to reveal the male chest that had always been there, hidden underneath.

Chapter Thirty

I don't know what I thought was going to happen the first time I went out after top surgery, but now that I'd taken off the whole disguise—the hair and the makeup and the excess body parts—I expected everyone to instantly see me. Which, of course, they didn't. It was early spring, and I'd been invited to a party hosted by a couple of art collectors whose foundation supported the Connecticut LGBTQ center. I walked through the front door, feeling like a million dollars in a pair of men's wool pants and a thin sweater that showed off my newly chiseled chest, and was greeted by a waiter bearing a silver tray of champagne flutes.

"Would you care for a drink, ma'am?" he asked.

My euphoria burst so quickly that for a moment I almost thought I might cry. Wouldn't waiters at a queer event be a little more clued-in that there might be some gender-incongruence among the guests? But I didn't correct him. I didn't want to have to tell everyone I was a man anymore, I wanted them to see it. What part of "I just removed my breasts" did people not understand? Every morning for the last three months I'd stood in front of my bathroom mirror, watching my newly male chest appear through the healing scars and fading bruises, but it still wasn't enough. The narrowness of my waist betrayed me, the curve of my hips, the pitch of my voice. In the eyes of the world, I was still a masculine-presenting woman.

I ran into the same problem when I took my shirt off at the beach that summer. At first it felt liberating, but as I sat on the sand talking with a friend, a middle-aged man surfaced out of the sea and started walking towards us. He was looking straight at me, as one does when one is walking up a beach, but as soon as he came within earshot he stopped. His mind was so busy trying to process the incongruence between what he was seeing—my male chest—and what he was hearing—my female voice—that he didn't realize he was staring until he noticed me staring back. He blinked, blushed, and hurried past.

I couldn't get the thought of testosterone out of my head. All day, every day, the ifs and buts, the pros and cons. If I took testosterone, people would finally read me as a man, but what kind of man would I be? I couldn't affect the sweet, campy charm of a gay man because I was attracted to women, and I couldn't affect the powerful, brooding charm of a straight man because I lacked the stature. My history as a woman gave me other qualities—sensitivity, loyalty, flexibility, patience—but were these virtues valuable in a man? I worried that trans men were just inferior versions of real men, that I'd go from feeling like a not-quite-good-enough woman to a not-quite-good-enough man.

It wasn't until the following February—over a year after my top surgery—that I finally made the decision, and in the end it was Alfie who gave me the clarity I needed. I was cooking dinner one evening, when he wandered into the kitchen and helped himself to a protein bar from the snack cupboard. "Mom, how many genders do you think there are?" he asked as he unwrapped it.

"An infinite number," I replied. "As many as there are personalities. As many as there are humans. We just don't have names for them all yet."

"What is gender, anyway?"

"I don't know. Nobody seems to know."

"Maybe there's no such thing as gender."

"That's what people say, that gender is a social construct. But dysphoria is real, and if dysphoria is what happens when your gender doesn't align with your sex, then gender must exist."

"But what if only sex is real?"

"What would that make me?"

"Someone whose sex doesn't align with their sex."

"But what does that make all the people who are nonbinary?"

"Maybe sex isn't real."

I smiled. "Now we're getting somewhere."

Alfie dropped his wrapper into the trash and wandered back out of the kitchen while I opened the fridge and got out a carton of milk. I put it down on the counter so hard that the cap popped off. Alfie had just hit the nail on the head. The answer had been in front of me all the time, but the simplicity of it had somehow got buried under all the theorizing. I'd lost myself in the elusive details of role and performance and expression, chasing my tail trying to explain my identity in a way that made sense, but all this conjecture about my gender had been nothing more than a distraction. My sex was the problem, not my gender. I knew exactly what my body was supposed to look like. All I had to do was pick up the phone.

I didn't have to wait months for an endocrinology appointment because I'd already moved to a family practice that
specialized in LGBTQ medicine, so within a week I was
sitting in the doctor's office, waiting for them to finish typing whatever it was they were typing into their computer.
Everyone who worked at the medical center was queer, from
the twink behind the receptionist's desk to the trans woman
taking prescriptions in the pharmacy to the doctor sitting in
front of me who had blue hair and used they/them pronouns.
I'd already given them the letter from my therapist confirming
my decision to transition, so now there was nothing standing
between me and a syringe full of testosterone except myself.

The doctor went through the formal medical stuff, and then
we turned to the potential side effects. My father still had a full
head of hair, so I probably wouldn't go bald; acne might be
an issue but it would only be temporary; mood swings would
be no worse than I'd experience during menopause; increased
aggression was unlikely if I stuck to the recommended dose.
Finally, the doctor explained that testosterone would increase
the size of my clitoris—that it would swell until it resembled a
tiny penis—and this change was irreversible. I tried to absorb
all this information. I wanted a smaller ass, bigger muscles,
and a deeper voice, I wanted to feel the rasp of stubble on my
chin, and I sure as hell wanted that tiny penis. What exactly
was it about testosterone that I didn't want?

"I can set you up with an appointment for your first shot
next week, if you think you're ready," the doctor suggested.

"Yes," I said. "Yes, I'm ready."

The voices were disembodied, indistinct; they hummed in
the air, swirling round from behind me as if coming from

somewhere just outside my peripheral vision. *Your existence is a violence against humanity.* I looked down to see the glinting barrel of a gun pointed at my groin. I could feel the hard steel pushing against my pelvis, my own finger pulling the curve of the trigger. *Nobody will ever love you again. You'll end up alone.*

I shot upright, wide-awake, the horror of the explosion filling the room. My hands clutched and smoothed the comforter, looking for something I'd dropped—the gun, where was the gun?—until I realized I was in my bedroom, the outline of the window coming into focus through the gloom.

I closed my eyes, waiting for my heart to stop racing. The voices weren't real. I didn't have to listen to what they were saying anymore. It was time to surrender, not to my internalized transphobia but to my body. It didn't matter whether I found love after I transitioned. I was a man, and I needed to live in the body of a man. If I didn't allow myself to do this, I would never exist, and I couldn't live with such a gaping hole in my life. Nobody else's love would be big enough to fill that void.

I hadn't realized how tightly I'd been clinging to the last shred of my femininity until I finally let go. Jaime had once suggested that my problem with being a man was tied to a fear that masculinity wasn't desirable, and it was only now that I understood how right she'd been. For the week leading up to my first testosterone shot I felt as if I were in free fall, rushing through the air at terrifying speed with no grip on anything to slow me down. I'd let go of my country, my wealth, my class, my heterosexuality, and finally now my gender, until I was nothing but a body spinning in space. The freedom felt too extreme. I waited to hit the ground, but the ground didn't appear. I wasn't falling, I was floating; I was finally free to be anything I wanted to be.

My first testosterone shot coincided with the beginning of the pandemic. I hadn't planned it that way, but when I realized we were going to be staying in lockdown indefinitely, it seemed like a thin silver lining around a large dark cloud. I told nobody except Maeve, Elisabeth, Bianca, and my immediate family. The kids were only mildly interested in this new leg of my journey—less concerned about whether I would end up with a beard and more concerned about when they could see their friends again—and now that I'd made the decision, I felt no fear. The first time I broke down sobbing in the bathroom, it wasn't because I was afraid nobody would love me if I were a man, it was because the schools had closed. I was a solo parent, I was completely outnumbered, and I was *definitely* not cut out to be a teacher. Stuck in a house with four teenagers who wanted to be anywhere but home, with no moments of silence, no quiet time ever, while the dog hair piled up in the corners because nobody had time to vacuum and the weeds overtook the backyard because nobody had time to garden, I wondered how long it would take before I completely lost my mind. I spent my days running from room to room in response to "Mom!" "Mom!" "Mom!" because I was the adult, so everyone expected me to know what the hell was going on and how to fix everything, which I clearly didn't. Nobody in the house seemed to know how to divide an improper fraction, and Lily's webcam kept shutting down, and suddenly there was a thing called Flipgrid and nobody knew what the fuck it was for, and I couldn't work out the difference between Stream and Classwork in Google Classroom, and Rose's entire Spanish section suddenly disappeared without a trace, and Alfie was bouncing off the ceilings because he wasn't getting enough exercise, and Freddie was hiding in his bat cave in the attic doing fuck-knows-what up there, and nobody was eating enough vegetables, and I missed my parents, and I needed a hug, which I clearly wasn't going to get from my kids, because they were teenagers and had developed some kind of magnetically repelling force around their bodies.

Meanwhile, the other Connecticut mothers were posting perfect pictures of their perfect children standing by their perfect desks with their hands on their hearts reciting the pledge of allegiance before starting their perfect homeschooling days, and never had I unfollowed so many people in such a short space of time. The fact that every Wednesday I was shooting forty milligrams of testosterone into my thigh seemed like one of the least noteworthy things in my life.

Eventually, we settled into a groove. The kids discovered that they didn't hate each other—or me—and we got a kitten, which helped. We started vacuuming again, and weeding the garden, and we painted the front hall bright orange and then decided it looked awful and painted it back to its original gray. My voice started to break—within a month my range had gone from Joni Mitchell to Donald Duck—but I kept my eye on the prize. I'd never been able to hit the low notes of the Beatles' "Norwegian Wood," and I felt like my voice would only truly be my own when I could.

One morning I noticed stray hairs sticking to my fingers while I was styling my hair. I ran my hand through the front of my hair again; more loose hairs fell into the bathroom sink. I felt a rush of adrenaline. I leaned forward with my hands on the counter and breathed deeply, trying to steady my racing heart. I remembered the long strands of hair lying in the bottom of the bathtub ten years earlier, the fear I'd felt when my hair was coming out in handfuls. But this was different. I rubbed a finger along my temples. My hairline was starting to recede, the irreversible changes everyone had warned me about were happening. I tried to imagine myself with long hair, with smooth skin and a soft voice again, but the thought filled me with horror. I waited for any feeling that I might be doing the wrong thing—that I might ever want to return to being a woman—but there was nothing. No doubt, no fear, no regret. The rush of adrenaline wasn't panic, it was excitement.

By November the changes in my body were becoming more noticeable. I'd started exercising rigorously, doing fifty push-ups every day. Top surgery had left me with a flat but bony chest, and no amount of exercise made any difference, but slowly I started to see muscles where before there had been only skin. Hair was sprouting everywhere—on my chin, my chest, my thighs, my bum, my toes—and my voice had dropped so much that although I could now reach the low notes in "Norwegian Wood," I couldn't reach the high ones.

I also started putting on weight and was surprised by how good it felt. I stopped worrying about the scales and ate when I felt hungry, which then led to the realization that I'd been starving myself for most of my life. A quick online search revealed that eating disorders were common among trans people—an attempt to combat dysphoria without the help of hormones—but now I understood that I hadn't just been trying to get rid of the weight around my hips and thighs because I'd wanted a male-shaped butt; I'd been trying to have less body.

Now my body was rebuilding itself—it was becoming thick, solid, and substantial—and every ounce of it made me happy. My flesh was the right flesh, my muscle was the right muscle, my weight was the right weight. I felt the dysphoria slip away as the testosterone started to change my body on a cellular level. I hadn't even had any mood swings and whipped through menopause in a matter of weeks. No more dieting, no more periods, and no hot flashes.

It was strange to hear everyone talk about the isolation of quarantine when I felt more depended on than ever. This was the first time I'd been with my kids twenty-four-seven since they were babies, and without their friends to talk to, they were forced to talk to me instead. So I began to get a more accurate picture of how each one felt about my transition. One morning while he was in the kitchen slicing a banana into the blender, Alfie asked me why, if clothes weren't gendered, I needed to wear men's clothes to feel like a man.

"You're a man. Would you feel comfortable wearing a dress?"

"No," Alfie responded. "But Harry Styles wears dresses and he's not trans."

"Maybe it's a confidence thing."

Alfie looked unconvinced. He turned on the blender, and I watched him mull the thought over in his head. "So, you're doing the same thing I'm doing, because you're a man like me?" he asked when he turned the blender off. "You're just wearing clothes that make you feel comfortable?"

"Pretty much."

Alfie wiggled the lid off the jar. "When Harry Styles wears a dress, everyone understands he's making a statement that he's cool enough to get away with it. But if I wore a dress it would make a completely different statement, like that I was queer or something." He poured the smoothie into a glass, and I watched the light bulb go on above his head. "It's not just about comfort, it's about communication. Your clothes tell people something about who you are."

Alfie dumped the blender jar in the sink, raised his smoothie at me in salute, and sauntered out of the kitchen. I turned on the faucet and filled the jar up with water before the remains of the smoothie dried onto the inside. My children were going to be okay. The world had tried to tell me that I couldn't care for myself and also for my children, that I couldn't be trans and queer and be a source of stability, that unless I was in a committed, long-term, monogamous relationship I couldn't provide them with the love and support they needed, but I no longer believed any of this. I didn't know who or what my children would become, but whatever my failings as a parent—and I knew there had been many—my children would walk out into the world armed with all the tools I'd once lacked: courage, curiosity, the confidence to form their own opinions and trust their own instincts. They'd already learned that life wouldn't always be easy, so they wouldn't be blindsided when things went wrong. They'd be able to change direction when a path they chose led to a dead end, and they'd know how to stand up for themselves—for who they were and what they believed in—wherever their lives ended up taking them. Their childhood had been messy and chaotic and unpredictable, but it had been real. They needed me and were embarrassed by me and blamed me for everything and frequently told me they hated me, and I wanted every part of it. The ferocity of my love for them had been the grounding force in my life. Everything I had, everything I'd done, everything I'd become, I owed to them.

Chapter Thirty-One

We'd been in lockdown for six months when I met Linc. Now that everything was online, I was able to attend events I'd never have been able to get to in person, so when one of my New York friends had a birthday party, all I had to do was throw together some dinner for the kids, change out of the sweatpants and T-shirt I'd been wearing for most of the week, and sit down at my computer.

It was a small gathering, and I was the last to arrive. The screen was mostly full of people I knew from my twelve-step group, but in the rectangle in the top right corner was an unfamiliar face. They had short silver hair, and when they smiled, their eyes creased up like butterfly wings. Their voice, when they spoke, was gentle and measured, as if they were used to operating at a pace a fraction slower than the rest of the world. It was soothing, like listening to someone recite poetry, or sing a lullaby. I looked at the name at the bottom of their window: *Linc, they/them*. I couldn't keep my eyes off them, and I realized that one of the benefits of Zoom was that I didn't have to.

When the party ended, I called the hostess and asked for Linc's number. I texted them the following evening while

I was cooking curry for the kids; they were also cooking curry, and we sent each other pictures of the ingredients on our kitchen counters to compare recipes. I asked what they did and where they were texting from; they told me they were a lens-based visual artist, and they lived in an artists' community in a converted warehouse in the Bronx. The conversation was fluid, easy, and undefined. I didn't try to explain why I'd reached out to them because I didn't know myself, and they didn't ask.

In mid-December I drove down to the Bronx to meet them. We went for a walk around Randall's Island because everything was still closed. It was dark, and the snow was deep. We were wearing masks, bundled up against the cold, and walking six feet apart, but I could feel the energy between us. As we walked, Linc paused periodically to point something out: the shadow the arches created as we walked through the underpass, seedpods clinging to the branches of a tree, the slant of moonlight on the water of the Hudson River.

"I have something I want to show you," they said as we neared a clearing. "Look, up there." They motioned up to the sky. "See that star there? And that one right next to it? That's Saturn and Jupiter. They're millions of miles apart but they look like they're almost touching."

We stood in the middle of the snow, heads bent back, staring up at the sky, two bodies mirroring the planets above our heads.

"This is the closest they've been in almost a hundred years," Linc said.

Neither of us knew quite how to end the evening, because we were social distancing, so I left the Bronx not knowing what we'd started or where it would go. But Linc kept texting me daily, so when Charles took the kids skiing for a few days after Christmas, I invited them to come and stay. We'd both taken tests, so we didn't have to wear masks, and we sat on the floor in the living room in front of the fire, eating olives and bruschetta and talking about our favorite artists and writers. Linc brought me a book of poetry and prose as a gift, a small volume written by a friend. I asked them to read me some, and they chose a story the poet had written about meeting the ghost of Marvin Gaye in a supermarket; how the ghost had persuaded her to dip her finger into a pot of honey, right there in the aisle, and explained that this was how she should approach love.

"I want to kiss," Linc read, their voice soft and low. "And I know a kiss is more than a kiss; I know it can come straight at you, or tease you, or speak to you and say I want you, but not just yet, I want you to wait until your wanting spills over my thigh."

Linc looked up at me. I waited, to see if the beating of my heart would slow down. They smiled, and their eyes creased up like butterfly wings. Curled up in bed with me later that night, Linc admitted that although they hadn't been sure where the afternoon would lead, they'd packed their tooth-brush, just in case. "I can stay for a few days if you'd like."

"I'd like that very much," I said.

Having Linc in my life changed the way I saw the world, and myself in it. They didn't want to put a label on what we were doing or who we were together, they wanted to take it one day at a time and see where it led. Linc had figured out the art to living in the moment. They slowed me down, allowed me to experience what was happening in the now rather than continually trying to project into the future. It was a shift I found surprisingly easy to make. I had no idea what the future might hold anyway, so there seemed to be little point in making plans for it anymore.

Since Linc and I had separate quarantine pods, we started meeting in art galleries in New York. Most of the galleries were empty because of the pandemic, which allowed us the privacy we needed to get to know each other. Walking through the rooms with Linc almost felt like dancing. An interlocking finger here, a stroke of my arm there, we'd move away from each other and come back together, a chin on my shoulder, a hand touching the back of my neck. The undefined nature of our relationship felt natural, and strangely familiar, as if it were a form of connection towards which I'd been gravitating without really noticing. Linc questioned things that I took for granted, and it opened my eyes.

The truth of Einstein's theory of relativity—that time isn't linear but contracts and expands—was something even those of us who weren't blessed with mathematical brains began to appreciate during the pandemic. The year we spent in full quarantine seems compressed in retrospect, but at the time the days elongated, leaving me with enough spare hours—apparently magically gifted by the universe—for this precious new relationship. Summer arrived and the lockdown regulations started to lift, which meant using the car again, but the radio had broken, so I drove it to a little audio store down the road to see if they could set me up with a new one.

"What can I do for you, sir?" the man behind the counter asked as I walked into the shop. I was momentarily startled. Nobody had called me sir before, not even when I was out with Linc. Since I'd been hidden under layers of winter clothes and wearing a mask, everyone had continued to assume I was

a woman. I explained what I was looking for, gesturing to
the car outside and waiting for him to correct himself. "I got
you, bro," he said, disappearing into the back of the shop.

I looked down at myself. I was wearing a pair of shorts,
below which were the unmistakable hairy knees and calves of
a man. My chest muscles had developed over the last twelve
months, so while you couldn't quite see my pecs, they were
clearly there, somewhere under my T-shirt. My forearms were
covered in tattoos, the backs of my hands veiny. The parts of
my neck and chin that were visible around the edges of my
mask were rough with stubble, and most importantly, my
voice, when I spoke, sounded gravely and low. The only thing
that might have betrayed my former gender was my height.

It turned out not to be a one-off event; I was now passing
universally. But recognition of my gender didn't end at being
called sir. People were treating me differently. While I'd never
doubted that we lived in a world that privileged men, it was
an entirely new experience to be on the receiving end. It
was all in the details—a male driver waiting to let me out
of a side road, a car mechanic treating me with respect, a
man acknowledging me with a nod on the street. It was
as if men could finally see me, which only made me even
more acutely aware of how blind to me they'd been before.
I was being treated differently by women too. Store clerks
smiled and bantered with me, seeing me as the cool dad, the
rare father who took his daughters shopping. The nurses in
the pediatric doctor's office talked to me kindly, assuming I
was the good guy taking the load off a busy mother. Female
baristas who'd previously ignored me now flirted with me,
whether because they were attracted to me or because appeas-
ing men had become a protection strategy, I didn't know. It

felt uncomfortable, and sometimes made me want to sink into my socks in shame. *Don't*, I wanted to say. *Please, don't.* I didn't want people to be nicer to me now that I was a man. I didn't want to be part of that narrative.

But the hardest adjustment was learning how to operate without the automatic embrace of the community I'd taken for granted all my life. However much I knew I wasn't a threat to women, it was clear that nobody else knew this anymore, and I hadn't realized how much I'd grown used to the solidarity that women reserved exclusively for each other until it was gone. When a lost child came up to me for help, her older sister pulled her away sharply, glaring at me with suspicion. When I parked in front of a house to answer a text, an elderly lady came out to tell me she'd call the police if I didn't leave. The way women touched each other casually during friendly conversation was now off-limits to me, which was particularly poignant because I'd spent so long trying to override my fear of nonsexual contact. Respect for women couldn't just be a feeling now, it had to take the form of actions, and those actions weren't transactional. My behavior mattered more than ever, because my allegiance to women could no longer be assumed.

And yet, I woke up every morning into a world that felt safer, even while the newspapers were telling me otherwise, even while the backlash against trans people grew. My default setting was now a consistent feeling of just being okay, as if my baseline had changed, and despite the consistency of this feeling, it surprised me daily. I'd got used to happiness being fleeting, something I had to grasp tightly before it slipped away, so I kept waiting for the other shoe to drop. But day after day I noticed the smallest things made me feel warm inside, sensory experiences I'd never been able to fully enjoy before because my dysphoria had messed so badly with my nervous system. The smell of basil or bath soap; hot butter dripping off a piece of toast; the warm weight of the dog leaning against me on the sofa. Common, everyday experiences that now felt vibrant with nostalgia, as if I were experiencing loss in reverse.

Occasionally I wondered whether this new sense of contentment was solely due to the fact that I was now living as a fully aligned human being, or whether it was partly due to the side effects of low-dose, everyday male privilege. I tried to separate the two, but it was sometimes hard to figure out how to enjoy being male without indulging the privilege of being male. I made some missteps in the early days. Robin and I had stayed in touch after our affair had ended, so when she came to play in a nearby city, I took Lily and Rose to see her perform. She invited them backstage afterwards and charmed their socks off, and when I went to pick Rose up from her guitar lesson the following week, her guitar teacher—an aging rocker with a gray ponytail and too-tight skinny jeans—came out of the rehearsal room with a new look of admiration on his face.

"Rose tells me you used to date Robin Blake?" he said. Before I could answer he raised his hand for a high five. "Put it there, bro. Respect."

Instinctively, without stopping to think what I was doing, I high-fived him back. He grinned, shot me a knowing look, and then disappeared back into the rehearsal room. I wrung my hand in disgust, realizing that I'd just participated in a moment of conquest-bonding with another man. I wanted to apologize to someone—to whom, to Robin?—but I knew it wouldn't achieve anything. I wasn't going to make the same mistake I'd made in my twenties by thinking that shame was a substitute for action. I wanted male friendships, I wanted the intimacy and camaraderie I'd seen between the bikers back in my twenties, but not if it came at the expense of women. I'd failed to use my privilege to support the queer community back then, and now that I'd been given a second chance, I wasn't going to mess it up.

Linc and I were sitting with the kids in the diner on the outskirts of our old town, waiting for our pancakes. It had been ten years since the motorcycle rally, but in the diner, nothing much had changed. The menu still offered the same selection of waffles and omelets, the booths were filled with the same middle-class white families. Even the waitresses didn't seem to have aged.

Across the table, Rose was licking the whipped cream from the top of her hot chocolate, her long hair falling across her face. Next to her, Lily was sitting back in the booth, her knees against the edge of the table, reading aloud the songs from her Spotify playlist. Alfie was probing Linc for more information about their upcoming exhibition, and Fred's seat was empty because he'd insisted on driving up separately but had turned off at the wrong exit and was now lost somewhere in the neighboring town.

It had been the kids' idea to have brunch here, partly because it was close to the Christmas store we visited every year to buy ornaments for the tree, but also because I wanted to show Linc where the kids had grown up. I stirred cream into my coffee while listening to snippets of Linc and Alfie's conversation. Linc had felt more like a friend than a lover for a while now, our relationship slowly evolving into something

more platonic. It seemed like such an easy and natural evo-
lution that I just let it happen. I didn't want to be contained,
even in a relationship. For the first time in my life, it felt good
not to belong to anyone. I hadn't anticipated the extent to
which having a solid identity would make me feel like I could
go anywhere and do anything, and my friendship with Linc
sat comfortably alongside this new sense of freedom. They
didn't treat me like a possession or a prize, they loved me
only for who I was, and to be loved this deeply just for being
myself felt infinitely more valuable than any love I'd had to
win by pretending to be someone else.

Lily put down her phone and picked up her coffee, and I
suddenly realized how grown-up my children had become.

"God, times have changed," I said. "Do you remember
when you couldn't sit still for more than five minutes?"

"We used to run around the parking lot while we were
waiting for the food."

"You let them run around the parking lot?" Linc asked.

"On the *sidewalk*," I said.

"*Mostly* on the sidewalk," Alfie said.

"And we used to steal the peppermints from the front desk,"
Rose added.

"You could only just reach."

"Wait, you knew?"

"You weren't exactly subtle, Rose."

Alfie looked out of the window towards the road. "Do you
remember the motorcycle rally?" he said.

Linc glanced at me, uncertain how much the kids knew
about that part of my history.

"What?" Lily asked, sensing something.

I shrugged and smiled. "That was the day I came out."

"You came out here? In this diner?" Rose asked.

"No, outside, by the road."

I explained how the motorcycles had been the catalyst for my eventual transition, which led to each of them trying to recall who first found out I was gay, and how they'd all reacted. Then they all told Linc the story about Alfie with the Pokémon cards, which was the only part everyone could remember.

"I'm going to get a phone charger from the car," Lily said, getting up. "Mom, don't let Alfie eat my pancakes if they come before I get back."

"We might have to start rethinking the 'Mom' thing at some stage," I commented as she walked away.

"Why?" Rose asked.

"Doesn't it feel a little odd when you're out in the middle of the street to yell 'Mom' at someone who's clearly a man?"

"We never yell 'Mom' at you in the middle of the street."

"No, I know, but if you *did*. Don't you think it would be a bit weird?"

"Never really thought about it," Rose admitted.

"Yeah, you're right, it's probably asking too much. I've already put you through quite a lot, haven't I?"

"Like what?" Alfie asked.

"Well, the divorce, and then coming out as gay, and then transitioning . . . and then after all that to demand you start calling me a different name . . . I mean, you've already nailed the pronouns, I don't want to push you too far."

Alfie sighed. "Look, Mom, I know you think you fucked us up, but you really didn't. It might have been a lot for you, but it really wasn't for us. We've got our friends and school, it really hasn't been that big of a deal. And we've got you. You're the mom-dad."

"The mom-dad?"

"Yeah, that's what Rose's friends call you. Like, 'Get the mom-dad to pick us up in the Mustang.' They think you're supercool."

"Seriously?"

"Where's my pancake? Did Alfie eat it?" Fred asked, appearing beside the table.

"Nobody ate your pancake; the food hasn't arrived yet."

"We were just talking about how cool Mom is."

"I think it's mostly the Mustang," I said.

"I don't know about cool, but your queerness probably saved me from QAnon," Fred replied, squeezing in next to his brother. He looked up and saw my face. "Come on, the amount of political shit I watch on YouTube? The algorithms would have sucked me into the alt-right by now."

"Are you kidding?"

"I'm deadly serious."

"Why's Mom laughing?" Lily asked, arriving back at the booth.

"Because he's the Queer Savior," Alfie said.

"I'll have that in my obituary, please."

The waitress arrived with our food, so we paused to argue over who had ordered what and to rearrange the plates so that each person got what they needed. Once the boys finished fighting over the maple syrup and we found Lily's lost fork and Linc did a head count of who needed more coffee, the waitress turned to me.

"Can I get you anything else, sir?" she asked.

"See?" I said as she walked away. "She'd think you were crazy if you called me Mom."

"We can't call you Dad, though, because Dad would have a fit," Lily said.

"And don't even start with Papa or Poppa or any stupid shit like that," Rose warned.

"I'm going to call you Bro," Alfie said.

"That would go down great with your teachers. *It's okay, I'll get my bro to sign the permission form.* Not really going to work, is it, Alfie?"

"Maybe you could call him by his first name?" Linc suggested. "It's not that unusual. Plenty of kids do it."

"Works for me," Fred said, tucking into his pancake.

"I am not a gender! I am a free man!" I said, despite being the only person at the table who watched 1960s British cult TV.

"Don't be weird, Oliver," Rose responded. And from that moment on, to everyone who knew me, that was my name.

Acknowledgments

This book would never have made it to print if a small group of people hadn't believed in it against the odds from the very beginning. First and foremost, thank you to my agent, Malaga Baldi. The day after you pulled my manuscript out of the slush pile you got knocked off your bicycle and ended up in hospital with a broken wrist; thank you for using your one good hand to type an email from your hospital bed asking me not to sign with anyone else before you finished reading. If it wasn't for your trust in me, your unwavering belief in this book, and your relentless perseverance in getting it published, this book wouldn't exist. We did this together, and I will always be grateful that I found you.

Roxane Gay, thank you for taking a chance on me, for prioritizing story over platform and message over marketability. You taught me so much about how to write, even before we met. Clear, concise instruction is my love language, and you are a master at it. I will always be grateful for your empathy and insight. Noah Rosenzweig, Clara Tamez, Alicia Burns, Amy Hundley, Deb Seager, and the rest of the team at Roxane Gay Books and Grove Atlantic, thank you for looking after me so well, and for making me feel supported as we got ready to put this book out into the world. Brian Ulicky and Aileen Boyle at Audere Media, thank you for spreading the word and helping to get this book into the hands of as many readers as possible, and Oliver Jeffers, thank you for making my dreams come true. I am so grateful to all of you.

Patrick McCord, you were the first person to read my early work, and you were convinced there was something there, even when I was writing utter crap. Your relentless focus on the good helped me persevere. Shelley Stenhouse, you took my writing to the next level; thank you for your friendship, your tutelage, and your excellent poetry. David Groff, you helped me figure out which parts of my story to focus on, and how to edit down the unwieldy manuscript that landed on your desk into something readable; thank you for helping me get it into good shape prior to submission. Parrish Turner, thank you for the supplementary feedback and suggestions. Sometimes we can't see what's right in front of us, and your additional perspective was invaluable.

To my cheerleaders, my early readers, my constant believers: I am so grateful for your patience, your kindness, your loyalty, and your support. Henrietta Weekes, Cara Buckley, Giselle Mazier, Susy Marples, Rachael Barraclough and Mark Earls—you are, always have been, and always will be, my best beloveds. I love each and every one of you with my whole heart. To the old friends who continued to stand by me through all the changes, and the new friends who made me feel seen and heard as I became myself: Lev Rose Water, Jojo Stephens, Richard Taylor, Sam Rudd, Jenny Vitulli, Patty Chamberlin, Kerri Gawreluk, Tara Kerner, Jen Spero, Katerina Hasiotis, Janet Waddell, Alice O'Malley, Bart Hoedemaker, Tom Arbron, Phoebe DuMaurier, Jody Mallory, Anthony

Varalli, Rose Allen, Mason Capozza, Chris Hornauer, Lestina Trainor, Jamie and Brandyn Cooper, Michael Cohen, Adrian Frandle, Ngina Lythcott, Byllye Avery, Julie Lythcott-Haims, Jo Fyffe, Rachel Bender, Wendell Steavenson, Scott and Jaime Durkee, Kristin Sabena, and Betsy Young. Thank you for letting me prioritize my kids and my writing over my social life, and for continuing to love me regardless. Jeffrey Lustman and Ady Ben-Israel, thank you for helping me with the uncovering. I wouldn't be who I am, or where I am, without you.

Mum and Dad, you are the true heroes of this story. Your ability to roll with the punches is nothing short of a miracle. You are an example to all parents everywhere, and I'm so grateful I get to call you mine. Ted, Antonia, Poppy, Oscar, India, Rufus, and Imogen, you're the most accepting (and most fun) family anyone could ask for. Thank you for teaching me the true meaning of unconditional love. And finally, my children. You are four of the best people who have ever walked this earth. Your combined power, resilience, compassion, and humor has carried us through all this. You are each a force to be reckoned with, you've made me the proudest parent in the world, and I hope, one day, to make you equally as proud. I love you best of all.